Making Gender Salient

Do gender quota laws – policies that mandate women's inclusion on parties' candidate slates – affect policy outcomes? *Making Gender Salient* tackles this crucial question by offering a new theory to understand when and how gender quota laws impact policy. Drawing on cross-national data from high-income democracies and a mixed-methods research design, the book argues that quotas lead to policy change for issues characterized by a gender gap in preferences, especially if these issues deviate from the usual left/right party-policy divide. The book focuses on one such issue, work–family policies, and finds that quotas shift work–family policies in the direction of gender equality. Substantive chapters show that quotas make gender more salient by giving women louder voices within parties, providing access to powerful ministerial roles, and encouraging male party leaders to compete on previously marginalized issues. The book concludes that quotas are one important way of facilitating congruence between women's policy preferences and actual policy outcomes.

Ana Catalano Weeks is an assistant professor in comparative politics in the Department of Politics, Languages and International Studies at the University of Bath.

Cambridge Studies in Gender and Politics

Cambridge Studies in Gender and Politics addresses theoretical, empirical, and normative issues at the intersection of politics and gender. Books in this series adopt incisive and comprehensive approaches to key research themes concerning the construction and impact of sex and gender, as well as their political and social consequences.

General Editors

Karen Beckwith, *Case Western Reserve University (Lead)*
Lisa Baldez, *Dartmouth College*
Christina Wolbrecht, *University of Notre Dame*

Editorial Advisory Board

Nancy Burns, *University of Michigan*
Matthew Evangelista, *Cornell University*
Nancy Hirschmann, *University of Pennsylvania*
Sarah Song, *University of California, Berkeley*
Ann Towns, *University of Gothenburg*
Aili Mari Tripp, *University of Wisconsin–Madison*
Georgina Waylen, *University of Manchester*

Books in the Series

J. Kevin Corder and Christina Wolbrecht, *Counting Women's Ballots*
Mala Htun, *Inclusion without Representation in Latin America*
Mala Htun and S. Laurel Weldon, *The Logics of Gender Justice*
Aili Mari Tripp, *Women and Power in Postconflict Africa*
Kristin N. Wylie, *Party Institutionalization and Women's Representation in Democratic Brazil*
Rachel E. Brulé, *Women, Power, and Property: The Paradox of Gender Equality Laws in India*

Making Gender Salient

From Gender Quota Laws to Policy

ANA CATALANO WEEKS

University of Bath

CAMBRIDGE
UNIVERSITY PRESS

CAMBRIDGE
UNIVERSITY PRESS

Shaftesbury Road, Cambridge CB2 8EA, United Kingdom

One Liberty Plaza, 20th Floor, New York, NY 10006, USA

477 Williamstown Road, Port Melbourne, VIC 3207, Australia

314–321, 3rd Floor, Plot 3, Splendor Forum, Jasola District Centre, New Delhi – 110025, India

103 Penang Road, #05–06/07, Visioncrest Commercial, Singapore 238467

Cambridge University Press is part of Cambridge University Press & Assessment, a department of the University of Cambridge.

We share the University's mission to contribute to society through the pursuit of education, learning and research at the highest international levels of excellence.

www.cambridge.org
Information on this title: www.cambridge.org/9781009158442

DOI: 10.1017/9781009158435

First published 2022
First paperback edition 2023

A catalogue record for this publication is available from the British Library

ISBN   978-1-009-16783-3   Hardback
ISBN   978-1-009-15844-2   Paperback

For Orla, Aidan, and Eloise with all my love

Contents

Figures

Tables

Acknowledgments

I have so many people to thank for their help with this book. I would like to start by thanking my mentor and dissertation committee member Lisa Baldez for her generous advice and support since my days as an undergraduate at Dartmouth College. Lisa has been an inspiration to me, and her insightful comments and suggestions have influenced my ideas in countless ways. My dissertation adviser Torben Iversen shaped my thinking about party politics, and I feel very lucky to have had the benefit of his incisive questions, feedback, and advice. Profound thanks also go to my other committee members, Nahomi Ichino and Jennifer Hochschild, for their thought-provoking comments and critiques that raised the standard of my research.

Many other friends and colleagues have offered helpful critiques, comments, and suggestions over the years. I am thankful especially to the "Brain Trust," Rachel Bernhard, Mona Morgan-Collins, and Soledad Prillaman for reading draft chapters and giving useful and constructive feedback. Thanks also go to the University of Bath's Gender and Sexuality Research Group and Nuffield College, Oxford, for sponsoring our workshops. I am thankful to Jenny Mansbridge for several illuminating conversations about representation and the concept of "uncrystallized interests." I am very grateful to Peter Allen, Colin Brown, Amanda Clayton, Miki Kittilson, Audrey Latura, Shom Mazumder, Jessica Preece, Johanna Rickne, Sparsha Saha, Øyvind Skorge, and Pär Zetterberg for their comments and critiques. Participants at various talks, workshops, and conferences – including Harvard University, the Harvard Kennedy

School's Women and Public Policy Program, the University of Bath, Dartmouth College, Nuffield College, Trinity College Dublin, the University of Cologne, the Empirical Study of Gender (EGEN) Research Network Vanderbilt workshop, and the American Political Science Association Annual Meetings 2016 and 2017 – provided stimulating questions and useful feedback on many parts of the book. I thank Danielle Roybal for her skillful research assistance on party attention to work–family policies and Kelley Friel for excellent copy edits on the draft manuscript. I am grateful to my editors at Cambridge University Press, Sara Doskow and Rachel Blaifeder, for their guidance through the publication process. I thank three anonymous reviewers of my manuscript for their detailed comments and suggestions, which improved the book immensely. I am fortunate that my book is among the important works in the Cambridge Studies in Gender and Politics series, and I thank series editors Karen Beckwith and Christina Wolbrecht for including it. Many thanks also to the talented Hazel McCoubrey for designing a beautiful cover, and to Sarah Childs for introducing us.

The fieldwork for this book could not have been conducted without the generous financial support from the Center for European Studies at Harvard, which funded my research in four countries. Profound thanks go to all of the politicians, bureaucrats, and activists who agreed to interviews and shared their experiences and views with me. Their insights were invaluable to informing my understanding of the effects of quota laws documented in this book.

Finally, I am very grateful to my friends and family for their encouragement and support throughout the long process of writing this book. Thank you to my mom (Louise) and dad (Michael) for giving me so many opportunities to grow and learn and raising me to believe I could achieve anything. Thanks to Marc, Ali, Maria, Peter, Sophie, Kim, Alison, and Emma for always cheering me on. Endless thanks to my husband Dominic who is my strongest supporter and best friend. This book is for our children Orla, Aidan, and Eloise. They made finishing this book challenging at times, but they also gave me a new understanding of the importance of the work–family policies I focus on in the book. Most importantly, they fill my life with joy. Their energy and creativity give me hope that the next generation will continue to make progress on a more inclusive and gender-equal future for all.

I

Introduction

Do gender quotas lead to policy change for women? More than sixty countries have passed gender quota laws, which require all political parties to include a minimum percentage of women on their candidate lists. Argentina passed the first such law in 1991, and they have increased exponentially since then: at least fifteen countries have followed suit in each subsequent decade (see Table 1.1). This growth is somewhat surprising because quota laws are highly controversial. Even the term "quota" has a negative connotation in many societies, leading many advocates to use terms like "parity" instead. Some proponents support quotas purely out of a sense of justice: women make up half the population, so they should be equally represented in parliaments. Others claim that quotas are necessary for symbolic reasons – that the historical absence of women in political institutions may be associated with perceptions that they are second-class citizens and the notion that politics is "men's domain." These arguments do not assert that women have a different set of policy preferences or act differently than men. Yet, in debates about quotas around the world, assumptions are often made about their impact on a set of loosely defined "women's issues." Many believe that increasing the number of women in politics will better address women's specific policy concerns.

Belgium adopted a quota law in 1995 requiring that no more than two-thirds of an electoral list consist of candidates of the same sex (it has since increased to 50 percent); parties with lists that do not comply are not eligible to appear on the ballot.[1] The share of women in parliament

---

[1] Law of May 24, 1994, "On promoting balanced distribution of men and women on the lists of candidates for the elections," *Belgisch Staatsblad*, July 1, 1994; Law of December 13, 2002, "On various changes to the electoral law," *Belgisch Staatsblad*, January 10, 2003.

TABLE 1.1 *Electoral quota law adoption (with current threshold) by decade*

No. of countries	1990	2000	2010
25		France (50%) Guyana (33%) Honduras (40%) Mexico (40%) Djibouti (25%) Niger (15%)	
20		Indonesia (30%) Macedonia (33%) Iraq (25%) Korea, Rep. (50%) Serbia (30%) Uzbekistan (30%)	Cabo Verde (50%) Guinea (30%) Algeria (31.7%) Congo (50%)
15	Argentina (30%) Italy (40%) Belgium (50%) Costa Rica (50%) Paraguay (50%)	Angola (30%) Liberia (30%) Timor-Leste (33%) Mauritania (33%) Portugal (40%)	Haiti (30%) Lesotho (50%) Mongolia (20%) Montenegro (30%) Poland (35%)
10	Bolivia (50%) Brazil (30%) Dominican Rep. (33%) Ecuador (50%) Panama (50%)	Slovenia (35%) Kyrgyzstan (30%) Nepal (33%) Senegal (50%) Spain (40%)	Tunisia (50%) Greece (33%) Ireland (30%) Libya (50%) Nicaragua (50%)
5	Peru (30%) Venezuela (40%) Bosnia & Herz. (40%) Armenia (20%) Colombia (30%)	Albania (30%) Croatia (40%) Burkina Faso (30%) Egypt (12%) Uruguay (37%)	El Salvador (30%) Togo (50%) Chile (40%) Vietnam (35%) Luxembourg (40%)

Notes: The table displays the decade in which electoral gender quota laws were first adopted in each country, followed by the current threshold of women required. The y-axis counts the number of quota law adoptions per decade. The countries at the top of each column adopted a quota law earlier in the decade than those lower down

has increased in Belgium from 12 percent in 1998 (before the quota law was first applied in the 1999 election) to 38 percent in 2019. In a personal interview with the author, one of the authors of the law, Christian democrat Senator Sabine de Bethune, asserted that the law has changed politics in the country:

My feeling is that more women in politics has broadened the political agenda, more things became politics. When I entered the political committee of my party, we were only 3 or 4 women in a committee of 60 people. Now we are more than half. When we tried to talk about child care, some men said what is this – and now we've changed it. It is one of the biggest budget points.[2]

Many of her colleagues agree. They bring up issues like child care and parental leave, gender quotas for corporate boards and in public administration, violence against women, and pensions equality. Flemish social democrat Renaat Landyut claims that, "The debates have changed... the difference between women and men that we didn't see as men – women have experienced it and so they could better point out the difficulties."[3] Some politicians also discuss changes to the culture of doing politics, suggesting that, "of course it changes attitudes, and the way people behave and so on."[4]

However, not everyone thinks quotas have made such a difference. Feminist activist and founder of the Women's University in Brussels Hedwige Peemans Poullet is disappointed with the lack of progress generated by Belgium's quota law. She explains, "a woman who is placed on the list because of the quota – does she represent women's interests or the political party? The parties make the lists, but we [feminists] thought that women candidates would come to the women's organizations and ask what was the agenda and relay that to the parties, but they did not do this."[5] French social democrat Yvan Mayeur also emphasizes the importance of party ideology over gender; he does not believe quotas have led to changes in social policy. He gives an example, "I am the president of the Social Affairs Commission of this parliament, and what I see is there is more difference between left and right than men and women. For instance I have four women from the N-VA, they are on the extreme right, and they are strongly against social measures."[6]

France adopted a quota law in 2000 requiring that 50 percent of the candidates on each party's list are women. The quota was controversial, and only passed after many years of sustained advocacy from the Socialist Party and other groups (Murray 2012). In the long debate about its merits, many supporters assumed that the proposed law would enhance the substantive representation of women's interests. For instance, an op-ed in *La Croix* claims that

[2] Personal interview, September 5, 2013, Brussels, Belgium.
[3] Renaat Landuyt, personal interview, September 23, 2013, Bruges, Belgium.
[4] Louis Tobback, personal interview, September 20, 2013, Leuven, Belgium.
[5] Hedwige Peemans Poullet, personal interview, October 4, 2013, Brussels, Belgium.
[6] Yvan Mayeur, personal interview, October 17, 2013, Brussels, Belgium

It [the quota law] also will help to put on the political agenda some different issues. On unemployment, for example, we get measures to help men who are unemployed. If there were more women in the Assembly, they would remind the Assembly that the unemployment rate is higher for women than for men. For many problems, issues concerning women would thus be taken into account more easily.[7]

Former Union for French Democracy (center-right) party secretary Anne-Marie Idrac supported the quota because "some of the most important concerns of women have not seen access to the political world. Women care much more about their jobs, their children and everyday safety, the environment, the reconciliation of working time and the family, solidarity between generations."[8]

Ireland passed a quota law in 2012 that required parties to include at least 30 percent women candidates on their ballots or face major funding cuts. The law was informed by a report on women's participation in politics published by the Justice Committee in 2009, which argues that "women bring different life experiences, priorities, knowledge and a different style of decision-making" to politics.[9] In an op-ed, first-time Fianna Fáil (centrist) candidate Laura Reid writes that she supports quotas and was motivated to run because "It will only be when a large enough proportion of elected representatives are female that challenges, interests and life experiences applicable to women will properly gain a voice and be represented."[10]

Italy has debated a quota law in parliament twice in recent years, in 2005–2006 and 2014–2015. In both cases, women Members of Parliament (MP) campaigned to include a gender quota in changes to the electoral law. While the first bill did not come to a vote because it was blocked by the majority, the more recent electoral reform of 2015 includes a 50 percent quota for women. In the debate about the quota in parliament, several women representatives made a connection between the

---

[7] "Pourquoi fallait-il inscrire la parité dans la Constitution?," *La Croix*, June 29, 1999, translation by Google Translate.
[8] "'Pour réparer l'injustice faite aux femmes, il faut modifier la Constitution' même s'il est triste d'en passer par là," *Liberation*, December 14, 1998, translation by Google Translate.
[9] Oireachtas Joint Committee on Justice, Equality, Defence and Women's Rights. 2009. "Women's Participation in Politics." www.oireachtas.ie/documents/committees30thdail/j-justiceedwr/reports_2008/20091105.pdf.
[10] "More female voices are needed in Irish politics to tackle societal imbalances," *The Journal.ie*, April 26, 2013.

historical lack of women in politics and inequality in Italian society. Annalisa Pannarale, a representative from the left-wing Left Ecology Freedom party, argued that the idea that quotas discriminate unfairly is a fallacy:

It is not true that women in this country can show what is their value and what is their quality, because there are no tools to do so. This is a country that must constantly address the gender pay gap, which sees the salaries of women drop lower and lower, this is a country that sees women in increasingly precarious contracts, where half of women do not work... where you must choose between a reproductive path or the possibility of a career.[11]

In the same debate, Paola Binetti, a representative from the Christian Democratic Union of Christian and Centre Democrats Party, suggested that persistent gender inequality is exactly why it is so important to have women in positions of political power:

The difficulty that women have balancing professional, or in this case political, engagement with family needs has been cited by many. But it is precisely for this reason that we want female presence at the highest decision-making levels; it is precisely for this reason that we hope that those policies for the family which have never been, come to be... there is a culture of thought and of difference that should be a positive enrichment for this parliament.[12]

These views are shared by the UN Committee established under the Convention on the Elimination of All Forms of Discrimination Against Women, which states: "the concept of democracy will have real and dynamic meaning and lasting effect only when political decision-making is shared by women and men and takes equal account of the interests of both."[13] These examples illustrate that quotas are often viewed as a way to promote women's inclusion as well as their political interests. Despite originating from women across the political spectrum, the themes communicated in these quotes share a striking commonality: most of them mention the need to represent women's unique life experiences, particularly the competing demands of work and family. Yet, we know very little about whether quotas produce meaningful policy change for

---

[11] Resoconto stenografico dell'Assemblea, Seduta 186 di lunedì 10 marzo 2014, author's translation.
[12] Resoconto stenografico dell'Assemblea, Seduta 186 di lunedì 10 marzo 2014, author's translation.
[13] CEDAW Committee, General Recommendation no. 23 (1997), para 14.

women. This book thus addresses a very practical policy question that has important implications for the quality of democracy: Do gender quota laws improve women's substantive representation?

1.1 THE PUZZLE: DO GENDER QUOTAS LEAD TO POLICY CHANGE?

There are three main types of political gender quotas: (1) voluntary party provisions ("party quotas"), which are often included in party statutes; (2) laws that require women to be elected (not just nominated) to certain positions ("political reservations"); and (3) laws that require all political parties to include a minimum percentage of women on their candidate lists ("quota laws"). While common in some countries, high-income Organisation for Economic Co-operation and Development (OECD) democracies do not have political reservations for women. This book focuses on quota laws because they oblige all parties in a country to comply, and thus have a greater potential for policy impact than party quotas. They also offer greater leverage to explore whether quotas truly bring about policy change, because they are imposed on some parties that did not support them.

As quotas have spread rapidly across the globe, a robust line of research has explored why gender quota laws are adopted and how they are implemented (Anderson & Swiss 2014; Araújo & García 2006; Baldez 2004; Bauer & Burnet 2013; Baum & Espírito-Santo 2012; Bjarnegård & Zetterberg 2014; Bush 2011; Fréchette, Maniquet, & Morelli 2008; Gatto N.d.; Htun & Jones 2002; Hughes, Krook, & Paxton 2015; Josefsson 2020; Krook 2009; Krook, Lovenduski, & Squires 2009; Meier 2012; Murray, Krook, & Opello 2012; Norris 2007; Palici di Suni 2012; Verge 2012; Weeks 2018). More recently, scholars have focused on the effects of quotas on women's access to political leadership roles (Barnes 2016; Kerevel 2019; Kerevel & Atkeson 2013; O'Brien & Rickne 2016), diversity in parliaments (Barnes & Holman 2020), and women's political participation and engagement (Barnes & Burchard 2013; Clayton 2015; Hinojosa & Kittilson 2020; Zetterberg 2009). Less attention has been paid to the question of whether gender quotas also enhance the substantive representation of women's interests.

There is good reason to think that quotas ought to matter. For instance, as the anecdotes from personal interviews and quota debates aforementioned illustrate, people often intuitively think that increasing the number of women in the legislature will make a difference. In addition, models of political competition and empirical studies of representation increasingly recognize the importance of identity and descriptive representation – the number of members of an identity group in political power – for the substantive representation of a group's interests. Citizen–candidate models suggest that politicians' personal preferences affect policy outcomes (Besley & Coate 1997; Osborne & Slivinski 1996). A growing empirical literature also suggests that politician identity – including race (Broockman 2013; Grose 2011), social class (Carnes 2012), and gender (Chattopadhyay & Duflo 2004), and learned behaviors like smoking (Burden 2007) – is relevant to policymaking. According to this view, politicians do not simply respond to incentives; their lived, gendered, raced, classed (etc.) experiences affect their priorities.

Gender and politics studies on women's descriptive and substantive representation have found that having more women in office often increases the representation of women's policy interests and preferences, although the specific institutional context conditions their degree of influence. Across different institutional contexts, prior research tends to find that women legislators give greater legislative attention to issues that are salient to women – such as children, the family, women's health, and social policy – than their male colleagues (Catalano 2009; Celis 2006; Childs & Withey 2004; Piscopo 2011; Swers 2005; Thomas 1994; Wängnerud 2005). In voting and policy outcomes, legislators are more constrained by institutional rules and norms, such as the role of individual legislators in the policymaking process and party discipline. For example, party is typically a more important determinant of roll-call votes than gender (Burrell 1994; Shwindt-Bayer & Corbetta 2004; Vega & Firestone 1995; Welch 1985).

As Wängnerud's (2009) review of women's descriptive and substantive representation highlights, connecting women's presence in office to actual policy outcomes is even more difficult: "the closer one gets to outcomes in citizens' everyday lives, the fewer empirical findings there are to report" (p. 63). Some studies of women's impact on policy outcomes find no evidence of significant effects (e.g., Ferreira & Gyourko 2011), or an effect only on some "gendered" policies but not others (Rehavi 2007). Yet, several prior studies show that women in office (especially those who hold cabinet-level posts) are linked to greater investment in child care and maternity leave (Atchison 2015; Atchison & Down 2009, 2019; Bratton & Ray 2002; Kittilson 2008), wage protection and equal wage polices (O'Regan 2000), and gender equality and preventing violence against women (Annesley, Engeli, & Gains 2015).

The findings from previous studies thus suggest that the relationship between women's descriptive and substantive representation is not deterministic: increasing the number of women legislators does not always translate into policy gains for women. This is partly because political parties may sometimes be incentivized to accommodate women's representative claims, but at other times might have rational reasons to ignore them. For instance, while parties may assess that it benefits them to support health care, they may be reluctant to support equal pay for fear of alienating men supporters. As Celis and Childs (2020) assert, traditional political parties have not comprehensively addressed women's issues because "the issues they prioritize are those that appeal to, or at least do not harm or repel, their established constituencies" (p. 13). Given the rapid rise of quotas and other measures to increase the representation of historically marginalized groups like women, identifying the conditions under which identity matters for policy change is critical to understanding the potential impact of such policies.

Studying the effect of gender quotas (what Dahlerup & Freidenvall 2005 calls the "fast track" to women's representation) is conceptually different from studying the impact of gradual increases in the number of women in parliament that occur over time without the help of a quota law. Quotas can either dampen or reinforce the representation of women's policy priorities. For example, they can make the political culture more accepting of women in politics, within both parliaments (Burnet 2011; Galligan, Clavero, & Calloni 2007; Xydias 2014) and among the general public (Allen & Cutts 2018; Beaman et al. 2009). They can also lead women elected via a quota to feel they have a mandate to act "for" women, making them especially likely to support women's policy interests (Franceschet & Piscopo 2008). However, women elected via a quota may feel stigmatized and seek to distance themselves from the law by avoiding women's issues (Franceschet & Piscopo 2008). Men politicians might resent them and try to prevent them from exercising political power (Hawkesworth 2003; Heath, Schwindt-Bayer, & Taylor-Robinson 2005). Quota laws also tend to increase the share of women across all parties, whereas gains in women's representation absent a quota tend to come from left-leaning parties, which are more likely to select women and put them in winnable positions (Caul 1999; Kittilson 2006).

Few studies have addressed the relationship between gender quota laws and policy outcomes across countries. Single-country case studies (e.g., in Argentina, Brazil, and Rwanda) provide valuable evidence of the link between quotas and outcomes such as women-friendly policy proposals, but the findings regarding whether quotas generate positive, lasting changes have been mixed (Devlin & Elgie 2008; Franceschet, Krook, & Piscopo 2012; Franceschet & Piscopo 2008; see Clayton 2021 for a review). For example, Franceschet and Piscopo (2008) show that gender quotas in Argentina increased the number of women's rights bills that were introduced into parliament (mostly by women), but these bills did not enjoy greater legislative success than before the quotas were introduced (see also Htun, Lacalle, & Micozzi (2013), who suggest that quotas actually made the approval of gender-related legislation less likely over time). At the provincial level in Argentina, Barnes (2016) finds that quotas, and associated increases in women legislators, can boost women's collaboration across parties particularly on issues concerning women, children, and families. Kerevel and Atkeson (2013) finds that after a quota law was implemented in Mexico women legislators are as successful as men at getting their bills passed, including bills related to gender equality.

The best evidence on the causal effect of quotas on policy outcomes comes from India. The country's constitution was amended in 1993 to require one-third of village council head positions to be randomly reserved for women. Analyses of this natural experiment seem to confirm the theory that gender quotas alter policy outcomes: women leaders were more likely to adopt laws and invest in resources that women favor – in this case, related to providing safe drinking water (Beaman et al. 2011; Chattopadhyay & Duflo 2003, 2004) – and they facilitate women's access to property rights (Brulé 2020). In high-income OECD democracies, where women have a different set of policy preferences and parties tend to exercise greater control over the behavior of individual representatives, the evidence of the quotas' impact is not as clear. For example, studies of the effects of quota laws in Spain and Italy find no evidence that quotas have significantly affected the size or allocation of local government expenditures in those countries (Bagues & Campa 2021; Rigon & Tanzi 2012).

Two studies consider the effect of quotas in a global context. Chen (2010) examines all types of quotas in over 100 countries and finds that those with quotas spend more on social welfare and health. Using more recent data, Clayton and Zetterberg (2018) find that quotas (again defined broadly) that lead to major increases in the number of women in office increase public spending on health, but not education. These studies provide initial evidence to support the argument that quotas shift policy outcomes in a global context. Building on this work, I narrow the scope to high-income OECD democracies and define clear expectations about which policies quotas ought to change in this context. Clayton and Zetter-berg (2018) purposefully avoid setting a priori expectations about policy change because in a global context in which women's preferences are not homogeneous, this would risk essentializing women's interests. I focus on rich OECD democracies because gender gaps in policy preferences are well established across this set of countries – for example, women prefer more spending on social policy, and as I will show are much more supportive of maternal employment – but not elsewhere.

1.2 THE ARGUMENT IN BRIEF

This book examines the relationship between gender quota laws and policy outcomes across high-income OECD democracies. The main argument focuses on understanding *when* and *how* quotas, and politician identity, are relevant to policy outcomes. It offers a new approach to studying women's substantive representation that takes into account not only the thorny question of how to define women's preferences but also how these preferences fit into the structure of mainstream party competition. I present a model of party incentives to address group-based demands that pinpoints the conditions under which such demands are either crystallized or ignored. Historically marginalized groups like women face high barriers to entry in politics, and their interests are especially likely to be ignored if they lie off the main left–right (class-based) dimension most parties still compete on today. This is because parties have few incentives to represent issues that detract from known positions or crosscut their constituencies – issues that divide men and women within parties. Quotas help overcome this mismatch between voter preferences and state policies – what I refer to as a "political market failure." When women's interests coincide with the left–right dimension, however, quotas are not needed for women's interests to be represented. Parties have every reason to take these issues up and gain women's votes by doing so.

Women's desire for more progressive work–family policies fits this criteria. Survey data show that perhaps the largest gender gap in preferences in rich OECD democracies relates to the issue of maternal employment (should mothers of young children work?). Women are far more supportive of mothers working than men, and the gender gap cuts across party lines. In other words, this issue unites women across parties, especially highly educated working women. The similarity in this gender gap across parties might seem surprising, but if we consider parties' track records on work–family issues it starts to make sense. Left-leaning parties have been criticized for their lack of attention to work–family policies, and center and right-leaning parties have been behind significant modernizing reforms in recent years. Parties often frame the issue differently – parties on the right might emphasize fertility or productivity, while those on the left are more likely to highlight gender equality – which blurs the lines of issue ownership (when it is addressed at all). Quotas, and increased numbers of women in office, can help correct this market failure and increase the likelihood that women's preferences are put on the political agenda and represented.

Quota laws influence policymaking in three main ways. First, they expand the leverage of women as factions within parties by increasing the number of women in office. After a quota law is implemented, an influx of women (especially a "critical mass") gives women more negotiating power to push their parties toward their collective preferences. Second, they increase the likelihood that women will be elevated to leadership roles in parties and government. Over time, quotas are likely to increase not just the number of women in parliament, but the number of women in government, who will have the power to reform policies directly. Third, they raise the salience of women's interests among men party elites, making it more likely that women's interests will be prioritized in office. An influx of women across parties and increased public attention to the role of women in politics (including media attention, particularly around election time) gives men elites new awareness of women's concerns and incentives to prioritize them.

I argue that what makes quotas different from a gradual increase in women's representation over time is that they raise the number of women *across parties*, especially on the right. This opens up a wide range of opportunities for change in parties across the political spectrum. In the cases I study, the parties most affected by gender quota laws are those on the right, which had no experience with voluntary quotas and few women in their ranks before the law. By tracing how parties on the left and right react and adapt to the inclusion of more women, the book reaches some novel conclusions about the scope of quotas' impacts. I observe the most dramatic changes to work–family positions in right-leaning parties, which previously espoused more traditional views about women's roles in the household.

1.3 METHODOLOGY

Investigating the link between gender quotas and policy outcomes requires an empirical approach that can distinguish between gender quotas, politician identity, and cultural and structural factors such as women's labor force participation and electoral rules. Moreover, any convincing explanation of policy change must be rooted in a solid understanding of both the role of identity and political decision-making processes at the internal party and national government levels. To accomplish all of these objectives effectively, this book employs a mixed-methods approach, using both statistical analysis and qualitative case studies. This approach offers the advantage of incorporating both the rigor and generality of statistical work and the causal narrative of case-based analysis. Cross-national statistical analyses establish key correlations, and careful robustness checks provide leverage for the causal interpretation of the results. Case studies assess the plausibility of observed statistical relationships between variables, and shed light on potential mechanisms.

The statistical analysis in this book aims for breadth of coverage in terms of both time periods and the number of countries included in the sample. The analysis includes over thirty years and twenty countries; coverage varies by chapter according to data availability for the dependent variable and key covariates. Extending the range of relevant dependent and explanatory variables as much as possible increases confidence in the model estimates and their potential generalizability. Large-N studies also have practical advantages, such as the ability to apply fixed effects and other advanced techniques. I restrict the sample to high-income OECD democracies because my theory is based on gender gaps in social policy preferences, which are well established in rich OECD democracies but not elsewhere. It is thus not clear that we should expect quotas, and politician identity, to influence similar policies in low- or middle-income countries. I explain this choice in further detail in Chapter 2.[14]

Statistical analysis establishes key associations between quotas and outcomes, but it cannot tell us much about the theorized causal chain linking the variables – especially since some of the mechanisms I identify are hard to operationalize with existing data. When possible, I provide statistical mediation tests to explore the indirect effect of quotas through women's representation. More frequently, however, I use case studies to disentangle the causal mechanisms at work. Matched-pair case studies compare quota and nonquota countries in detail, checking the credibility of the statistical results and examining how the processes leading to policy change compare to the mechanisms laid out in the theory. Matched-pair case selection accomplishes two key goals. First, "most-similar"

[14] "The data and replication files to reproduce quantitative analysis in the book can be found at: https://doi.org/10.7910/DVN/OBGENQ."

cases can serve as mutual counterfactuals. They provide a framework for thinking about what would have happened, all else equal, if a key treatment variable (passage of a quota law) had not occurred (Tarrow 2010). Second, matched pairs can also be used to unpack the process by which outcomes came about in each case (George & Bennett 2005; Tarrow 2010). This parallel process tracing provides important leverage for exploring causal mechanisms, which are often complex. In the next section I introduce the cases, including details on how they were selected and relevant country background information.

1.3.1   The Cases: Belgium and Austria, Portugal and Italy

Throughout the book, I use evidence from two sets of matched-pair case studies that are similar in most respects except that one country adopted a quota law and the other country did not. I chose these cases in two stages. First, I selected the "quota countries" of Belgium and Portugal because quota laws led to increases in the percentage of women in office in both countries, but in very different contexts and time periods.

Belgium's quota law was first implemented in the election of 1999. Over time it generated a large increase in the share of women elected. Figure 1.1 displays trends in women's representation in the country, before and after the law came into effect (dark solid line). The figure also shows a counterfactual version of Belgium if it had not implemented a quota law (dark dashed line). The counterfactual is approximated by a weighted average of "control" countries that have the same pre-quota characteristics (e.g., women's representation, economic development, and women's labor force participation), and thus share similar backgrounds. I use synthetic control methods to estimate the counterfactual version of Belgium (Abadie & Gardeazabal 2003; Abadie, Diamond, & Hainmueller 2014).[15]

Figure 1.1 shows that the counterfactual produced from synthetic predictions (dark dashed line) is very similar to the real trend (solid line) in women's representation before the quota law was passed. It is also clear that the "counterfactual Belgium" predicts that levels of women's representation would be lower had the country not adopted a quota law. Immediately after the law was implemented, the two lines (actual and synthetic trends in representation) begin to diverge noticeably.

---

[15] All technical details are presented in the Appendix to Chapter 1, including tables showing the comparison of pretreatment characteristics of Belgium and its synthetic version, the weights of each control country composing synthetic countries, and placebo tests to assess the robustness of the results.

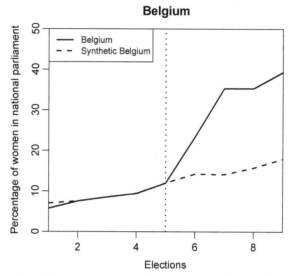

FIGURE I.I Trends in the percentage of women in parliament: Belgium versus counterfactual Belgium

Notes: Synthetic counterfactuals are based on analysis conducted using Synth for R (Abadie, Diamond, & Hainmueller 2011).

While women's representation in the counterfactual (no quota) version continues to increase slowly, the real trend (with quota) increases sharply. The discrepancy between these lines suggests that the quota law had a large positive effect on women's representation in Belgium. Only two elections after the law's passage, women's representation is estimated to have increased by more than 20 percentage points. This is likely due to the strength of the law. From 2002 it requires parties to nominate 50 percent women, the first two positions on the list must alternate by gender (known as a "zipper" list), and compliance is required for the list to be accepted. Belgium thus has a very effective quota law that has been in place for over twenty years (see also Górecki & Pierzgalski 2022 who replicate these findings for the case of Belgium).

Portugal implemented a gender quota law more recently (2009) with somewhat weaker provisions. The quota threshold is 33 percent with mandated gender alternation on the party lists, and compliance is not required for lists to be accepted (parties instead face financial penalties). It is thus no surprise that Portugal's law has had smaller estimated effects than Belgium's. Figure 1.2 shows trends in women's representation over time for Portugal before and after the quota law was implemented (dark solid line), along with the counterfactual (nonquota) version trends (dark

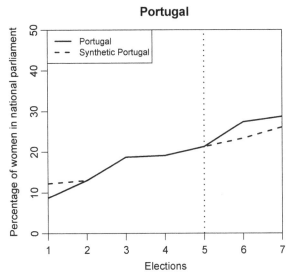

FIGURE 1.2 Trends in the percentage of women in parliament: Portugal versus counterfactual Portugal

Notes: Synthetic counterfactuals are based on analysis conducted using Synth for R (Abadie, Diamond, & Hainmueller 2011).

dashed line) estimated using synthetic control methods. As in the case of Belgium, this counterfactual version approximates levels of women's representation before the quota law was implemented in Portugal very closely. A sharp increase in the trend line occurs after the law came into effect, but the increase is smaller than in Belgium. After one election with the quota, the share of women elected increased by 4 percent; this dropped to 3 percent after two elections with the law in place. The increase is thus relatively small, although still larger than the growth expected to occur without a quota. It is worth noting that the aggregate share of women elected shown here hides large increases concentrated among parties on the right (I discuss this more in subsequent chapters). Moreover, just outside the period of comparison here, in the third election after Portugal's quota law (2015), the share of women again jumped to 35 percent.

Overall, these figures suggest that the strength of the law greatly influences its expected effects, but even weaker laws produce noticeable effects. The cases of Belgium and Portugal thus provide variation in the effectiveness of quotas on women's representation as well as the duration of use. They also advance the evidence base from high-income OECD democracies, where quota laws are on the rise, when so far much of the literature has focused on low- or middle-income countries like India.[16]

Next, I used statistical matching to select pairs for Belgium and Portugal. Statistical matching offers a transparent and systematic way to select cases when there are many relevant variables (Nielsen 2014). Methodologists are increasingly advocating matching to select paired cases (Gerring 2006; Nielsen 2014; Seawright & Gerring 2008; Tarrow 2010), and although it is a relatively new technique, several studies have employed it successfully (Genovese, Wassmann, & Schneider 2014; Glynn & Ichino 2014; Lyall 2014; Madrigal, Alpízar, & Schlüter 2011). The goal for the matched pairs (counterfactual cases) is that they should be similar to quota countries, particularly with regard to potential confounders – variables that might correlate with both quota adoption and policy outcomes related to women's interests. The matching procedure successfully identifies nonquota matches for both Belgium and Portugal. Belgium is matched to Austria, and Portugal to Italy.[17]

Belgium and Austria are both considered social democratic welfare states. They had very similar levels of economic development and women's labor force participation in the time period just before a quota was adopted in Belgium in 1994 (see Appendix Table A1.1). Before the Belgian quota law, both had relatively few women in office, but particularly Belgium (9 percent, compared to Austria's 22 percent). The two countries have similar electoral systems: both had closed-list PR systems with medium-sized districts (fourteen to twenty legislators are elected per district, on average) in the early 1990s.[18] Both countries have a strong history of Catholicism; 89 and 90 percent of the population identified as Catholic in 1980 in Austria and Belgium, respectively. Both also had political parties with voluntary quota laws, including the socialist SPÖ in Austria and the Flemish Christian democrats and social democrats in Belgium. Finally, Austria is one of the only high-income OECD democracies that has unsuccessfully proposed a quota law: the national parliament proposed a quota following the 1994 elections but it failed to pass in 1999

---

[16] I considered studying other quota countries, like France. However, France's quota law was implemented around the same time as Belgium's law (2002), and it was less effective at increasing the number of women in office, at least at first (Murray 2012).

[17] Further details about the matching procedure can be found in the Appendix to Chapter 1, including a discussion of the selection of matching variables, similarities and differences between the countries, and tables showing the data used (Tables A1.1 and A1.2).

[18] After 1995 Belgium adopted several changes to increase the importance of preference votes, so it is now considered to have an open-list system.

(Köpl 2005). This suggests that it is a particularly good counterfactual for the case of Belgium.

Portugal and Italy are Southern European countries that had similarly low levels of women in office before the Portuguese quota law was adopted in 2006 (21 and 10 percent, respectively; see Appendix Table A1.2). The electoral systems at the time were similar: both had closed-list PR systems and multimember districts. Catholicism is also very strong in both countries. The main left-wing parties in both countries had a voluntary party quota at the time (the Democrats of the Left in Italy and the Socialist Party in Portugal). The match is less close on the economy and women's employment. Italy is a higher-income country, but in Portugal a greater percentage of women are active in the labor market. However, since both of these factors are hypothesized to lead to greater levels of women's representation and higher social spending, the bias from the mismatch ought to even out. Finally, I have extra confidence in this match because – as in the case of Austria – a quota law was proposed in Italy around the same time as in Portugal but did not pass at the time.

I conducted fieldwork in all four countries from September 2013 to May 2014, interviewing a total of sixty-four key political actors. The goal was to gain knowledge about the determinants of policy outcomes in key areas of interest to women, especially work–family policies, including the role of quotas. I used a nonrandom strategy to select interviewees, deliberately choosing subjects who could offer the best evidence on the topic of quota adoption and policymaking. This includes party leaders, cabinet members, politicians, social partners, and activists with a track record of engagement on work–family policies. I interviewed twelve men and fifty-two women, a gender imbalance that reflects women's disproportionate interest and involvement in work–family policies and quotas. I spoke to men party leaders in both "treated" countries, Belgium and Portugal. Following best practice for interview research in political science (Bleich & Pekkanen 2013), full details about the sampling procedure and interview research methods, including a table of all interviews sought, obtained, and declined, are included in the Appendix (Table A1.3).

Data from these interviews are used throughout the book, but especially in Chapter 6, which focuses on how quotas lead to policy change for women. The interviews shed important light on factors that influence outcomes that are very difficult to measure or observe using existing quantitative data. This includes the views and underlying motivations of key actors, their experiences and actions directed at policy change, and the barriers they perceive to that change. Pairing the interviews with party and government documents, parliamentary proceedings, and newspaper coverage of policy debates, I provide new insights into the mechanisms that link quota laws to policy change. The interviews also help confirm the main findings of the quantitative analysis – do key political actors agree on the impact of quotas?

While it is very difficult to derive valid causal inferences from qualitative comparative research, the concept of causality as a counterfactual effect that I employ in the book's case study approach offers significant benefits for the validity and reliability of the findings (Plümper, Troeger, & Neumayer 2019). One potential problem with using interview data is that interviewees could give inaccurate information – either because they misremember or for strategic reasons (e.g., to portray their actions in a more positive light; Mosley 2013). While this misgiving can never be totally overcome, I take steps to control for this "measurement error" by being careful to convey any divergences in opinion and checking for confirmation of claims across segments of the sample frame (e.g., different parties and genders).

1.4 PLAN OF THE BOOK

The rest of this book is organized as follows. Chapter 2 provides a detailed overview of the book's theory of quotas, identity, and policy change. The chapter also develops a theory about the conditions under which gender quotas are most likely to be consequential for policy outcomes. Building on Mansbridge's concept of "uncrystallized interests" (Mansbridge 1999), my explanation focuses on the alignment of group interests with the main political cleavages in a society. I suggest that quotas ought to matter especially when group interests cut across mainstream left–right dimensions, and highlight several reasons why parties are deterred from advancing these interests if they do not have members of the group in office.

While women's preferences for policies that are well defined along party lines can be accommodated without a quota, parties have little incentive to prioritize issues that divide men and women within the party. Quotas increase the number of women in office as well as the probability that cross-cutting interests will be placed on the political agenda and taken up by parties. Quota policies also increase public awareness of and support for women in politics, which cues party elites to prioritize women's concerns in order to raise their visibility on these issues and claim credit from women constituents. I clarify key assumptions, the scope of the project, and expected external validity.

To explain the impact of quotas on policies of concern to women, it is first necessary to define women's policy preferences. Chapter 3 defines expectations about which policies we ought to expect to change following quota implementation in rich OECD democracies. Many previous studies, as well as commonsense understandings, define women's preferences a priori as conforming to stereotypes about women. My approach provides an inductive measure of women's policy preferences as the issues characterized by the largest differences in opinion between men and women. I use survey data to explore the size and direction of gender gaps in preferences on a large number of specific policy issues across nineteen OECD democracies over three decades. I find that while women prefer more spending than men on issues like health care, unemployment benefits, and inequality, no significant gender gaps emerge on other issues often perceived to be gendered, like education or military spending. The largest gender gaps in preferences exist over the issue of maternal employment: women are roughly 10 percentage points more progressive than men on this issue, and the gender gap has been growing over time. Women are also significantly more likely to prioritize work–family issues (calling it their "most important" issue in the election) than men.

Further, I show that gender gaps on the issue of maternal employment are not explained by partisan ideology. Factor analysis illustrates that preferences for maternal employment and government intervention in society (fundamental to the class-based left–right dimension in politics) are distinct issue dimensions. Gender is also a significant determinant of preferences regarding maternal employment *within* political parties across the left and right. Women have particularly strong preferences for maternal employment that do not coincide with the main left–right dimension in politics. I therefore focus on maternal employment and associated work–family policies as key outcomes of interest in the rest of the book.

Chapters 4 and 5 turn to the key question of this book: do quotas affect policy outcomes? These chapters provide cross-country evidence that they do in high-income OECD democracies. This involves two distinct components. First, how do quotas shape the substance of party agendas? Second, how do quotas affect the outcome of policies more broadly? Chapter 4 explores the relationship between quotas and political party priorities using manifesto data. I examine positive party attention to equality (including gender equality) and welfare state expansion, and then use hand-coded data from the four cases (Belgium, Austria, Portugal, and Italy) to take a closer look at the impact of quotas on different work–family policies. These issues are all characterized by a gender gap in preferences (women are more progressive in their views), but equality and work–family issues can be considered off the main left–right dimension, while welfare expansion is not. Using matching and regression methods with a panel dataset of parties in rich OECD democracies, I find that parties in countries that implement a quota law devote more positive attention to equality issues in their manifestos than similar parties in countries without a quota. No change is found for party priorities related to welfare state expansion. Evidence from the four country cases suggests that quotas lead to shifts in party attention to different work–family policies in the direction of women's preferences (more attention to child care and leave that promotes gender equality, less to cash transfers that encourage women to stay at home).

Chapter 5 tackles the question of whether quotas lead to real policy shifts. While the party position-taking stage is an important part of the policymaking process, most people ultimately judge political representation by actual policy outputs. Do quotas lead to real policy change? Using time-series, cross-national data for twenty-two high-income OECD democracies from 1980 to 2016, I examine family policy spending and composition. In line with women's preferences, I find that implementing a quota law shifts the composition of leave policies toward those that support working mothers and encourage fathers to take part in child care – namely shared parental and father-specific leave – and decrease spending on family allowances, which instead encourage women to stay at home. Specifically, quotas are linked to an additional nineteen weeks of leave that promotes gender equality (paid parental and father-specific leave over maternity-only leave). These effects are greater in countries with a larger increase (or "shock") of women elected after a quota law. No change is found for spending on issues with no gender gap in preferences, or where there is a gender gap but issues align with the main left–right dimension in politics. In short, quotas matter, although not for every issue. In line with women's preferences, gender quotas facilitate important policy shifts that support both working mothers and fathers to balance work and family.

Chapter 6 offers an explanation for why these effects occur – *how* do quotas lead to policy change in the direction of women's preferences? It draws on qualitative evidence from countries that are otherwise similar but differ on passing a quota law (Belgium and Austria, and Portugal and Italy). I first develop the logic of three potential mechanisms through which quotas could shift national-level work–family policies for women: factions, ministers, and salience. I argue that electoral quota laws amplify all three mechanisms: they increase the number of women across parties, and especially on the right, where parties have not already embraced other affirmative action measures. Quotas regenerate party demographics across the political spectrum – opening up more opportunities for change – and men across parties have to confront this change. This shift, in addition to the added salience the quota law brings to gender equality in the public and among elites, makes the effect of quotas unique from the effects of descriptive representation absent a quota.

Using evidence from the four cases, I compare key maternity, paternity, and parental leave policy legislation, tracing the origins and motivations of reforms and their links to quota adoption. I find that the relative strength of different mechanisms depends on the institutional context: where parliament is a path to government (Belgium), quotas lead to more women in ministerial portfolios that cover work–family policies. When it is not (Portugal), quotas have nonetheless led to women coordinating across parties within committees, and more women on the right have shifted their parties' positions on work–family issues. The counterfactual cases of Austria and Italy instead offer evidence of backsliding or the absence of significant policy change, particularly when women are not represented well and when parties on the far right gain government power.

Chapter 7 examines the implications of my approach to policy representation for the use of quotas to achieve gender equality, and for forms of identity beyond gender. First, the adoption of gender quota laws has important policy implications for work–family and related issues – policies that affect everyone, not just women. Second, by providing new insights into *when* and *how* identity matters, the book demonstrates that descriptive representation may be more consequential than is often assumed, even in the context of strong parties and parliamentary democracies. We just need to know where (and on which issues) to look for effects. My proposed theoretical framework can help explain why certain policy demands are likely to be underrepresented, and determine whether mechanisms to increase group representation in office might help. The chapter concludes by discussing several promising lines of future inquiry to advance knowledge in the field. Overall, the findings suggest *not* that quotas are a panacea, but that they help women across parties give voice to shared interests, and bring in new men allies to share the work of gender equality.

When Do Quotas Matter? A Theory of the Substantive Representation of Cross-Cutting Interests

The United States is one of the only countries in the world that has no federal paid parental leave, despite widespread support, particularly among women. According to a 2016 poll by the National Partnership for Women & Families, 66 percent of men and 85 percent of women would support a law to create a national paid family and medical leave fund.[1] In the 2016 election, for the first time, both major-party presidential candidates put forward paid maternity or parental leave policies. Former US President Donald Trump failed to pass a paid family leave bill, although his daughter Ivanka lobbied for a plan throughout his time in office. While Democrats say they are committed to introducing paid family leave, the issue took up only two sentences in its 2016 platform (compared to four paragraphs on providing affordable higher education, another relatively new issue). Republicans and Democrats thus now support paid family leave, although they disagree on the details of how to pay for it – but it still hasn't been prioritized. This chapter addresses two key, related puzzles that can shed light on why. First, why do some group-based demands go un- or underrepresented in politics? Second, when can gender quotas, and increased numbers of women in office, lead to policy change for women?

Women's policy preferences can be considered one of a set of new policy demands that have risen out of the transition to a service economy and changing values in postindustrial democracies. Some of these new demands have been incorporated into the political agendas in several

---

[1] www.nationalpartnership.org/news-room/press-releases/new-poll-as-the-nations-unpaid-leave-law-turns-23-nearly-four-in-five-agree-its-important-for-paid-family-and-medical-leave-to-be-next.html

democracies – for example, "new left" and ecological parties have gained power in many countries – but others have not. For example, there is a substantial unmet and gendered public demand for work–family policies (Gingrich & Ansell 2015; Morgan 2013). The spatial theory of party and voter behavior – originally made famous by Downs (1957) but also at the heart of more recent work on parties (Adams, Merrill, & Grofman 2005; Enelow & Hinich 1984; Meguid 2005; Persson & Tabellini 2005) – assumes that interests expressed by citizens get represented in politics. According to this logic, political parties gain power by addressing citizens' policy concerns and minimizing the distance between themselves and voters. Yet, many issues never make it onto the political agenda. In this chapter, I argue that the mechanism of quotas calls attention to these "uncrystallized" issues that are otherwise likely to be ignored (Mansbridge 1999).

The main argument of this book has two parts. First, I explain why some group-based demands go unrepresented by political parties. Then, I explain how quotas can encourage parties to address these issues. Understanding why some issues are underrepresented in the first place is a key part of my theory about how quotas lead to policy change, and so I begin with this question. Bringing together the literatures on gender and politics and political economy, I argue that political parties' incentives are key to understanding why some group-based demands are ignored – and why quotas are likely to have the biggest impact on these demands. I propose a model of party incentives to address group-based demands, which suggests that when new policy demands cut across the main left–right policy dimension and the group demanding change faces high barriers to entry in politics, these issues are often ignored. Parties have few incentives to address issues that do not align with the main left–right dimension in politics because they distract from their core issues and divide key constituencies. If the groups that support these issues are underrepresented in parliamentary parties and lack the resources to form a new party, the result is what I call a political market failure: The issue remains off the agenda, despite high group-based demand.

The second part of my argument suggests that gender quotas can help place women's policy interests on parties' agendas. Such quotas prevent the political dominance of men and signal a new commitment to gender-related concerns. They provide a way to bypass the traditional barriers to entry that leave women underrepresented in parties and parliaments. They also increase the number of women in legislatures *across parties*, which is important because, compared to increases in women's representation absent a quota, which tend to come from parties on the left, quotas generate more opportunities for women to shift the agendas of center and right-wing parties. When more women are elected to represent all parties, they can act as factions within their parties to negotiate for policy change. Women also become more likely to ascend to key leadership roles and become "critical actors" for change. Finally, quotas increase the salience of gender equality in politics, cueing party leaders to pay more attention to women's interests. When women are more equally represented in politics and parties are incentivized to compete on gender equality, we should expect to see policy change on the issues that women prioritize. I expect to see the largest change on issues that are both (1) characterized by a gender gap (women prefer them more than men) and (2) cut across the left–right dimension. This is because parties have strong incentives to represent women's interests that already coincide with their core ideology, without a quota.

The chapter proceeds as follows. Building on the literatures on representation, political parties, and gender and politics, in Section 2.1, I discuss how some issues gain representation (and why some do not). In Section 2.2, I present a new model of party incentives to address group-based demands. This model expands on Mansbridge's (1999) concept of "uncrystallized interests" and proposes that some issues are uncrystallized because of who is demanding them and where they fall on the main left–right political spectrum. Section 2.3 discusses how quotas can help overcome these obstacles by increasing the number of women representatives across parties and elevating gender equality issues to the national stage. In this section, I also broadly define "policy change" as the political decision-making process that leads to public policy outputs. This process involves an intricate chain of ideas, institutions, and actors, including voters, representatives, parties, and governments (Sabatier & Weible 2014). I discuss three main mechanisms through which quotas lead to policy change – factions, ministers, and salience. In Section 2.4, I outline the key assumptions on which this book's theory rests and discuss the extent to which it can be applied beyond high-income OECD democracies.

2.1 THE REPRESENTATION OF EMERGING ISSUES

The conventional starting point for thinking about policy representation is a one-dimensional spatial model in which the policy space is defined by the labor–capital conflict over economic issues. Traditional partisan politics theory holds that programmatic parties are representatives of social constituencies that are broadly defined in terms of industrial classes. In Lipset and Rokkan's (1967) classic theory, economic cleavages between the working class and upper class/business provide a basic framework for party competition and the formation of many mass party systems.[2] These cleavages became institutionalized ("frozen"); class was the most salient source of electoral competition until very recently. Importantly for women, when these cleavages were defined, they were based on a full-time male "breadwinner" model in which women stayed at home to look after the family. Thus, policies to support families often sought to uphold the income of the man as the primary earner – for example, employment-based entitlement systems rather than individualized benefit systems and public care services (Esping-Andersen 1999, 2002).[3]

Since the 1970s, high-income OECD democracies have transitioned into postindustrial societies. The growth of the service sector and women's entry into the labor force coincided with important cultural value changes that emphasized equality and individualization over materialist and security concerns (Inglehart 2008). The literature on comparative welfare states has recently posited that new issues are emerging to challenge traditional one-dimensional models of party competition (Beramendi et al. 2015; Häusermann 2006, 2010; Kitschelt 1994; Kriesi 1998). These studies maintain that class is still important (Allan & Scruggs 2004; Bartolini & Mair 2007; Benoit et al. 2006), but other issues have eclipsed economic interests. Electoral constituencies and voter interests have changed in recent decades: More high-skilled middle-class voters support left-leaning parties, while more working-class voters back right-wing, anti-immigration parties.

Prior research has demonstrated the relevance of several cleavages other than (industrial) class, such as environmentalism (Kitschelt 1988), anti-immigration (Bornschier 2010), labor market insiders and outsiders (Rueda 2005), and social and cultural professionals (Kriesi 1998). Crucially, gender has also become a relevant cleavage as the male breadwinner model has become increasingly out of touch with new social structures and values – notably the rise of women's employment, the decline in marriage rates, and changing attitudes toward gender roles in society (Edlund

---

[2] Other salient divisions in society, such as religion or urban/rural, led noneconomic cleavages to be more pronounced in some countries.

[3] Note that a "pure" breadwinner model never existed; working-class women often could not afford to stay out of the paid labor force (Pfau-Effinger 2004). However, it described the reality for the middle and upper working classes in many Western countries; it was also aspirational (Lewis 1992).

& Pande 2002; Esping-Andersen 1999; Iversen & Rosenbluth 2010). The
major issue facing women in postindustrial societies is reconciling their
increased labor force participation with continuing to do the bulk of care
work within the family (Lewis 1992; Orloff 1993). While some countries
have initiated major reforms to address this work–family balance, such
as child care resources and parental leave, the pace of change has been
very slow (Gingrich & Ansell 2015; Morgan 2013).

How have parties responded to these emerging issues, particularly with
regard to gender-related policies? The rise of "niche" parties – such as
far-right, green, and regional parties, characterized by their rejection of
the traditional class-based dimension of politics – has transformed party
systems. Niche parties have gained seats in parliaments and participated
in governments. They can influence the positions of mainstream parties
even by winning a small number of seats. In her work on mainstream
party responses to the rise of niche parties, Meguid (2005, 2008) highlights three strategies mainstream parties can use to deal with emerging
issues – advocate a similar stance in hopes of drawing voters away from
the threatening new party (accommodating strategy), ignore the issue, or
increase their opposition to the new issue (adversarial strategy). Mainstream parties base their choice of strategy on: (1) their position on the
left–right spectrum vis-à-vis the niche party and (2) their recent electoral
fortunes. In Meguid's model, mainstream parties are not pressured to
address the issue until a new party enters to make the issue dimension
salient. Otherwise, mainstream parties can continue to ignore an emerging issue without fear of consequences at the polls. This is important
for emerging issues related to gender, because women's parties tend to
be small and have trouble attracting the necessary resources to grow (I
discuss this problem in more detail Section 2.2).

Explanations of the representation of emerging issues also highlight
the role of institutions and party organization as two key factors that
determine the extent to which parties and states are able to modernize
to meet the challenges of postindustrial society. For example, electoral
constituency shifts mean that programmatic parties have had to recon-
ceptualize their core voters, and party systems that have shifted away
from the "class-mass" model have been more successful at pivoting to do
this (Kitschelt 2000b). Multiparty systems are more compatible with the
development of secondary cleavages, such as Christian democratic parties
in continental Europe (Van Kersbergen 2003), agrarian parties in Nordic
countries (Manow 2009), and left-libertarian parties in the Netherlands
and Austria (Kitschelt 1988). Another strand of literature shows that

the emergence of new needs and values in society can lead to cross-class alliances, bringing together groups that support reforms for different reasons (Häusermann 2006; Rueda 2005). These coalitions are more easily forged in consensual democracies, as Häusermann (2010) demonstrates in the case of pension reform.

Yet these arguments are somewhat unsatisfying because they cannot explain why reforms in the work–family area have been relatively anemic compared to other policy areas, especially outside of Scandinavia. For example, Gingrich and Ansell (2015) show that in many countries, women strongly support government spending on child care and work–life policies but do not feel that existing policies support it: They describe this as "a substantial, often untapped, public demand" (p. 290). It is notable that explanations of Nordic work–family generosity from the gender and politics literature stress the role of women's political agency (Lambert 2008; Skeije 1993) as well as institutional factors. For example, in Sweden, women social democrats such as Alva Myrdal, a prominent politician and the first chair of the World Organization of Early Childhood Education, played a key role in shaping the party's policies on the expansion of public child care (Bergqvist & Jungar 2000; Hwang & Broberg 1992). Morgan's (2006, 2013) work on family policies in continental Europe, where women's political representation has been much lower than the Nordic states, also suggests that politician ("critical actor") identity has played an important role in major changes. This leaves an unresolved puzzle: If new needs and values are emerging in a society, which of these cleavages will become politically salient in a given context? To solve this puzzle, I argue later, we need to consider who is demanding change (the role of group-based identity) and how the issue aligns with society's main ideological cleavage.

2.2   WHY ARE SOME ISSUES IGNORED? A MODEL OF PARTY INCENTIVES TO REPRESENT GROUP-BASED DEMANDS

The main argument about why some group demands remain under represented by parties proceeds as follows. Policy demands are translated into political articulation and outcomes based on whether the policy demand comes from groups that face high barriers to entry in politics and how group demands map onto a society's main left–right political cleavages. I understand political parties to have electoral incentives as well as commitments to ideology and preferences that are not necessarily unitary or stable. They must also respond to the evolving preferences of activists within the party (Kitschelt 1994), and these preferences are influenced by identity.

The first fundamental question is whether a group with new (or under-represented) policy demands faces systemic barriers to entry in politics. Barriers to entry are defined by both historical processes of exclusion and institutions. For example, women and ethnic minorities in many societies were historically prohibited from participating in politics, and they face ongoing challenges that relate to structural racism and sexism in society. This includes both higher costs associated with running for office (comparative lack of time and resources) and discrimination in being selected (Anzia & Berry 2011; Barber et al. 2016; Bernhard, Shames, & Teele 2021; Bird 2005; Fox & Lawless 2004; Lawless & Fox 2005; Lovenduski & Norris 1993; Rule 1987; Rule & Zimmerman 1994; Verba, Schlozman, & Brady 1995). Electing more women requires electing fewer men, and studies show that men elites are most willing to include women when it is likely to generate tangible benefits for them. Valdini's (2019) theory of the "inclusion calculation" suggests that in certain moments, such as after corruption crises and in decaying democracies, the benefit of women's inclusion can outweigh the threat to men's power.

Discrimination need not be so calculated; for example, party selectorates could avoid choosing women because they are, statistically speaking, less likely to invest in long, uninterrupted careers (Iversen & Rosenbluth 2010). Party leaders might unconsciously prefer candidates like themselves and/or have few members of the group in their professional networks (Crowder-Meyer 2013; Fox & Lawless 2010; Kanter 1977; Niven 1998; Sanbonmatsu 2006). Countries with proportional representation electoral systems might be better able to facilitate the entry of marginalized groups because smaller, niche parties can win seats, different qualities in candidates are rewarded (party loyalists rather than long tenure), and parties are conscious of presenting a more "balanced" list of candidates (Iversen & Rosenbluth 2010). Previous studies show that proportional representation increases the share of women legislators elected to office (Kittilson & Schwindt-Bayer 2012; Paxton, Hughes, & Barnes 2020; Rule 1987; Thames 2017; ?), but this effect does not necessarily extend to geographically concentrated ethnic groups (Ruedin 2009).

Groups that do not face high barriers to entry have access to resources and opportunities that allow them to participate in politics, mobilize, and even form new political parties if existing parties do not sufficiently represent their views. Groups that face high barriers to entry do not have the same means to put new issues on the political agenda. For example, forming new parties requires even more effort and resources than participating in existing parties and interest groups (Kitschelt 1988). Regardless of how parties are conceived – if they are seen as expressions of social cleavages or groups of "intense policy demanders" (Bawn et al. 2012) – dominant identity groups shape the main lines of party competition.

In practice, individuals have intersectional interests. For example, within groups of workers, there are men and women who both want more redistribution. Women workers might also want equal pay in addition to more redistribution, but men workers may not want to focus on that. How should a workers' party respond? In order to maximize their votes and avoid internal tension, the party ought to double down on the issues that can appeal to all constituents and continue to nominate candidates committed to these broad issues (Bawn et al. 2012, p. 574). This example describes the experience of women in unions and left-leaning parties in many countries. Unions have traditionally defended the wages of male breadwinners and have opposed some measures designed to promote women's employment, for fear that new issues might compete with the importance of class-based concerns (Gelb 1989; Huber & Stephens 2001). Communists also traditionally rejected feminism because it was seen to undermine the class struggle (new Reform Communists consider patriarchy to be a separate form of oppression; Keith & Verge 2016). Center-left parties were also guilty of ignoring gender equality in favor of class: This is the heart of feminist critiques of the welfare state that the "historic class compromise rested on a series of gender and racial-ethnic exclusions" (Fraser 2012, p. 5).

Returning to the example at the start of this chapter, an important reason that the United States lacks paid parental leave is that women remain underrepresented in Congress, and parties have few incentives to address these issues without their presence. The share of women in Congress in 2021 is the highest it has ever been, but women still comprise just over one-quarter (27 percent) of members. Progress on leave has historically been blocked due in no small part to the male-dominated Republican Party's views that it would be too costly or disruptive to businesses. Recently, women on the left (Kirsten Gillibrand, Rosa DeLauro, Ayanna Pressley, etc.) and right (Ivanka Trump, Kyrsten Sinema, Elise Stefanik, etc.) have been leading the fight for paid leave, with some men colleagues as well. In 2019, Ivanka Trump said her ideal plan would "go beyond" what Republicans were discussing to also include paid leave for caregiving and personal health conditions (Gontcharova 2018). She commented, "As a mother myself, of three young children, I know how hard it is to work while raising a family. ... Policies that allow women with children to thrive should not be novelties, they should be the norm."[4] This sounds remarkably similar to Democratic Senator Gillibrand's comments on the matter: "Very few members of Congress, I suspect, have dropped a child off at day care. Very few members of Congress know exactly how much daycare costs, because they didn't pay those bills. And so for a lot of members of Congress, they don't relate to the issue."[5] Women are more likely to agree on the need for paid leave and are more likely to prioritize it than men.

When historically disadvantaged groups become more equally represented in politics, we should expect to see policy change on the issues that these groups prioritize. There are several issues on which the preferences of historically disadvantaged groups do not diverge from those of dominant groups; in this case, no policy change is expected. But when there are significant gaps in policy preferences, policy ought to shift in the direction of disadvantaged group interests after their numbers increase. For example, lower levels of income and education are associated with more support for redistribution (Finseraas 2009; Lloren, Rosset, & Wüest 2015; Rueda & Pontusson 2010; Svallfors 1997); immigrant groups prefer less-restrictionist immigration policies (Mughan & Paxton 2006; Scheve & Slaughter 2001); and women favor more spending on a range of social policies compared to men across high-income OECD democracies, even controlling for class and party (Edlund & Pande 2002; Huber & Stephens 2000; Iversen & Soskice 2001; Lott & Kenny 1999; Svallfors 1997). As Chapter 3 illustrates, women are also far more supportive of maternal employment than men.

I expect the representation of disadvantaged groups to be *especially* likely to lead to policy change on issues that cut across the main left–right party dimension. This is the second key component of my argument. When issue demands coincide with existing party preferences, disadvantaged groups are likely to find allies within the established political system to represent their interests. Political parties can be effective vehicles for representing new demands related to these issues. However, when

---

[4] Ivanka Trump, Speech at the Republican Convention 2016. Transcript available at: https://time.com/4417579/republican-convention-ivanka-trump-transcript/.
[5] Senator Gillibrand interview with *Salon* magazine, February 9, 2015 (Walsh 2015).

demands cut across political parties and split their constituencies, parties have little incentive to represent them. While there is empirical evidence that voter positions now line up along two dimensions – one class-based and the other social and increasingly focused on immigration (Häusermann & Kriesi 2015; Kriesi et al. 2006, 2008) – it is less clear that parties actually compete on multiple dimensions. Van der Brug and Van Spanje (2009) find that party positions are still mainly structured by one left–right dimension that takes into account both economic and social issues (Van der Brug & Van Spanje 2009; see also Alonso & da Fonseca 2012; Budge 2001; Fuchs et al. 1990; Marks et al. 2006).

There are two reasons for parties to avoid cross-cutting demands. First, prioritizing these issues would likely cause further divisions within a party, which could lose votes as a result (Ferrara & Weishaupt 2004; Parsons & Weber 2011). As Downs (1957, pp. 110–111) argued, since parties depend on an existing constituency and are constrained by their ideological reputation, they seek to avoid exacerbating internal tensions. Second, parties cannot compete on all issues in every election. Thus, they are likely to focus on issues in which they enjoy an advantage ("issue ownership") and ignore or equivocate on those that are perceived to be difficult or unimportant (Budge, Robertson, & Hearl 1987; Rovny 2012). While voters' preferences are multidimensional, parties often compete on a single left–right "super-dimension" that incorporates only some of this diversity in preferences (Thomassen 2012). Therefore, unless the issue of women's interests in work–family policies is taken up by mainstream parties that establish clear and separate positions, it is unlikely to be represented at all.

When disadvantaged groups do gain descriptive representation, they are in a unique position to shift the salience and position of issues that the party might otherwise avoid. As Mansbridge (1999, 2015) originally argued, the level of "crystallization" of an issue is crucial in determining whether descriptive representation leads to substantive representation. She says: "In some historical moments, citizen interests on a given set of issues are relatively uncrystallized. The issues have not been on the agenda long... and political parties are not organized around them" (Mansbridge 1999, p. 643).

Mansbridge goes on to suggest that in situations in which an uncrystallized interest is up for debate, the best way to have your substantive interests represented is to choose a representative whose descriptive characteristics match your own on the issues you expect to emerge. The basic logic is that politicians rely at least in part on their own judgments to decide what issues to support and how to vote, and these judgments are informed by their identity and lived experiences. Without descriptive representatives pressing for change or a gendered institution cueing parties to compete on women's interests, parties prefer to maintain the status quo.

How do we know whether an issue is crystallized or not? In her work on the link between descriptive and substantive representation among the working class, Mansbridge (2015) argues that working-class voters are less likely to need descriptive representatives in politics compared to women or ethnic minorities because "political battles have been fought over class issues since Aristotle" (p. 263). In other words, working-class interests ought to be very well crystallized, perhaps the most crystallized in political history. While political parties have clear incentives to represent these issues, descriptive representatives may be even more committed (Carnes 2012). Issues are crystallized when they are taken up and expressed by parties; that often means when they become part of the left–right dimension. The same logic of party incentives within left–right competition explains both why some issues remain underrepresented and when descriptive representation is likely to matter most. One theoretical contribution of this book is to operationalize "uncrystallized interests" by locating group-based preferences that cut across the main left–right dimension in a society. This can help us determine when quotas and descriptive representation ought to matter most.

Table 2.1 cross-tabulates policy issues by the issue type (on the main left–right dimension or not) and the status of the group demanding change (low or high barriers to entry). It yields four ideal-type policy representation alternatives (shown in italics) and highlights an example of each. The top-left cell represents the traditional one-dimensional model of the policy space, in which the working class and wealthy diverge on economic interests. Mainstream parties have clear incentives to represent this issue, which has traditionally defined their ideological profiles. High-income individuals face particularly low barriers to entry in politics; elected officials increasingly tend to be drawn from white-collar professions and the business community (Pontusson 2015). Thus, high-income interests in keeping taxation and spending low are likely to be well represented in politics.

The bottom-left cell represents emerging policy demands that coincide with the main left–right dimension but are supported by groups that face high barriers to entry in politics. An example is women's preferences for more redistribution, which align with the interests of the working class.

TABLE 2.1 *The representation of policy demands*

		Left–right dimension		New parties emerge
	Issues well represented	On	Off	
Barriers to entry	Low	Low redistribution (high income)	Environment (environmentalists)	
	High	High redistribution (women)	Work–family conciliation (women)	
	Dealignment/ realignment			Political market failure

Notes: Cells show policy demands followed by the group demanding policy change in parentheses. The table shows four ideal-type policy representation alternatives and highlights an example of each.

These interests can and have been represented by parties without necessarily needing women's descriptive representation – that is, the process of women's realignment from right to left in postindustrial democracies, followed by parties competing to attract women voters. Some of the earliest studies on the gender gap in voting from the 1950s found that women disproportionately supported conservative and Christian democratic parties (Duverger 1955; Lipset 1960); they started moving to the left in the 1960s. As I discuss in Chapter 3, this shift has been attributed to several factors including the rise of non-marriage and divorce and the increase in women's employment in postindustrial labor markets. When marriage was the only secure livelihood for women, they were more likely to support parties that "shore up the strength and sanctity of family values" (Iversen & Rosenbluth 2010, p. 113). Over time, women became more vulnerable to income loss through divorce or non-marriage and, due to structural discrimination, were overrepresented in low-paid jobs. To compete for women's votes, left-wing parties could shore up the welfare state and public employment. Lott and Kenny's work shows that the growth of the welfare state was influenced by women voters (Lott & Kenny 1999; see also Abrams & Settle 1999; Bertocchi 2011; Miller 2008).

The top-right cell represents the opposite scenario: emerging policy demands that do not coincide with the main left–right dimension but are supported by groups that face low barriers to entry in politics. An example is environmental concerns, an issue associated with rising post-materialist values in recent decades. Environmentalists struggled to work within mainstream parties and were initially ignored. Social democratic parties found it difficult to address the issue given an electorate of blue-collar workers and young, post-materialist voters, while conservative parties were divided between business and a new, liberal middle-class electorate. As a result, green parties emerged in the 1970s to represent these interests, using the mantra: "We are neither Left nor Right, we are out in front" (Dalton 2009).

Importantly, environmentalists – mostly well educated and middle class – had the resources and opportunities necessary to form these new parties (Kitschelt 1988). Because environmentalists faced low barriers to entry in politics, they could successfully compete with mainstream parties. Many mainstream parties only began to incorporate environmental concerns into their agendas after green parties became a significant threat – which is consistent with how mainstream parties have responded to the rise of anti-immigration parties (Harmel & Svåsand 1997; Meguid 2005; Norris 2005). Many argue that these issues are no longer orthogonal but have become part of the main left–right political space (Dalton 2009; Spoon, Hobolt, & De Vries 2014).

The bottom-right cell of Table 2.1 represents political market failure – that is, a salient political interest that is underrepresented in the mainstream policy space. In this scenario, groups that face high barriers to entry in politics have policy concerns that lie off the main left–right dimension. The example I use is women's interests in work–family conciliation policies like paid parental leave and child care. Like environmental issues, work–family policies might detract from traditional class-based concerns, so mainstream parties have few incentives to represent them. Moreover, as I will show, the gender gap in preferences on maternal employment cuts across partisan identities. Across left and right parties, women support mothers of young children working significantly more than men do. Parties are therefore likely to downplay the issue because it could exacerbate internal divisions.

Work–family policies are not clearly identifiable with either left- or right-wing parties. Ideologically, the issue seems to be a fear that gender will compete with traditional class concerns. Indeed, left-leaning parties have been criticized for their indifference to problems facing working mothers (Perrigo 1996; Von Wahl 2006). The right is not clearly opposed to investing in these policies; it has been influential in making work–

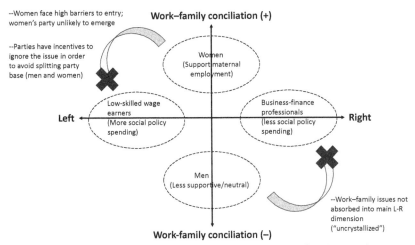

FIGURE 2.1 Party avoidance of orthogonal issues (work–family conciliation)

family policies more progressive in several cases, such as Germany and Austria's recent reforms led by Christian democratic parties. In their work on women's descriptive and substantive representation across parties in high-income democracies, Espírito-Santo, Freire, and Serra-Silva (2020) suggest that issues that disproportionately affect women, including reconciling work and family life, "have always been polarized within Christian democratic parties" in some countries (p. 231). Opposing parties often ground their support for work–family policies in different normative frameworks. Parties on the right and center-right take a market-oriented approach, describing such policies in the context of the need for continued fertility and economic productivity, while those on the left are more likely to frame the issue as one of gender equality. In other words, parties in many countries have not articulated distinct and opposing positions on the issue: they are relatively "uncrystallized."

Why don't women form parties to address these concerns, as environmentalists did? There are relatively few examples of women's parties, none of which has enjoyed significant electoral success (Cowell-Meyers 2016b).[6] Women face high barriers to entry in politics, and forming a party is even more difficult than participating in the established party framework. Japan has one of the largest women's parties. The People's Political Network (*Netto*) runs in local elections in big cities and

[6] A well-known example is Iceland's Women's Alliance Party, which entered parliament in the 1980s. At its highest point (1987) it gained 10 percent of the seats in parliament.

surrounding suburban areas; while all of its candidates are women, the top leaders are all men (Shin 2016). Research on women's parties in other countries shows that a lack of resources, including low salaries, an inability to hire staff, and lack of support beyond membership (e.g., in the business community or unions) represent serious obstacles preventing women's parties from thriving (Cowell-Meyers 2016a). By contrast, while women now tend to make up a large share of green party members and voters (Dolezal 2010), at their founding most green parliamentary parties and leadership were men dominated (e.g., in Germany see Kolinsky 1988, in France see Cole & Doherty 1995).

Perhaps more importantly, women's parties are an unlikely electoral threat because women's interests are largely heterogeneous, which might be considered another barrier to entry. As the next chapter shows, on many issues men and women have the same interests, or women's interests correspond to existing party ideologies. It is unclear that women's preferences on the issue of maternal employment (or other specific issues) are enough to outweigh the numerous other issues that are well represented in the established party system. They have been in the past: for example, women's suffrage was an issue salient enough for women to successfully organize around. Morgan-Collins (2019) found that when a strong women's suffrage movement was present, newly enfranchised women in the United States were successful at voting out incumbents who did not share their interests (in this case, the issues included children and public schools, and prohibition). Absent a fight for fundamental rights, women's heterogeneity on a range of key issues means women's-only parties struggle to attract large constituencies (see also Htun, Lacalle, & Micozzi 2013 for an argument that shared oppression is what unites women as an identity group).

This also explains why women do not tend to punish parties at the polls. When mainstream parties exclude cross-cutting issues from the agenda, and women are unlikely to form a party with sufficient resources to threaten the mainstream, there are few political alternatives. Figure 2.1 illustrates the political space when parties are faced with an orthogonal issue, but no electoral threat from a new party or movement emerging (work–family conciliation). Absent a shift in the lines of party competition, the gendered demand for work–family policies ought to remain largely underrepresented in politics. It is better for parties to avoid these issues than to risk splitting their voter base and drawing attention away from core issues. In summary, some issues remain off the agenda ("uncrystallized") because they are supported by groups that lack political power and the issues do not align well with existing left–right ideology, giving parties strategic reasons to ignore them.

2.3   THE EFFECTS OF QUOTAS

Increased descriptive representation is likely to influence all policies that an historically disadvantaged group prioritizes (the bottom row in Table 2.1). Adding more descriptive representatives to political parties gives them more opportunities to place their preferences onto mainstream party agendas. However, I expect descriptive representation to be associated with greater changes to policies that cut across the main left–right dimension (bottom-right cell of Table 2.1). This is because parties are unlikely to represent these interests at all, absent descriptive representation of the relevant groups. Parties are likely to have *already* taken up other preferences that coincide with the main left–right dimension in order to maximize their electoral gains. Insofar as these preferences coincide with the main left–right dimension, parties have incentives to address them, making the added value of descriptive representatives less significant on these issues.

The discussion so far has emphasized the role of gender identity as a potential determinant of policy outcomes, but it has not explained how quotas as a gendered institution can influence change. This question is particularly important in high-income OECD democracies, where most countries that have passed a quota law have parliamentary systems. This is perhaps the "most difficult" institutional setting because scholars have historically assumed that the primary mechanism of representation is the unitary political party (Barnes 1977; Dalton 1985; Esaiasson & Heidar 2000; Sartori 1968). In parliamentary systems, decision-making is highly institutionalized and party discipline is strong, so individual politicians have less power to influence outcomes. In this section, I propose three main mechanisms through which quotas, and the increased numbers of women across the political spectrum that they produce, will lead to policy change. In subsequent chapters, I elaborate on how these mechanisms apply at different stages of the policymaking process, using case studies to explore their plausibility.

I expect that quotas will impact policymaking through three key mechanisms – factions, ministers, and salience. The first two are both related to increasing the number of women in parties. Women have greater

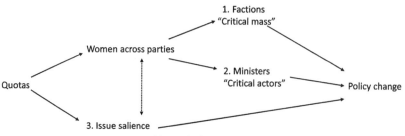

FIGURE 2.2 Causal logic linking quotas to policy change

bargaining power within parties and direct influence over policies as their numbers in parliamentary parties and government increase. The third mechanism (salience) can directly link quotas to policy change by incentivizing men party elites to compete on gender equality issues, but salience is also likely heightened or lowered by the extent to which quotas increase the number of women in political parties around men party elites. Figure 2.2 illustrates the causal logic of these three mechanisms and each is described later in turn.

The first mechanism, *factions*, is now commonplace in many party systems (Greene & Haber 2014; Harmel et al. 1995), and internal ideological conflict can explain why parties might not shift their policy positions to maximize the women's vote share. For example, conservative Catholic factions might make parties more reluctant to adopt progressive initiatives with regard to gender and the family (Celis 2007; Morgan 2006). Strong women's sections, women's committees, or other informal groups or networks are often key to shifting party agendas toward women's interests (Allen & Childs 2019; Kittilson 2011), although even without a formal or informal group women can work together to achieve change (e.g., in parliamentary committees). To explain changing Christian Democratic Union (CDU) policies toward women in Germany, Wiliarty (2010) suggests that internal interest group politics were critical – namely, the strength and position of the women's section in the party, the Women's Union. The CDU Women's Union was able to pass paid parental leave in the 1980s because the group was united behind the policy goal and held a position in the dominant party coalition. Even when the Women's Union did not have a position in the dominant party coalition in the 1990s, it was able to pass a law guaranteeing all children a place in a state-funded Kindergarten by mobilizing other key groups and carefully framing the need for child care as related to the party's opposition to abortion.

There are many other examples of women organizing within parties to successfully change policy for women – especially related to work–family policies. For example, women in the UK Conservative Party successfully lobbied the party leadership to emphasize education spending and child care packages in the 2001 electoral program (Lovenduski 2001). Similarly, the women's section of the Dutch Christian democratic party "challenged the party's longstanding traditionalism and favored measures that promoted women's economic independence and greater choice in matters of child care and work" (Morgan 2006, p. 91). A "critical mass" of women that is created within a party after a quota law is implemented could have more leverage to push the party to shift positions or simply prioritize existing positions related to women's interests (Kanter 1977). In a more gender-balanced environment (many scholars use the 30 percent women benchmark), women may be encouraged to speak out on behalf of women's interests, and men may be more open to their views.

The second mechanism, *ministers*, focuses on the role of women in ministries that shape work–family policies in particular – typically labor, social affairs, or gender equality portfolios. It is based on the logic that increasing the number of women in parties makes it more likely that they will advance to positions of power in the government and party leadership, where they can influence policies more directly. While the factions mechanism focuses more on critical mass, the ministers mechanism suggests that quotas make it more likely that "critical actors" will be appointed (Childs & Krook 2009; Krook 2015). As Annesley and Gains (2010) point out, the core executive in government is "the most significant venue for achieving the substantive representation of women" (p. 909).

An important point with regard to both the factions and ministers mechanisms is that quota laws tend to increase the number of women legislators *across parties*. In many countries (e.g., Portugal), quotas increase the share of women more in parties on the right (including center-right Christian democratic parties) than those on the left – which often had voluntary quotas already. This leads to a more balanced level of women across parties than gradual growth absent a quota, which is most often driven by left-leaning parties. While left-wing parties have been linked to a range of feminist policy outcomes, for example, reproductive rights and equal employment policies (Htun & Weldon 2018; Huber & Stephens 2000; Mazur 2002), recent scholarship highlights the role of women in Christian democrat and conservative parties in promoting policy change for women (Celis & Childs 2014; Morgan 2013; O'Brien 2018; Xydias

2013). O'Brien (2018) finds that the link between women's descriptive representation in the parliamentary party and women-related terms in the party's manifesto is strongest within Christian democratic parties. Similarly, in their study of ten European countries, Celis and Erzeel (2015) find that MPs in liberal, conservative, and Christian democratic parties make up a significant share of legislators promoting women's issues. Connecting this back to my expectations about maternal employment as an orthogonal issue, this means that quotas bring in more (educated, working) women MPs and ministers on the right who are likely to introduce new approaches to work–family policies to their previously men-dominated parties. Compared to increases in representation without a quota, quotas open up more opportunities for change within parties across the political spectrum.

The third mechanism, *salience*, focuses on the changing incentives of men political elites after the implementation of a quota law. In previous work, I show that increasing competition between and within parties can lead men elites to support gender quota legislation (Weeks 2018). Where there is a rising party on the left or conflict over candidate selection between local and central party leaders, quotas can be a useful strategic tool to unify the party and increase its electoral competitiveness. Competition thus cannot be said to be exogenously imparted by the quota law, at least not completely. However, adopting and implementing a quota law exposes political elites across all relevant parties (including those that did not support it) to increasing competition on gender equality. It raises the salience of gender equality by putting it on the national agenda, increases media attention and scrutiny, and ultimately puts pressure on men elites to increase the amount of attention the party devotes to women and their interests. In line with previous research which finds that increasing competition within and between parties can open doors for reforms that benefit women (Baldez 2004; Teele 2018; Weeks 2018; Weeks et al. Forthcoming), I argue that one way in which quotas affect political outcomes is by increasing the salience of gender-related issues and cueing party leaders across the political spectrum to prioritize them.

Regardless of the number of women in office, parties might interpret the growing support for women in politics signaled by the adoption of a quota law as a cue to better represent women's interests and claim credit from women constituents (Mayhew 1974). Quotas can put women's political issues on the radar of men elites who may not have appreciated the importance of certain policies to women, even if the party had taken "women-friendly" policy positions in the past. As Laver explains, "there is a clear distinction between a person's position on an issue and how salient he or she feels this issue is" (Laver et al. 2003, p. 70). Clayton and Zetterberg (2018) point out that all legislators who have voted on quota adoption have been exposed to new gendered debates about representation, often hearing from women's organizations and women party activists. As a consequence, they suggest that the quota itself sends important cues to politicians about women's policy priorities: "the introduction of quota policies may draw attention to gender equality issues more broadly and thus to issues prioritized by women citizens" (p. 919).

Previous studies offer examples of gender quotas increasing the salience of women's representation among both the general public and elites. For example, studies of political party quotas in Germany find that they raise legislators' attention to women's interests (including men legislators), possibly because "candidate selection processes that include quotas socialize legislators into awareness of gendered inequalities" (Xydias 2014, p. 11; see also Xydias 2007). In their analysis of public opinion before and after an electoral quota law was implemented in Uruguay, Hinojosa and Kittilson (2020) find that women citizens notice an improvement in the descriptive representation of women after the law is implemented (even if the majority still believe it is too low). Their interviews with elites confirm that the quota was believed to have had important effects by many politicians. One interviewee claimed that, "If it weren't for the quota law the topic of women's participation in politics wouldn't have been part of the debate" (cited in text, p. 87). News articles often mentioned the quota, for example, circulating numerous photographs of the women who were newly elected to parliament. These visible gains in women's representation are linked to increases in women citizens' political interest and knowledge. Finally, corporate board quotas have been found to exert similar salience effects among company leadership. Latura and Weeks (Forthcoming) find that corporate board quotas significantly increase attention to gender equality issues in workplace policies, and significant effects are observed even before more women enter boards.

Building on these findings, I expect that quotas signal the importance of gender equality and women's preferences. Even parties that were openly opposed to the quota might feel an added incentive to highlight and/or develop their policy positions to address these issues as a sort of defense mechanism, so as to not to appear outdated. When it comes to addressing such issues, men party leaders benefit from the advantage of "gendered leeway": while women politicians are expected to address women's issues and can be blamed for not doing so, men politicians are not and get credit if they do (Bergqvist, Bjarnegård, & Zetterberg 2018). Thus, men leaders, "are in a position that allows them to let strategic concerns play into their decisions about when to engage in women's substantive representation" (Höhmann & Nugent 2021, p. 5).

As Figure 2.2 shows (dotted line), rising issue salience could directly link quotas to policy change, but the effect of salience might be heightened even more with increasing numbers of women in the party and cabinet. The physical presence of more women in parties is likely to reinforce the message that women's interests matter. Finally, policy changes that are aligned with women's preferences could have their own effects on future outcomes by creating new constituencies (e.g., users of shared parental leave, women in the workforce), increasing demand further and setting in motion a chain of greater policy responsiveness on these issues. I explore these dynamics further in the empirical chapters.

How are these three mechanisms likely to play out over time? Quota laws do not always immediately increase the numbers of women in parliamentary parties. Previous studies suggest that strong enforcement mechanisms, like requiring parties to comply with the quota law for electoral lists to be accepted and requiring parties to alternate men and women on the party lists, enhance quota laws' effectiveness (Schwindt-Bayer 2009). Over time, my interviews suggest that even those parties that did not vote for the law become more likely to comply with it. For example, in a personal interview Portuguese center-right (PSD) MP José Mendes Bota told me that, "after all these years, nobody else is now opposing the law... it became natural."[7] It might take even more time for quota laws to increase women ministers, because political experience is often a prerequisite for being considered for cabinet appointments, especially in parliamentary democracies (Annesley, Beckwith, & Franceschet 2019). I thus expect the mechanisms of factions and ministers to link quotas to policy change over the long term.

While quota laws do not always increase women in political parties right away, they increase the salience of the issue of gender inequality immediately. Legislators in all parties, even those that did not agree with the quota law, are exposed to a national debate about women's representation and increased public attention to – and support for – the issue. Studies suggest that gender quotas attract media attention to (the lack of)

---

[7] José Mendes Bota, personal interview, November 7, 2013, Lisbon, Portugal.

women in politics (Sacchet 2008; Sénac-Slawinski 2008), and that quotas can change public opinion about the role of women in politics in a positive direction (Beaman et al. 2009; Burnet 2011). Such shifts in media attention and public attitudes are likely to affect the incentives and strategies of party leaders. Specifically, elites might use party manifestos to associate the party with women's policy concerns in order to raise their visibility on these issues and claim credit from women constituents (Mayhew 1974). It is also possible that changing norms are internalized by party elites themselves (who come to believe that more balanced representation is normatively appropriate), regardless of electoral incentives. Therefore, I expect that the mechanism of salience links gender quota laws to policy agenda change in the short term.

In summary, gender quotas are most likely to influence policies that are preferred by women across parties – issues that are characterized by a gender gap and also cut across the main left–right dimension in politics. Thus I expect quotas to lead to changes in policies related to helping mothers of young children return to work – an issue that meets both of these criteria – but not, for example, overall social spending, an issue characterized by a gender gap but which is also squarely on the left–right dimension.

2.4 ASSUMPTIONS AND SCOPE

As described earlier, the logic of policy change makes three main assumptions about the relationship between gendered preferences, politician identity, and policymaking power. I discuss each assumption in turn before concluding with a discussion of the extent to which I believe this theory applies beyond rich OECD countries.

First, women elected to office are assumed to have the same general preferences as women in the general public. Research comparing elite and mass preferences finds that there is congruence between the preferences of women politicians and citizens (Campbell, Childs, & Lovenduski 2010; Clayton et al. 2019; Wängnerud 2000). Campbell, Childs, and Lovenduski (2010) conclude that in the United Kingdom, "in terms of attitudes to traditional gender roles, on average men and women differ, and women representatives are more like women voters and male representatives are more like male voters" (p. 194). However, it is also true that women elected to parliament are likely to be more educated than average women in the population (e.g., Besley, Pande, & Rao 2005; Matthews 1984; Norris 1995). In general, I expect that this means women MPs will be even more likely to prioritize women's concerns for work–family conciliation because gender gaps on maternal employment increase with the level of education (see Chapter 3). However, this does raise concerns about whether quotas – and increased numbers of educated, professional, and most likely privileged women – can represent the interests of women in general.

Second, the gender gaps in preferences that I measure are assumed to apply to women as a group, which ignores potential intersections of gender and other forms of identity like race and class. To measure gender gaps in preferences, I use a dichotomous variable of gender identity. However, it is important to acknowledge that women are not a homogeneous group and that there might be important variations in preferences among women. I try to overcome some of these problems by testing whether gender differences in preferences persist even after controlling for other social categories like age, class, and occupational status, but unfortunately data are not available for other identities of interest such as ethnic minority status across democracies. My results suggest that more women than men, across a variety of subgroups, support maternal employment. Because women and men have different preferences, increasing the number of women in parliament should increase the average presence of attitudes that are favorable to women's preferences. Still, it is possible that gender gaps on specific policy questions, like support for family allowances, might not be consistent across different social groups (e.g., class), and we lack good comparative data on these questions. If this is the case, trade-offs may emerge in which educated, professional women benefit at the expense of lower-income women. I consider potential differences within the broad category of women further in the relevant empirical chapters.

Finally, the women elected to office as a result of a quota law are assumed to have power equal to that of their peers. My theory of policy change expects that women elected after a quota law is passed will have sufficient agency within the party to advocate for their interests. Although the notion that quotas will lead to less qualified candidates is common, the empirical literature rejects these arguments. Quotas are not associated with lower candidate quality (Allen, Cutts, & Campbell 2016; Murray 2010; O'Brien 2012); in fact, women elected via a quota have been found to be more qualified than their peers on several measures (Besley et al. 2017; Weeks & Baldez 2015). Another concern is that quotas could create "token" women who are marginalized and play little role in the legislative process (Bauer & Britton 2006). Again, most evidence suggests that this is not the case; women elected via quotas do not seem to confront more obstacles than other women in parliament, as we would expect if they were mere placeholders (Devlin & Elgie 2008; Kerevel & Atkeson 2013; Xydias 2009; Zetterberg 2008; but see Clayton, Josefsson, & Wang 2014). One caveat is that women elected via a quota are more likely than their peers to be newcomers to national parliaments (Weeks & Baldez 2015), and for any newcomer it takes time to build up a reputation and seniority within the party. My model of policy change is sensitive to these concerns. It predicts that women MPs will lead to policy shifts primarily through the leverage that added numbers give them to lobby party leaders for change. In subsequent chapters I use case studies to investigate the plausibility of this mechanism, and I also explore whether quotas lead to more women in positions of power over time.

As for the scope of the theory, I expect my model of quotas and policy change to hold in parliamentary systems with strong parties. It could thus apply to many countries outside of high-income OECD democracies, provided there are significant gender gaps in policy preferences. The dynamics of party politics and policymaking in parliamentary and presidential systems vary considerably. Parties are less disciplined in presidential/majoritarian systems, which gives individual representatives more power to propose bills and affect the party's agenda (Carey 2007; Shugart 1998). In this context of weak parties, the argument that quotas influence policy change by giving women more leverage within the party would not be appropriate. The stages of the policymaking process are different, and thus require different approaches. For example, in parliamentary systems it is important to consider party-level policy change, such as manifesto promises, whereas in presidential/majoritarian systems bill proposals and roll-call votes are likely to be more important.

Finally, quotas and other mechanisms designed to increase the number of women in politics are only one method of advancing women's substantive interests. Social movements, transnational networks and policy diffusion, and macro-level variables like culture and socioeconomic development are all important mechanisms that have been linked to changes in women's interests and preferences. In subsequent chapters I account for some of these variables as potential confounders of the relationship between quota adoption and policy change. For example, in Chapter 5 I discuss the role of women's movements in driving quota adoption or work–family policy change, and conclude that women's movements do not play a strong role in the high-income OECD democracies under consideration here. Future research should directly compare the effects of quotas or women in parliament to these other factors on a range of issues to broaden the theory about identity and policy change, and make it more precise (Wängnerud 2009).

The following Chapters 4, 5, and 6 build on and test these theoretical insights using data from parties and governments in wealthy OECD democracies. But first, Chapter 3 explores the empirical question of women's preferences. It provides initial evidence that supports my expectations about the preferences of women, and the alignment of these preferences with the main left–right policy dimension in high-income OECD democracies.

3

What Do Women Want? Gender Gaps in Preferences

What are women's preferences? How can we measure them? A large literature in gender and politics focuses on the meaning and measurement of women's political interests and preferences – after all, "we need to know what women want before we can assess how well politicians represent them" (Baldez 2011). There is no consensus on which specific policies should be identified as "women's," and scholars often use terms like "women's interests" and "women's issues" interchangeably to describe a set of policies that women ought to favor. Some question whether "women's interests" exist at all, given the vast heterogeneity within this group (Weldon 2002; Young 1997), and those that do study this concept base their definitions on a wide variety of criteria. Some scholars rely on feminist theory, defining a women's interest as one that promotes women's rights and equality, such as reproductive rights (Franceschet & Piscopo 2008; Htun, Lacalle, & Micozzi 2013). Others use women's interest group demands as a reasonable proxy for women's interests; these often overlap with feminist issues (Swers 1998; Washington 2008) but not always (e.g., see Schreiber 2002 on conservative women's groups). Finally some authors define women's interests as those that were traditionally part of the private sphere, and thus women's domain, including policies related to education, children, and families (Funk & Philips 2019; Sapiro 1981; Swers 2005).

These definitions each have important strengths. For example, as Dovi (2007) argues, feminist policies (those that promote gender equality and the elimination of gender hierarchies) are an objective good regardless of what men and women think about them. Studying support for feminist policies and the conditions under which they are adopted is thus important for furthering the quality of our democracies. However, not all women are feminist, and feminist issues are not always supported by women any more than they are by than men. Abortion is a good example. It fits the criteria of many definitions of women's interests: it is the subject of feminist theory about women's rights and autonomy, women's interest groups often focus on it, and it is intimately linked to women's bodies. Yet, it does not fit the criteria of a gender gap in preferences.

Survey data from the United States typically shows no difference in men's and women's opinions on abortion; in some recent years men have reported being more supportive of abortion with no limits than women (Smith & Son 2013). Partisan differences, however, are large (Adams 1997). For example, Barnes and Cassese (2017) shows no gender gap on abortion among Republican voters. This means that while progressive change to liberalize abortion policy in the United States would represent the preferences of left-leaning voters, it would not necessarily represent the preferences of all women. While fewer studies address attitudes toward abortion outside of the United States (where the issue is especially politically polarizing), analysis of gender differences in support for abortion using data from the World Values Survey does not reveal significant gender gaps in Western Europe. Indeed, in the Netherlands and Spain the opposite trend is observed (men are more accepting than women) (Loll & Hall 2019).

Beckwith's (2011, 2014) theoretical distinction between women's *interests*, *issues*, and *preferences* provides a useful framework for measuring gender gaps. She defines *interests* as fundamental to women's life chances. Since identifying interests requires women's autonomy and political participation, it is a normative judgment. The absence of women in positions of political power, especially those from non-majority groups (race, class, and so on), makes identifying interests very difficult. As Beckwith (2011) describes, men's dominance in politics "constitutes a context of *political drag* on the identification of women's interests" (p. 425, emphasis in original) – that is, if women are not organizing around an issue, we cannot simply assume it is because it is not considered a "woman's interest." One example of a normative interest that unites women across subgroups and over time is being free from violence. *Issues* are strategic choices that emphasize components of interest as points of mobilization, such as legislation that criminalizes domestic violence. Finally, *preferences* are discrete and limited alternatives that actors choose from. For example, these could include preference alternatives over the role of the state in criminalizing domestic violence, the consequences that should incur, and so forth.

In this book, I am primarily concerned with women's *preferences*. I advocate an inductive approach to defining women's (rather than feminist) preferences based on gender gaps in survey data. This approach addresses recent concerns that women's interests are context dependent, rather than defined a priori and stable over time (Celis 2008; Smooth 2011). It gives women agency, and takes conservative claims to represent women seriously. As Childs and Celis (2018) explain, existing theories of women's substantive representation often conflate this notion with *feminist* substantive representation. Combining these concepts limits our understanding of representation because, as the previous discussion of preferences on reproductive rights illustrates, women on the right often do not identify with feminist claims. An inductive approach allows me to measure not only whether the issue is characterized by a gender gap in preferences, but whether this gender gap cuts across parties. This is a critical component of my theory, because I argue that gender quotas have the unique advantage of increasing the number of women legislators across parties. I thus expect quotas to influence policies that women prefer, conditional on these policy preferences existing among women as a group within both left- and right-leaning parties.

In this chapter I map gender gaps in preferences across a variety of issues, which provides evidence of women's strong and orthogonal preferences for maternal employment. I then connect the findings from survey data to the literature on the determinants of work–family policies, which suggests that descriptive representation is a more important determinant of work–family policy change than party ideology. Together, the findings build empirical support for the expectation that gender quotas ought to matter, particularly for work–family policies that encourage maternal employment.

3.1 WOMEN'S SHIFT TO THE LEFT

While women are not a monolithic group, there is substantial evidence that women and men have different preferences on at least a subset of issues in rich OECD democracies. Some of the earliest studies from the 1920s to 1950s found that women tended to vote along with their husbands or in some cases more conservatively (Corder & Wolbrecht 2016; Duverger 1955; Lipset 1960). Women now support left-wing parties in greater numbers (Abendschön & Steinmetz 2014; Edlund & Pande 2002; Emmenegger & Manow 2014; Giger 2009; Inglehart & Norris 2000; Norris 2003; Studlar, McAllister, & Hayes 1998) – particularly young cohorts of women (Shorrocks 2018). One recent study (using 2008 survey

data) finds that the only countries in Western Europe that are *not* characterized by the modern gender gap (women further to the left than men)
are Ireland and Portugal (Abendschön & Steinmetz 2014).

Related to the gender gap in voting, a large and consistent literature shows that women prefer more social spending and redistribution
than men in high-income OECD democracies (Alesina & Giuliano 2011;
Dallinger 2010; Eger & Breznau 2017; Iversen & Soskice 2001; Svallfors 1997). There are even gender gaps on welfare and social spending
within right-wing voters (e.g., Barnes & Cassese 2017). These gender
gaps are thought to be very much related to the shift from an industrial
to postindustrial society. The modern gender gap might reflect the decline
of marriage, the rise in the divorce rate, and corresponding higher poverty rates for women in recent years, or women's increasing labor force
participation and associated need for affordable care services (Edlund &
Pande 2002; Iversen & Rosenbluth 2010). Both theories suggest that, due
to historical discrimination and the structure of markets in rich OECD
democracies, women benefit more than men from government spending.

There is no similar consensus on gender gaps in preferences outside
of rich OECD democracies, where the issue has received less attention and the political context is often very different. Survey data from
Latin America reveals the persistence of "traditional" gender gaps in
voting (women voting to the right of men) and women identifying themselves as more ideologically conservative than men (Morgan 2015).
Many formerly communist countries also still exhibit the traditional
gender gap in voting, like Slovakia, the Czech Republic, and Poland
(Abendschön & Steinmetz 2014). Where state capacity to provide large-
scale welfare programs is low, and political parties are not necessarily
organized around redistribution as the main left-right cleavage, it is
unlikely the same gender gaps in preferences would emerge. In these
contexts, studies have focused on gender gaps in preferences for local
level goods and services. For example, in Pakistan and India men and
women tend to prioritize goods and services that benefit them more;
women prioritize drinking water, while men are more likely to prioritize roads (Chattopadhyay & Duflo 2004; Kahn 2021; Prillaman 2021).
In African countries, also, women are more likely to prioritize drinking
water and poverty alleviation than men (Gottlieb, Grossman, & Robinson 2016). More work is needed to unpack gender gaps around the
world, but I focus on high-income OECD democracies here because
the well-established gender gaps provide a good context for testing my
theory.

While the gender gap over redistribution in rich OECD democracies is well known, less attention has been paid to the gender gap in specific policy preferences, especially in comparative perspective. That is, studies tend to examine one policy area at a time rather than compare the gender gap across policies.[1] For example, Iversen and Rosenbluth (2006) provide evidence of a large gender gap in support for public employment (women are more supportive than men) that is conditioned by a country's skill system and divorce rates. While gender is not their main focus, Busemeyer and Neimanns (2017) show that women prefer greater government responsibility for public child care services. Women are also more likely than men to perceive gender inequalities (e.g., to believe that equality between the sexes has not gone far enough), and tend to be more supportive of the women's movement (Campbell, Childs, & Lovenduski 2010; Hayes, McAllister, & Studlar 2000; Simon & Landis 1989).

3.2 MAPPING GENDER GAPS

In order to identify the policy areas with the largest gender gaps in preferences, I analyze survey data from four waves of the International Social Survey Programme's (ISSP) Role of Government survey (1985, 1990, 1996, and 2006) and four waves of the ISSP's Family and Changing Gender Roles survey (1988, 1994, 2002, and 2012). The ISSP offers perhaps the best comparable data on attitudes toward specific social policies. The Role of Government survey covers attitudes toward government spending in different areas, as well as attitudes toward the government's broader role in society. The Family and Changing Gender Roles survey covers attitudes toward the employment of women and mothers. Across both surveys, my sample includes over 140,000 respondents from nineteen countries. Both survey modules are designed to be nationally representative, gathering stratified random samples of adult respondents from each country.[2] Appendix Table A3.1 lists which countries and years are included in each survey wave.

---

[1] Exceptions include Barnes and Cassesse (2017), who compare gender gaps on a wide range of issues within the United States, and Gottlieb, Grossman, and Robinson (2016), who analyze gender gaps in policy prioritization in African countries.

[2] Sampling procedures differ for the individual countries and over time, with partly simple, partly multistage stratified random samples of respondents typically aged eighteen years old and older. Data collection methods include face-to-face interviews, mail surveys, telephone interviews, self-completed questionnaires, and web surveys. For further information, please see www.gesis.org/en/issp

Survey respondents are asked about their level of support for different policies and statements, and are typically given a Likert scale to respond. For example, in the Role of Government survey respondents are asked whether they would like to see more or less government spending in different areas, and can respond on a 5-point scale from "Much more" to "Much less" or "Can't choose." I coded each question as a binary variable, where support for a policy (e.g., "much more" and "more" spending on a policy) equals 1, and 0 otherwise. While this removes information about the intensity of preferences, it has the advantage of providing a simple measure of support for a policy that can be compared across genders. Table 3.1 presents a summary of the survey items and question wording.

To describe and compare average (pooled) gender gaps in preferences, I estimate ordinary least squares (OLS) regressions with country and survey round fixed effects separately for each survey item. Survey weights are included. Following previous work, I deliberately do not control for other covariates such as labor market participation, marital status, or education (Gottlieb, Grossman, & Robinson 2016). As Sen and Wasow (2016) note, these covariates would all be considered "post-treatment" because they occur after gender identity has been "assigned" (typically at birth). Gender gaps in preferences likely reflect women's differential wealth, labor force participation, and other factors. Controlling for these other variables is thus likely to dilute the "effects" (differences in preferences) that gender identity is associated with.

Figure 3.1 presents the estimated "effects" of gender on the likelihood of supporting various policies. In line with previous findings, the figure confirms that women prefer greater attention to and spending on many social policies compared to men, including whether the government should provide a job, reduce inequality, and spend more on health care (gender gaps in the range of 4 to 6 percentage points). However, the largest gender differences in preferences by far are found on the issue of maternal employment, which features an 8 to 9 percentage point gap between women and men. For example, on average 39 percent of women disagree with the statement that "a preschool child is likely to suffer if his or her mother works," compared to 30 percent of men. Similarly, 45 percent of women disagree that "a job is alright, but what women really want is home and children," compared to 37 percent of men. By contrast, there are very small or insignificant gender gaps on spending on education, defense, and the environment – even though these issues are also often considered to be gendered.

TABLE 3.1 *Survey items included in the analysis*

Survey: ISSP Role of Government	Question Wording
	Here are some things the government might do for the economy. Please show which actions you are in favor of and which you are against.
Cut spending	Cuts in government spending.
	Listed below are various areas of government spending. Please show whether you would like to see more or less government spending in each area. Remember that if you say "much more," it might require a tax increase to pay for it.
Spend more: culture	Culture and the arts
Spend more: defense	The military and defense
Spend more: education	Education
Spend more: environment	The environment
Spend more: health	Health
Spend more: law enforcement	The police and law enforcement
Spend more: retirement	Old age pensions
Spend more: unemployment	Unemployment benefits
	On the whole, do you think it should be or should not be the government's responsibility to:
Control prices	Keep prices under control
Provide a job	Provide a job for everyone who wants one
Reduce inequality	Reduce income differences between the rich and poor

Survey: ISSP Family and Changing Gender Roles	Question Wording
	To what extent do you agree or disagree ...?
Man's job money, woman's job house (disagree)	A man's job is to earn money; a woman's job is to look after the home and family
PreK child suffers (disagree)	A preschool child is likely to suffer if his or her mother works
Women prefer home (disagree)	A job is all right, but what most women really want is a home and children
Working mother warm	A working mother can establish just as warm and secure a relationship with her children as a mother who does not work

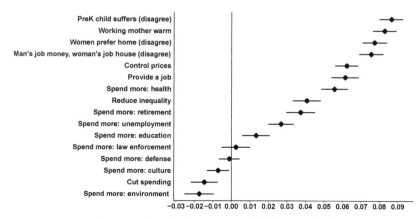

FIGURE 3.1 Impact of gender (woman) on likelihood of policy support
Notes: OLS analysis with country and year fixed effects, 95% confidence intervals (CIs).
Data from ISSP Role of Government, Family and Changing Gender Roles surveys
(1985–2012). Survey weights are included.

Figure 3.2 summarizes the gender gap in preferences toward maternal employment by country, using the survey question about whether a preschool child is likely to suffer if his or her mother works. The average share of women who disagree with the statement is included in parentheses following the country name. To map differences across countries, I compiled the average gender gap for this question by country using seven different cross-national surveys from 1988 to 2012. Because not all countries of interest are included in the four waves of the ISSP Family and Changing Gender Roles survey, I supplement the data with three waves of the European Values Study (EVS) (1990, 1999, and 2008).[3] For each country in each survey-year, I calculate the mean level of support for maternal employment for men and women as well as the gender gap (women support minus men support). Survey weights are employed. I then average all available data (mean levels of support and gender gaps) for each country.

Looking at between-country variation, there are large gender gaps in Scandinavia and many "liberal" welfare states such as Australia and the United States. Continental Europe, including Germany, France, and the Netherlands, has more moderate gaps. Southern Europe exhibits smaller

---

[3] The European Values Study consists of a core questionnaire repeated over time surveyed on representative samples of the resident adult population in each country. The ISSP and EVS both ask whether respondents agree or disagree with the statement: "A pre-school child is likely to suffer if his or her mother works" (the wording is identical).

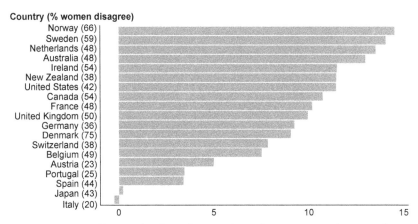

FIGURE 3.2 Country-level gender gaps in preferences toward maternal employment

Notes: Values indicate the average share of women who disagree minus the share of men who disagree with the following statement: "A pre-school child is likely to suffer if his or her mother works." The figure in parentheses after the country name on the left is the average share of women who disagree with the statement. Data come from the ISSP Changing Gender Roles surveys in 1988, 1994, 2002, and 2012 and the European Values Study rounds from 1990, 1999, and 2008. Survey weights are employed. All available data are averaged for each country.

gender gaps, but they have increased over time – a trend that applies to many countries in the sample. For example, in Portugal the gender gap in preferences for maternal employment increased from 2 to 6.5 percent from 1990 to 1999 (EVS data). Analysis of the impact of gender on support for maternal employment within each ISSP survey wave (retaining country fixed effects) finds that the gender gap has slowly increased over time. While both men and women are becoming more progressive on the issue (they are more likely to disagree over time), women are becoming more progressive more quickly, which generates a widening gender gap. In 1988, 21 percent of men and 28.5 percent of women disagreed with the statement that a preschool child would suffer if his or her mother works (7.5-point gap). By 2002, these figures reached 32 percent for men and 42 percent for women (10-point gap). In 2012, the gap narrowed slightly to 37 percent of men and 46 percent of women (9-point gap).

The gap in preferences also increases with education level. Gender gaps in support for maternal employment increase from 8 percent among those with up to secondary-level education to 14 percent among those with some postsecondary education and above (ISSP data, all survey rounds included). Overall levels of support are also higher among those with

Party (% women disagree)

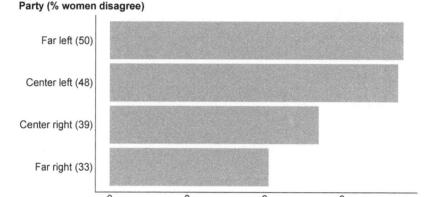

FIGURE 3.3 Gender gaps for maternal employment by party affiliation
Notes: Gender gaps by country-specific party affiliation. Data come from the ISSP
Changing Gender Roles survey rounds in 1988, 1994, 2002, and 2012. Survey weights are
included. The figures illustrate the share of women minus the share of men who disagree
with the statement "A pre-school child is likely to suffer if his or her mother works."

higher levels of education, with the highest levels of support from highly
educated women. A majority of highly educated women (59 percent)
disagree that a preschool child will suffer if his or her mother works,
compared to only 45 percent of highly educated men. Because women in
political power are likely to be well educated, this is all the more reason
to believe that they will be likely to prioritize these issues in office.

Distinct differences between men and women persist across political party lines. Figure 3.3 illustrates the gender gap in preferences for
maternal employment by party affiliation (ISSP data, all survey rounds
included). Respondents were asked which party they voted for in the
last parliamentary election, and the ISSP codes the country-specific party
responses into categories of far left, mainstream left, far right, and mainstream right for cross-national comparison. Figure 3.3 shows that the
gender gap in support for maternal employment cuts across parties. The
average gap within both far and mainstream left parties is 11 percent,
compared to 8 percent among those voting for mainstream right parties
and 6 percent among far-right voters.

As one might expect, overall levels of support for maternal employment are highest among far-left voters and they decline systematically
moving from left to right. Still, significant gender gaps persist on this
issue even among those furthest to the right. The gender gap in support
for maternal employment among far-right voters increases significantly

from 6 points overall to 13 points in the highly educated subsample
(n = 172 respondents, about 10 percent of the total voting far right in
the ISSP data): 53 percent of women versus 40 percent of men in this subsample disagree that a preschool child will suffer. Further country-level
analysis using 2002 ISSP data confirms that while the relative size of gender gaps within parties varies across countries, the gaps persist across left
and right. In many countries (e.g., Sweden) no party differences are visible at all. In others, such as Spain, Ireland, and Denmark, gender gaps are
larger among those voting for mainstream right parties compared to the
left. And in some countries – the United Kingdom, Australia, and Norway – the opposite is seen, with larger gender gaps on the left. Overall, the
gender gap in support for maternal employment is persistent and strong
regardless of party identification.

Finally, another way of looking at gender gaps is to consider the policy priorities of men and women. The analysis so far has established
gender gaps in *preferences*, but not in the prioritization of political
issues. To investigate gender gaps in policy priorities, I use data from
the third round of the Comparative Study of Electoral Systems (CSES)
survey (2006–2011). The CSES consists of nationally representative surveys conducted shortly before or after national elections, and round
3 includes the question, "What has been the most important issue to
you personally in this election?" This is usually an open-ended question, and the CSES country teams code the responses into different
categories. I analyze data from nine countries that include some kind of
work–family issue in their category coding of the most important issue
question: Canada, Denmark, Japan, the Netherlands, Norway, Portugal,
Spain, Sweden, and Switzerland.[4] Because the question asks about the

---

[4] I include the following codes for each country in the binary variable for work–family
policies: (1) Canada – code 62, "Family benefits, childcare funding & programs"; (2)
Denmark – code 132, "Families with children/ child care"; (3) Japan – code 22, "Birth
dearth"; (4) the Netherlands – code 104, "Family policy/childcare"; (5) Norway – codes
31, "Kindergartens," 32, "Cash benefit for families with small children," 35, "(Other)
child and family issues"; (6) Portugal – code 18, " Support for the elderly, children and
other groups"; (7) Spain – code 16, "Family policy"; (8) Sweden – codes 43, "Care,"
85, "Family policy/child care," 86, "Child-care allowance," 89, "Parents' insurance,"
92, "Daycare centre"; (9) and Switzerland – code 46, "Family policy." The following countries are not included in the analysis because they either offer a closed list
of policy categories to respondents that does not include work–family issues or they
code responses into categories that do not include a specific work–family policy issue
(but might include a broader category like social policies): Australia, France, Germany,
Ireland, New Zealand, United States. I drop responses listed as: other problem (not
specifiable), no problem, refused, don't know, and missing.

"most important" issue (a relative measure), this is a hard test for work–family policy priorities. The top categories listed typically include the economy, health, education, taxes, and employment. Undoubtedly, issues like personal health, economic well-being, and security likely take priority over issues related to combining work and family life, even if work–family issues are still considered important. Still, the data offer some useful leverage over the question of the extent to which the prioritization of work–family issues is gendered.

Overall, out of the nearly 18,000 respondents in these nine countries, 2.4 percent (436, 305 of whom were women) reported that work–family issues are the most important to them, rising to 3.9 percent (718, 487 women) if we also consider responses to the second-most important issue question (all frequencies employ survey weights). While the share of respondents who cite work–family issues as their most important concern in the election is small, there are large gender gaps in the likelihood of indicating that a work–family policy is the most important.

Of respondents who mention work–family issues as their most important concern in the election, 70 percent are women. Of those who mention work–family issues as the most or second-most important, 67 percent are women. Thus, women are 2.3 times more likely than men to say that a work–family issue is the most important – a large gender gap. Among women, 5.2 percent list a work–family issue as their most important or second-most important issue, compared to 2.6 percent of men. This data confirms that gender gaps in preferences also extend to the prioritization of work–family issues. In the next section, I conduct empirical tests to confirm that preferences regarding maternal employment are a unique underlying dimension that is uncorrelated with the traditional left–right dimension.

3.3 TESTS OF MATERNAL EMPLOYMENT AS A CROSS-CUTTING ISSUE

So far, the survey data demonstrate that women and men have different preferences on a range of social policies: women prefer more spending/government support than men, and the gender gap is largest for the issue of maternal employment. Women are also more likely to prioritize work–family policies than men. The fact that gaps persist across party lines suggests that this issue does not align with the main left–right dimension in politics. I confirm this interpretation in two ways. First, factor analysis tests for the existence of a latent "maternal employment" dimension, distinct from typical left–right issues in politics. Second, regression models assess the relationship between gender, partisanship, and policy preferences, all else equal. These tests allow me to confirm whether gender gaps in attitudes toward maternal employment persist within parties even after controlling for other factors, which I would expect if my argument about the orthogonality of this issue holds.

Factor analysis is a method that reduces a large amount of data into a smaller number of dimensions, or "factors," based on the patterns observed in the data. It shows how variables in the data are related to one another, highlighting the underlying structure of the data. In this case, factor analysis can provide evidence about whether attitudes toward government intervention (left–right politics) and attitudes toward maternal employment are part of the same underlying response pattern, or whether they form separate and distinct issue dimensions, as I argue.

To test whether attitudes toward maternal employment are orthogonal to the traditional left–right dimension in politics, we need a dataset with items that tap into both of these issue areas. The EVS is a good fit for this purpose, as it is one of the only surveys that asks about both issues. Unfortunately, none of the ISSP waves include questions related to both the traditional left–right dimension and maternal employment in the same survey; however, I return to the ISSP data in subsequent regression models. The EVS data includes nineteen countries (Austria, Belgium, Denmark, Finland, France, Germany, Great Britain, Greece, Iceland, Ireland, Italy, Luxembourg, Netherlands, Norway, Portugal, Spain, Sweden, Switzerland, United States) over three survey waves: 1990, 1999, and 2008. The data includes three items typically identified with the traditional left–right dimension in politics, and three related to maternal employment.[5] Table 3.2 lists these items. A benefit of this data is that these questions are comparable to each other: the items included to measure the left–right dimension and maternal employment all capture attitudes toward social phenomenon, rather than specific policy preferences (which are not available over time for maternal employment). For ease of interpretation, items are coded such that higher scores indicate stronger preferences.

Following best practice for identifying a latent dimension in preexisting survey data, I divide the survey sample in half and run separate analyses

---

[5] The same three "left–right" variables have been used to measure attitudes toward government intervention in other studies (e.g., Pitlik & Kouba 2015). Variables related to working women were not included if they did not refer to motherhood or children specifically, for example, "Having a job is the best way for a woman to be an independent person."

TABLE 3.2 *Preference dimensions in the EVS, 1990–2008: exploratory factor analysis*

Variable	Survey item	Factor 1: Maternal employment	Factor 2: Left–right
Expected to load on Factor 1:			
PreK child suffers	A preschool child is likely to suffer if his or her mother works	0.77	−0.31
Working mom relationship	A working mother can establish just as warm and secure a relationship with her children as a mother who does not work	**0.69**	−0.24
Women: job versus home	A job is alright but what most women really want is a home and children	**0.64**	−0.28
Expected to load on Factor 2:			
State responsibility	People should take more responsibility to provide for themselves versus the government should take more responsibility to ensure that everyone is provided for	0.26	**0.67**
Government ownership	Private ownership of business should be increased versus government ownership of business should be increased	0.36	**0.65**
Competition	Competition is good. It stimulates people to work hard and develop new ideas versus competition is harmful. It brings out the worst in people	0.27	**0.68**
	Eigenvalue	1.75	1.58
	Proportion of shared variance explained	29.1	26.3

N = 23,813 (sample 1)

Note: Cell entries are factor loadings obtained from a principal component analysis; those greater than 0.5 are highlighted in bold. The first three items are preceded by the text, "People talk about the changing roles of men and women today. For each of the following statements I read out, can you tell me how much you agree with each. Please use the responses on this card" (range from Agree Strongly to Disagree Strongly). The last three items are preceded by the text, "Now I'd like you to tell me your views on various issues. How would you place your views on this scale? 1 means you agree completely with the statement on the left; 10 means you agree completely with the statement on the right; and if your views fall somewhere in between, you can choose any number in between."

on each subsample. I first perform an exploratory factor analysis (EFA) on one-half of the data to test the plausibility of a two-factor solution by letting survey items freely load on any latent factors (1, 2, or more) in the data. I then perform a confirmatory factor analysis (CFA) on the second half of the data. The CFA returns a more reliable estimate of correlations between latent dimensions (Cavaillé & Trump 2015; Matsunaga 2015; Osborne & Costello 2009).

I perform the EFA using a principal-components extraction method that identifies two main dimensions: (1) the first three variables have high factor loadings and (2) only the last variable items have high, and about equally large, factor loadings.[6] These two factors explain 55 percent of the shared variance. As Table 3.2 shows, the factor loadings conform to expectations. Items that load on Factor 1, which I call "Maternal Employment," emphasize working mothers, while those that load onto Factor 2, "Left–Right," emphasize government intervention. The results of the initial EFA are thus consistent with the interpretation that preferences regarding maternal employment are orthogonal to the standard left–right dimension in politics.

Since all of the variables load highly on only one component (above 0.6), it makes sense to keep them all in the subsequent CFA analysis. Unlike the EFA, the CFA imposes a preconceived structure on the data. It is used to confirm the underlying factor structure identified in the EFA. I conduct the CFA analysis on the second half of the survey sample, and the results match the two-factor pattern found in the EFA. Table 3.3 reports the factor loadings as well as a set of indicators of the "goodness of fit" of the overall model. All of the factor loadings were significant by conventional standards and load to expected factors. The model returns a factor correlation of 0.06, which supports the expectation that the dimensions are mostly orthogonal. The fit indicators suggest the model does a good job of explaining the covariance among the observed variables.

As a robustness check, I also ran separate CFA analyses to determine whether the two-dimensional hypothesis holds for each survey wave in the data, and for each individual country. The model holds for each survey wave with no significant variation in factor loadings. The covariance between factors has decreased over time, from 0.11 in 1990 to −0.05 in

---

[6] Other extraction methods, for example, maximum likelihood, yield very similar results. The results are also robust to using a polychoric correlation matrix, adapted to ordinal variables. The diagnostic scree test shows that after two components, Eigenvalues of subsequent factors drop significantly, providing additional support for retaining two dimensions (Osborne & Costello 2009).

TABLE 3.3 *Preference dimensions in the EVS, 1990–2008: confirmatory factor analysis*

Variable	Survey item	Factor 1: Maternal employment	Factor 2: Left–right
PreK child suffers	A preschool child is likely to suffer if his or her mother works	**0.86**	
Working mom relationship	A working mother can establish just as warm and secure a relationship with her children as a mother who does not work	**0.50**	
Women: job versus home	A job is alright but what most women really want is a home and children	0.44	
State responsibility	People should take more responsibility to provide for themselves versus the government should take more responsibility to ensure that everyone is provided for		**0.52**
Government ownership	Private ownership of business should be increased versus government ownership of business should be increased		**0.62**
Competition	Competition is good. It stimulates people to work hard and develop new ideas versus competition is harmful. It brings out the worst in people		**0.53**
Correlation coefficient between factors		0.06	
RMSEA		0.02	
CFI		0.99	
TLI		0.99	

N = 23,813 (sample 2)

Note: Cell entries are factor loadings from CFA; loadings greater than 0.5 highlighted in bold. The recommended cutoffs are as follows: RMSEA (0.06), TLI (0.95), and CFI (0.95; Hu & Bentler 1999).

2008. The model also holds for every country in the analysis, although factor loadings and covariance between factors differ slightly by country. Overall, the factor analyses show that the data does not support a unidimensional view of attitudes toward government intervention and maternal employment. Instead, preferences toward maternal employment form a distinct issue dimension.

Another way of investigating this question is to consider the significance of gender identity as a determinant of preferences among supporters of the same political party bloc (left or right), controlling for other factors. I argue that after a quota law is implemented, we should expect changes on issues that are characterized by a gender gap, especially if these issues cut across partisan identities. If women's preferences for maternal employment are orthogonal to the left–right dimension, then gender ought to be a significant determinant of preferences even among those who support the same type of political party.

I estimate probit models of policy preferences based on gender and a set of controls, using data from the ISSP's 2002 Family and Changing Gender Roles Survey. All models are estimated twice – once using the subset of respondents who say they support left-wing parties, and once with the subset of respondents who support right-wing parties. The dependent variable is a binary measure that takes a value of 1 if the respondent agrees (or disagrees when stated) with the question, and 0 otherwise. The notes under Figure 3.4 contain details on the survey questions. *Woman* is a binary variable that equals 1 if the respondent is a woman, and 0 for man. Party affiliation is measured using a question that asks respondents to place themselves on a left–right political spectrum. *Left* includes those responding that they place themselves on the far left, left, or center left, and *Right* includes those who place themselves in the categories of far right or right, conservative. The analysis includes a battery of individual-level controls that have been shown to influence policy preferences: age, education, social class (self-reported), supervisory position, self-employment, unemployment, part-time employment, public sector employment, not in the labor force, retirement status, and rural residence (Cusack, Iversen, & Rehm 2006; Svallfors 1997). Survey weights are employed.[7]

---

[7] The countries included in the analysis are: Australia, Austria, Belgium, Denmark, France, Germany, Ireland, Japan, Netherlands, New Zealand, Norway, Portugal, Spain, Sweden, Switzerland, United Kingdom, United States.

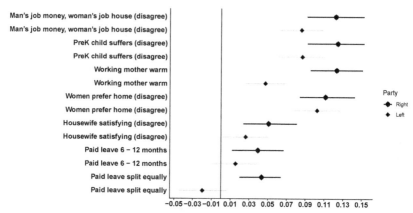

FIGURE 3.4 Marginal effects of gender (woman) on preferences within parties
Plots show marginal effects with 95% CIs, calculated from probit models of policy preferences based on gender and a set of controls, using data from the ISSP's 2002 Family and Changing Gender Roles Survey, and the 2012 Family and Changing Gender Roles Survey (paid leave items only). Analysis carried out using the Zelig package for R v 4.0.3.
(Imai, King, & Lau 2009).
Survey questions (from top to bottom):
(1) A man's job is to earn money; a woman's job is to look after the home and family (disagree).
(2) A preschool child is likely to suffer if his or her mother works (disagree).
(3) A working mother can establish just as warm and secure a relationship with her children as a mother who does not work.
(4) A job is all right, but what most women really want is a home and children (disagree).
(5) Being a housewife is just as fulfilling as working for pay (disagree).
(6) Consider a couple who both work full time and now have a newborn child. One of them stops working for some time to care for their child. Do you think there should be paid leave available and, if so, for how long? (six to twelve months).
(7) Still thinking about the same couple, if both are in a similar work situation and are eligible for paid leave, how should this paid leave period be divided between the mother and the father? (Mother and father half).

Because the coefficients of probit models have little substantive meaning on their own, I present the marginal effects in Figure 3.4. The plots show the estimated marginal effect (with 95% CIs) on the probability that a respondent will express support given a one-unit increase in the value of the predictor variable (e.g., going from man to woman), holding all other variables at their sample mean. The dark (light) bars indicate marginal effects within right- (left-)wing parties.

The results reveal empirical patterns consistent with the argument that gender preferences for maternal employment are orthogonal to the main left–right dimension in politics. As expected, women are associated with large and significant increases in support for maternal employment, even within parties and controlling for other variables correlated with gender. The figure shows significant gender gaps within respondents who identify with both left- and right-wing parties. Gender gaps are often larger among respondents on the right. For example, there is a 12 percentage point gender gap among right-wing respondents on the question of mutually exclusive gender roles (disagreement with the statement "A man's job is to earn money; a woman's job is to look after the home and family"), compared to an 8.5-point gap among those on the left. Similarly, the gender gap on the question of whether a working mother can have just as warm a relationship with her children is characterized by a larger gender gap within the right (12 points) than the left (5 points), controlling for other factors. For both of these questions, mean levels of support are higher on the left, but women are more progressive within each party bloc and have moved further from their men peers on the right.

One potential concern is that attitudes toward maternal employment are not a specific policy preference. To address this concern, I include two survey questions related to paid leave from the 2012 ISSP survey: "Do you think paid parental leave should be available, and if so for how long?" and "How should the paid leave period be divided between the mother and the father?" These questions are not perfect, since they do not specify, for example, how well leave should be compensated, or whether it should be gender-neutral parental leave versus specific maternity or paternity leave, but they represent a policy nonetheless. Responses to the first question are coded 1 if the respondent says that paid leave should be available for between six and twelve months (since it is generally agreed that relatively short, well-paid leave of less than one year is best for encouraging maternal employment), and 0 otherwise. Responses to the second question are coded 1 if the respondent says that paid leave periods should be divided equally between the mother and the father (given that both are eligible).

Figure 3.4 shows that within both party blocs, women are more likely to support paid leave, even controlling for other covariates. Women are associated with a 4 percent increase in support (compared to men) for paid leave among right-wing respondents, and a 1.5 percent increase among respondents who support left-wing parties (the gap among left-wing respondents is not significant). The gender gap is smaller for paid leave support compared to some other questions related to maternal employment, but again the question is relatively vague and does not ask about components that women are likely to favor like pay and incentives for fathers. Right-wing women are also more likely than right-wing men to believe that paid leave should be split equally by the mother and father. The gender gap among right-wing respondents is 4.3 points, while the gender gap among left-wing respondents is negative, but not significant.

Across the majority of models shown in Figure 3.4, gender is a consistent, positive determinant of support for maternal employment within political parties. While we lack time series, cross-national data on specific policies like gender-neutral and well-paid parental leave, the questions that we do have on paid leave from the 2012 ISSP data confirm similar gender gaps within right-wing parties especially on specific policies to the ones we see on attitudes toward maternal employment. Data from individual country cases often demonstrates similar gender patterns on specific policies related to work–family reconciliation. For example, in 2020 a representative survey of Swiss voters found that support for a proposed reform to institute ten days of paid paternity leave was higher among women (67 percent) than men (60 percent).[8] An important pattern across these models is that women on the right, in particular, are often further apart from the men in their parties with regard to views on maternal employment compared to those within left-wing parties. This will be relevant later in the story, as quota laws increase the number of women legislators, especially in parties on the right.

In summary, women are more supportive of maternal employment than men; they prioritize it more, and this preference does not coincide with attitudes toward left–right (government intervention) issues in politics. Connecting women's preferences on this orthogonal issue back to policy change, the empirical evidence to date finds a strong relationship between women's descriptive representation and policies like child care and paid leave (which promote maternal employment), but little evidence that left party power matters (Bratton & Ray 2002; Htun & Weldon 2018; Kittilson 2008; Lambert 2008; but see Bonoli & Reber 2010). By contrast, evidence on whether women's descriptive representation increases overall social spending is mixed; some find increases in overall levels of spending (Bolzendahl 2009; Bolzendahl & Brooks 2007; Holman 2014), while others do not (Clayton & Zetterberg 2018; Ferreira & Gyourko 2011; Funk & Gathmann 2008; Rehavi 2007). Reassuringly, the data presented here showing women's strong,

---

[8] The survey was carried out on behalf of the Swiss Broadcasting Corporation (SRG SSR) by the research institute gfs.bern. www.srf.ch/news/abstimmung-27-september-2020/vaterschaftsurlaub/abstimmungsumfrage-viel-zustimmung-fuer-zwei-wochen-papi-urlaub

cross-party preference for supporting working mothers reinforces the existing empirical evidence that highlights the role of gender over party.

3.4 CONCLUSION

Defining women's preferences is a crucial first step toward analyzing women's substantive representation in politics. Getting the definition wrong risks missing or understating women's impact once in office and the role of quotas (among other factors) in shifting policies for women. It means that we might be overlooking appropriate and relevant dependent variables. Many studies of women's substantive representation define policy demands *not* by gaps in public preferences but based on other criteria, such as feminist theory about women's rights and equality. Nor do most previous studies consider where women's policy demands fall on the main left–right dimension in politics. These approaches fail to seriously consider women's views, which are context dependent, and political parties' important role in mediating the representation of these views. The contribution of this chapter is to define and operationalize an inductive approach to determining women's preferences in politics, defined by gender gaps and where they fall in the left–right political space.

This chapter provides empirical tests of the theoretical expectation that maternal employment, and associated work–family policies, is likely to be a particularly important issue to women as a group. Using survey data, I show that women and men have different preferences on a range of social policy issues, including health, unemployment, and inequality. However, one of the largest gender gaps in rich OECD democracies exists over the issue of maternal employment, and this gender gap cuts across partisan identities. It constitutes a separate underlying attitude dimension from the main left–right, economic dimension. Quotas ought to matter most for these cross-cutting issues, because politicians – who are biased based on their own gendered lived experiences – can push parties to address issues they would rather ignore. Prior research on leave and child care policies confirms the importance of women's descriptive representation over party power.

It is important to note that maternal employment is only one potential "uncrystallized" issue, and I focus on it here because we happen to have good, comparative data on it. Many other issues that could feature significant gaps in preferences go unarticulated on questionnaires – a further symptom of their lack of crystallization in mainstream politics. For example, sexual harassment and violence against women was not on political agendas until relatively recently, and the issue arguably cuts across class and social dimensions due to gender-based differences in preferences (Mansbridge 1999). A Eurobarometer survey from 2010 shows that 73 percent of women believe that tougher laws to combat violence against women would be "very useful," compared to 65 percent of men (8-point gap). Further, while 86 percent of women believe that domestic violence against women should always be punishable, only 79 percent of men agree (7-point gap).[9] Another issue I expect to generate large, cross-cutting gender gaps is gender quotas themselves – which are often supported by women across parties. While cross-national data on support for political quota laws is not available, a 2011 Eurobarometer survey on corporate board quotas finds that 52 percent of women support fifty-fifty quotas for corporate boards, compared to 38 percent of men (14-point gap).[10] I return to the topic of how political gender quotas might facilitate the expansion of quotas to other sectors in the concluding chapter.

To summarize, this chapter suggests that gender quotas will have a greater impact on policies related to maternal employment (helping mothers return to work) than overall social spending, health, unemployment, or other policies clearly on the left–right spectrum in politics. My analysis of public opinion data in wealthy OECD democracies suggests that the biggest gap between men's and women's views is on the issue of whether mothers should work: women, on average, are 9 points more supportive than men. Moreover, this gender gap cuts across parties: it thus meets a key criterion of my argument about when quotas ought to matter. If my argument about the impact of quotas is correct, then we would expect them to lead to stronger policies that incentivize mothers to return to work – like shared parental leave and use-it-or-lose-it paternity leave – and decreases in policies that discourage maternal employment – like extended maternity-only leaves and family allowances. In the next chapters I evaluate this argument using both time-series cross-sectional data and matched-pair case studies. I first turn to the question of whether (and how) quotas shift agenda setting within parties.

---

[9] Eurobarometer 73.2: Humanitarian Aid, Domestic Violence against Women, and Mental Well-Being, February–March 2010.
[10] Eurobarometer 76.1: Financial and Economic Crisis, Financial Services, Corruption, Development Aid, and Gender Equality, September 2011.

4

The First Stage of Policy Change: The Effects of Quotas on Party Priorities

I had to fight to have a chapter in the [party] program for instance. For gender equality…I wrote it, and then I presented it, there were no questions, no one made any comments. And it was one of the texts since the beginning everybody said, OK, that text is OK. So after that I had to proofread it myself to see if there were any mistakes or so on. I don't think anybody read it.

–Viviane Teitelbaum, Belgian politician (Mouvement Réformateur, MR)[1]

The issues of inequality are now a political problem. Even people of the right wing that didn't agree with the [quota] law, they now talk about the effects, how they will affect women, of several measures that are adopted by the government.

–Maria de Belém, Portuguese politician (Partido Socialista, PS)[2]

The first step in policy change is shifting the party's political agenda. Do gender quota laws influence parties' policy agendas? And if so, how? This chapter explores the effects of quotas on party priorities, an early but critical stage of the policymaking process.[3] Party agendas are crucial because they set the bounds for future policy change. Some theorists maintain that agenda setting is the most important measure of political power (Bachrach & Baratz 1962; Gaventa 1982). Just as they are underrepresented in parliaments, women have also traditionally been blocked from the upper echelons of party leadership, who typically make the final decisions about party positions (Kittilson 2006; Reynolds 1999; Rule 1994). Can gender quotas shift these dynamics and help put women's interests on the agenda?

Chapter 2 suggests that after a quota law has been implemented, we should expect change on issues characterized by a large gap between

---

[1] Personal interview, October 23, 2013, Brussels, Belgium.
[2] Personal interview, November 7, 2013, Lisbon, Portugal.
[3] Some of the arguments presented here first appeared in Weeks 2019.

women's and men's views, especially if these issues cut across the main left–right party dimension. Here, I test this hypothesis by exploring whether quotas increase parties' attention to women's policy concerns, focusing on gender equality and work–family policies. The previous quotations both suggest that after a quota law has been implemented, parties have good reason to increase attention to women's policy concerns – either because women themselves push for the inclusion of gender equality in the party program (as in the first quote from liberal party politician Teitelbaum) or because party leaders come to see gender equality as a "political problem" that they can no longer ignore (second quote from social democrat politician de Belém).

I use a mixed-methods approach that combines (1) quantitative analysis of party attention to equality in their manifestos across rich OECD democracies with (2) quantitative and qualitative analysis of party attention to work–family policies in my two matched pair cases (Belgium and Austria, and Portugal and Italy). Party manifestos provide one indication of the relative "crystallization" of a political issue. They help determine whether the issue is well established, or whether it is "surfacing and evolving rapidly on the political agenda" (Mansbridge 1999, p. 644), as Mansbridge suggests is common for issues related to gender. The first quantitative analysis uses data from the Comparative Manifesto Project (MARPOR; Budge 2001; Klingemann 2006; Volkens et al. 2016) to assess the effects of quotas on party attention to gender equality (a cross-cutting issue for women) and welfare state expansion (a left–right issue).

The MARPOR data include gender equality in their "Equality: Positive" category. Welfare state expansion is a fundamental issue structuring the left–right divide over politics in most countries, which is still typically class based. Parties have well-defined positions on these issues, and they might be particularly sticky given the constraints of ideological reputation and issue ownership (Budge, Robertson, & Hearl 1987; Downs 1957). The issue of gender equality, and equality for underprivileged groups (beyond class) more broadly, has not traditionally structured party competition. In line with my main theory, I thus expect that quotas are likely to increase positive party attention to equality concerns but not welfare state expansion. I use statistical matching and a difference-in-difference approach, which compares "treated" parties in countries that pass a quota law to "control" parties that do not, to test this claim. The MARPOR data allow an analysis of the impact of quotas on party priorities over a relatively short time period: up to three election-years. In Chapter 2, I make the case that short-term effects of quota laws are likely driven by increased salience, because it can take time for political parties to comply with gender quota laws (which may not have strong enforcement mechanisms). I provide an initial test of whether women MPs in political parties drive the link between quotas and policy priorities, or whether the effect is instead independent of women MPs, through mediation analysis.

The MARPOR dataset is the most comprehensive source available measuring party attention to different issues across countries and over time. It enables a comparative analysis of the effects of quota laws across a large sample of rich OECD democracies. However, the MARPOR data are not very well suited to measuring attention to women's specific policy preferences. For example, it does not include a coding category for work–family policies. I therefore supplement the MARPOR analysis with original data on party attention to different work–family policies in four countries – Belgium, Austria, Portugal, and Italy. As I discuss in Chapter 3, maternal employment is characterized by a large gender gap, with women more supportive than men, and this gap cuts across parties. It thus fits the criteria of a policy that women prefer that is relatively "uncrystallized."

I hand code party manifesto data based on attention to work–family policies across all four cases (Belgium, Austria, Portugal, and Italy) from 1990 to 2018. I use these data to compare trends in attention to different types of policies (including family allowances, child care, and different types of parental leave policies) across countries that did and did not pass a quota law. The descriptive results from these four countries confirm that parties in countries that implemented a quota law start paying more attention to policies that encourage maternal employment like child care, shared parental leave, and paternity leave after the law comes into effect. Parties in countries that did *not* adopt such a law continue to focus a great deal on policies that tend to shore up the male breadwinner model, including cash transfers like family allowances and tax breaks, and do not focus on paternity leave. This second set of findings sets the stage for an in-depth analysis of leave policy change in these four countries in Chapters 5 and 6.

The chapter proceeds as follows. First, I review the literature on party agenda setting and specify the issues we should expect parties to turn their attention to after a quota law has been passed. I test the link between quotas and party agendas using mixed methods to analyze comparative manifesto data, which allows me to assess both how much attention parties devote to different issues and the content of their agendas. The results present consistent evidence that quotas increase party attention to women's interests, but only if those interests are not well aligned with traditional left–right ideology. I conclude with a summary and discussion of future research implications.

4.1   PARTY AGENDA SETTING AND GENDER QUOTAS

Party positions, as set out in manifestos, represent an early but crucial stage in the policy process: they set the agenda. The winning party's manifesto provides a program for it to follow; it can also be used to hold the party accountable once in office. While parties are not bound by the contents of their manifestos, behavior in office generally correlates with manifesto promises (Klingemann et al. 1994; Mansergh & Thomson 2007; Naurin 2014; Walgrave, Varone, & Dumont 2006). Previous work suggests that parties are more likely to keep their campaign pledges when they have more control over the government, but even parties in opposition can fulfill pledges (Thomson et al. 2012). Manifesto decisions are significant not just for the party's electoral success, but because they dictate the topics of political debate in a society. They have important implications for the quality of political representation afforded to women (and other groups).

Prior studies suggest that parties change their positions in response to environmental factors such as shifts in public opinion (Adams et al. 2004, 2006; Ezrow 2007; McDonald & Budge 2005), economic conditions (Adams, Haupt, & Stoll 2009; Burgoon 2012; Haupt 2010), and how the party performed in the last election (Somer-Topcu 2009). Only a handful of studies have focused on the impact of women on party positions, and to the best of my knowledge this study is the first to consider the role of gender quotas on party attention to women's preferences for work–family policies. Notably, Kittilson (2011) finds that the share of women and existence of women's organizations in the party are associated with increased attention to equality, but not welfare or education, in party platforms. More recently, Greene and O'Brien (2016) find that parties with a higher proportion of women are associated with an increased diversity of issues in the manifesto, and tend to shift leftward. Informed by this literature, the main contribution of this chapter is to measure the effect of quotas, and associated increases in women's representation, on party priorities.

Overall, there is good reason to think that quotas, and a numerical increase in women's presence, will affect at least a subset of issues.

Evidence from studies of legislative behavior suggests that the agenda-setting stage is particularly important for women policymakers. Previous research consistently finds that women raise new issues that are important to women as a group and show greater commitment to these issues in the policy process (e.g., through bill initiation and debate), even if they differ on the specific policy details (e.g., Catalano 2009; Shwindt-Bayer & Corbetta 2004; Skjeie 1991; Swers 2002; Thomas 1994). Women might be especially influential early on in the policymaking process, when decisions about whether certain issues reach the agenda at all are made. Unlike previous studies, the theory of quotas and policy change outlined in Chapter 2 suggests that quotas will lead to policy change for issues characterized by a gender gap in preferences, especially if these issues are off the main left–right party dimension. This is the main relationship I test in this chapter.

Which issues should we expect parties to turn their attention to after a quota law comes into effect? My theory suggests that expectations about policy change should be guided by gender differences in policy preferences. Once the quota law is in place, we should expect to see change only on those issues on which men's and women's views differ. Chapter 3 demonstrates that there are large gender gaps on many issues. For instance, women prefer more social spending and government intervention on policies including health care, unemployment, and inequality, and are more supportive of working mothers.

The theory outlined in Chapter 2 suggests that quotas are likely to influence all policies that women as a group prioritize, but particularly those that are off the main left–right dimension. Chapter 3 establishes that maternal employment and associated work–family policies fit this criterion. Welfare state expansion is an issue that structures the fundamental, class-based political cleavage in most rich OECD countries. Parties have well-defined positions on these issues, and they might be particularly sticky given the constraints of ideological reputation and issue ownership (Budge, Robertson, & Hearl 1987; Downs 1957). I thus expect quotas to increase attention to maternal employment and associated work–family policies, but not to affect party attention to welfare expansion.

The issue of equality for underprivileged groups (beyond class) has not traditionally structured party competition. Parties might therefore prefer to ignore or downplay the issue unless factions within the party or changing public opinion force them to address it. Some evidence suggests that attitudes toward equality are characterized by gender gaps within political parties, although the category of equality is admittedly broad, and more research is needed across countries. For example, Barnes and Cassese (2017) find within-party gender differences on the issue of gay rights in the United States; women are more supportive than men within the Republican Party. In a survey of elite attitudes in the United Kingdom, Campbell, Childs, and Lovenduski (2010) find that within the Conservative and Labour parties, women are more likely than men to feel strongly that there should be more women MPs and are significantly more in favor of equality guarantees. I thus expect that quotas will increase political party attention to equality.

The next two sections discuss the empirical analysis of quotas and party priorities. I first examine the broad categories of welfare state expansion and equality, and then narrow the focus to support for work–family policies that promote gender equality.

4.2   COMPARATIVE MANIFESTO DATA AND METHODS

In the first stage of analysis, I analyze party priorities using MARPOR party manifesto data. MARPOR measures parties' positions on particular policy issues using information from their election-year manifestos. Its coders match up "quasi-sentences" (which can be a full sentence, a clause, or a bullet point) in each manifesto with a category of policy. Each category is standardized by taking the total number of quasi-sentences coded in the same document as a base. The resulting percentage serves as a measure of the party's policy priorities (Budge 2001; Klingemann 2006; Volkens et al. 2016). Manifestos are only coded in election-years (observations are not retained between elections).[4] The full dataset includes 132 parties in twenty-one countries from 1969 to 2011.[5]

The discussion so far suggests that we should observe a relationship between quota laws and party attention to women's policy preferences. However, quota laws are not randomly assigned to countries, and the concern related to causal inference is that countries that adopt quota laws, or parties that propose them, may be self-selecting based on some observable or unobservable factors. To address these potential

---

[4] Many scholars have criticized the MARPOR data for how it estimates policy positions and scales the data into L–R positions; however, because this chapter evaluates change in relative policy emphasis over time (what the data were originally intended for), these concerns are not as relevant (Gemenis 2013).
[5] The countries included are: Australia, Austria, Belgium, Canada, Denmark, Finland, France, Germany, Great Britain, Greece, Ireland, Italy, Japan, Luxembourg, the Netherlands, New Zealand, Norway, Portugal, Spain, Sweden, and the United States.

endogeneity bias concerns, I use statistical matching to preprocess the data and match parties in countries that have adopted a quota law to those in countries with no quota (Ho et al. 2007). The goal of matching is to reduce the imbalance of potential confounders between "treated" and "control" groups (Stuart 2010). More balanced data more closely approximates data that might have resulted from a randomized experiment, which reduces model dependence and enhances the argument for causal inference (Ho et al. 2007; Imai, King, & Stuart 2008; King & Nielsen 2016). The Appendix to Chapter 4 details the matching procedure. Each matched pair consists of a party in a country that has implemented a quota law, and a similar party in a country that has not.

Using the pruned dataset, I then employ a difference-in-differences approach by estimating regression models that include both party- (which in linear combination are equal to country-) and year fixed effects. The coefficient estimates measure the link between quota laws and party priorities over time, relative to parties that have not been affected by a quota law. The "treated" group is parties in countries that have passed a quota law, and the "control" is matched parties in countries without such a quota law. Fixed-effects models control for any party- or country-specific omitted variables (observable and unobservable) that are constant over time – a potentially large source of omitted variable bias.

The baseline model with party and year fixed effects can be written as:

$$Y_{it} = \beta_1 Quota\ Law_{it} + \beta_2 Z_{it} + \alpha_i + \eta_t + \mu_{it}$$

where Y_{it} is the outcome of interest which measures the priorities of party i in year t; *Quota Law* is a dummy variable equal to 1 after the implementation of a quota law and 0 otherwise, and β_1 is the coefficient for this main independent variable; Z_{it} represents a vector of covariates, and β_2 the coefficients for these covariates; α_i and η_t are party and year fixed effects, respectively; and μ_{it} is the error term. All right-hand-side variables are lagged by one election-year because party manifestos are written before the election. I use robust standard errors clustered by election to address the concern that unobserved election-specific factors may influence all parties' policy priorities in a given election, leading to correlated errors among the parties standing in that election (Rogers 1994; Williams 2000).

4.2.1 Dependent Variables

The main dependent variables are the share of the party manifesto devoted to two MARPOR policy categories capturing women's preferences: (1) *Equality* and (2) *Welfare State Expansion*. *Equality* includes any mention of social justice and the need for the fair treatment of all people, including an end to sex-based discrimination, as well as equality for other underprivileged groups including those based on race, class, sexuality, and disability (code 503). Examples are, "Promote equal opportunities" (Portugal Socialist Party 2011) and "Recent figures from Eurostat show that the gender pay gap in Belgium between men and women still averages 17 percent. The government within the framework of its powers and the social partners for their part must close the gap" (Belgium Flemish Christian Democrats 2007, both sentences coded as 503). While this category is broad, it reflects women's interests in attention to gender equality.

Welfare State Expansion includes favorable mentions of the need to introduce, maintain, or expand any social service or social security scheme, and support for social services such as child care, health care, retirement, and unemployment benefits (code 504). Examples are, "Guarantee public social security" (Portugal Socialist Party 2011) and "Guaranteeing a healthy life, with a living environment that is protected for the future, but also with good and affordable healthcare for every person" (Belgium Flemish Christian Democrats 2007). Note that while child care (a policy expected to increase maternal employment) is included in welfare state expansion, so are a range of other social spending items that are *not* expected to increase maternal employment, like health care and pensions. Therefore, the welfare state expansion category best reflects women's broad interest in increased social spending generally (an issue on the left–right dimension). MARPOR sometimes codes child care in the equality category, if it is discussed in the context of gender equality. It is thus not possible to isolate attention to child care in the MARPOR data. In Section 4 of this chapter, I use hand-coded manifesto data to examine the question of party attention to child care and other work–family policies.

4.2.2 Independent Variable

The key independent variable is *Quota Law*, a binary variable coded "1" for parties in countries that have a national quota law, after the law was implemented (including and after the first election in which the quota was in operation). Five countries in my dataset have passed a quota law: Italy (since repealed), Belgium, France, Spain, and Portugal. Because these laws are relatively recent (their first use in elections ranges from 1994 in Italy to 2009 in Portugal) and it was necessary to lag this variable, the parties included in this study had a quota law for up to three consecutive election-years.[6] Thus, the results capture the short-term effects of a quota law.

4.2.3   Control Variables

I control for several variables that could be linked to both quota adoption and party agenda change (potential confounders). I include a measure of *Party Quota*, because voluntary gender quotas are potentially linked to both quota adoption through a "contagion" mechanism (Meier 2004) and increased attention to women's concerns (Henig 2002; Matland 2005).[7] I also control for *Log(GDP per capita)* and *Women's Labor Force Participation*, both of which are hypothesized to transform sex roles and attitudes toward women as societies shift away from materialist values (Inglehart & Norris 2000; Norris 1985). Rising incomes and women's entry into previously male-dominated jobs influence attitudes toward gender equality in society, including receptiveness to women in politics (and, potentially, quota laws). Women's labor force participation also ought to increase demand for policies that help balance work and family demands (Bonoli & Reber 2010). The fixed effects account for many potentially important time-invariant confounders that would otherwise be included, including party family, electoral system, and a country's history of religious conservatism.

I include two other variables that are not potential confounders in order to increase model accuracy. *Vote Share* is included because smaller, niche parties might be more likely to take up special issues such as equality: they are not constrained by a history of emphasizing traditional left–right issues (Kittilson 2011). I also control for *Effective Number of Parties* because party systems with more parties might be more responsive to new issues than two-party systems, where there is less likely to be competitive diffusion (Kittilson 2011; Matland & Studlar 1996). Appendix

---

[6] In the matched data, of the twenty parties in the sample that were subject to a gender quota law, observations are included for all twenty in the first election-year (year of implementation), for nineteen in the first election-year after implementation, and for six in the second election-year after implementation.

[7] Note that *Quota Law* and *Party Quota* are not strongly correlated; the Pearson correlation coefficient is 0.26.

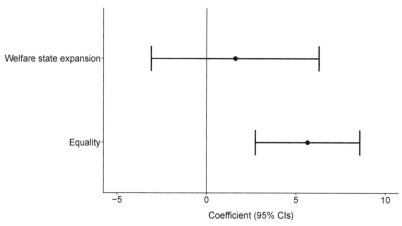

FIGURE 4.1 Effect of quota law on party priorities

Notes: The figure illustrates the regression results reported in Appendix Table A4.3 Models 1 and 2, regressing party priorities on quota implementation. Models include controls, party and year fixed effects, and robust standard errors clustered around election.

Table A4.1 reports the summary statistics for all parameters used in the analysis, as well as details about the data sources.

4.3 GENDER QUOTAS AND PARTY ATTENTION TO EQUALITY AND WELFARE EXPANSION

Figure 4.1 displays the main results of models regressing party priorities on quota implementation. Throughout the book, I use coefficient plots and marginal effects plots to display key results visually, with full regression tables available in the Appendix. The effects shown here come from models that control for omitted variable bias both over time and across political parties, and should be interpreted to estimate within-party changes in treatment. The analysis uses matched data; analysis using the full dataset returns similar results (see Weeks (2019) for this analysis). The results show that after a quota is implemented, parties shift their positions on equality, but not welfare state expansion.

The coefficient of 5.6 on *Quota Law* indicates that a one-unit change in *Quota Law*, that is, going from not having a quota to implementing a quota, is associated with a 5.6-percentage-point increase in positive party attention to equality. For example, a party that devotes 5 percent of its manifesto to equality issues (the mean) before a quota law is passed would be expected to allocate double this amount – 10.6 percent – to equality after it is implemented. Using regression without matching, the effect of a quota law is slightly smaller (4 percent increase). However, as previously discussed, because the matching results rely less on untestable modelling assumptions (such as which parametric model to choose), I believe they are more credible.

Parties that pass a quota law are no more likely to prioritize welfare state expansion than those without such a law. This suggests that quota laws do not lead parties to change positions on more traditional issues like welfare, which have long been fundamental to left–right politics (Allan & Scruggs 2004; Bartolini & Mair 2007; Benoit & Laver 2006; Lipset & Rokkan 1967). This finding aligns with evidence from Kittilson's (2011) study of women in parties and party priorities, which demonstrates that the share of women is a significant determinant of positive mentions of equality in the manifesto, but not welfare state expansion.

Do increases in the number of women MPs in political parties drive the link between quotas and policy priorities? In order to understand more about the mechanism driving agenda shifts, I investigate whether the relationship between quotas and prioritizing equality is indirect (driven by increases in the number of women in the party) or instead driven by the quota law itself and the increased emphasis on equality issues (direct). If the effect of the quota law is due to the increased salience of equality concerns, I would expect the impact of a quota on equality to be independent of the share of women in the party. To explore the indirect effect of increased women's representation generated by a quota law, I follow Kenny and et al.'s three steps for validating mediation effects: (1) show that the causal variable is correlated with the outcome; (2) demonstrate that the causal variable is correlated with the mediator; (3) for partial/complete mediation, show that the effect of the causal variable on the outcome while controlling for the mediator is reduced/zero (Baron & Kenny 1986; Judd & Kenny 1981, 2010). In the next paragraph I describe each step in turn.

In the first step, I establish that the causal variable is correlated with the outcome. Previous results (illustrated in Figure 4.1) establish that the causal variable (*Quota Law*) is related to the outcome of positive attention to equality. In a second step, I test whether the causal variable is correlated with the mediator. Appendix Table A4.3 Model 3 shows no evidence that the causal variable *Quota Law* is correlated with the mediator, *Women in Party*. The coefficient is negative although not statistically significant at conventional levels. This result is somewhat unexpected, since most research shows that quota laws increase women's representation at the national level (Hughes 2011; Paxton & Hughes 2015; Paxton, Hughes, & Painter 2010). Still, an important finding is that policy design matters; higher thresholds, placement mandates, and strict enforcement mechanisms have been shown to enhance quota effectiveness (Schwindt-Bayer 2009). Both France and Portugal fine parties rather than require compliance to run candidates. In France, parties notoriously shirked the quota for years and opted to pay a fine instead (Fréchette, Maniquet, & Morelli 2008; Murray, Krook, & Opello 2012).

While the Spanish law requires compliance with the gender quota for list submission, women in the country were well represented before the quota's introduction. Prior research has illustrated how parties in Spain got around the quota in creative ways, for example, by nominating women in lower positions on the ballot (Esteve-Volart & Bagues 2012). Given these examples, differences between findings using party- and national-level data could be attributed to country contexts (weak laws, and the relatively short time period of available post-quota data). The results might also suggest that smaller, less electorally relevant parties in particular are not complying with the new regulations. This is not due to the lagged quota variable (which does not capture effects in the year of quota implementation): as an additional test I run models that do not lag the right-side variables, and the results do not change. These results suggest that, on average, quotas had only minimal short-term effects on women within parties in this set of countries. In Chapter 6, which covers a longer time period through 2019, I show that gender quotas increased women within all parties in Belgium and among right-leaning parties (center-right and Christian democrats) in Portugal. Additionally, analysis of a longer time period (1985 to 2018) and including more parties and countries than the matched data here, finds that gender quota laws are associated with a significant increase in women in parliamentary parties (Weeks et al. Forthcoming).

The final step in the mediation demonstrates that including the mediator *Women in Party* does not reduce the size of the effect of *Quota Law* at all: Model 4 of Appendix Table A4.3 shows that the size of the effect of quotas on party attention to equality is virtually unchanged from original models that do not include *Women in Party*. Nor does causal mediation analysis using the potential outcomes framework (Imai, Keele,

& Tingley 2010) show evidence of indirect effects.[8] I also fit models including the variable *Quota Shock*, defined as the change in women's descriptive representation following quota implementation (rather than operationalizing quota as a binary variable; O'Brien & Rickne 2016). While the quota shock variable has a large range (-40 to 50), the mean is close to zero (0.6), again suggesting that overall quotas in these countries had a minimal short-term impact on women in the party. The coefficient on *Quota Shock* is close to zero and not significant at conventional levels in these models (see Appendix Table A4.5 Models 1 and 2).

This suggests that quota laws have a direct short-term effect on party priorities that is not channeled through increases in the number of women in the party. In line with the expectations of my theory, quota laws cue parties to devote more positive attention to equality issues in the short term. Given that they have not increased the number of women in this sample of parties, it is no surprise that the effect of quotas is not driven by women. Of course, this could change over the long term and as quota laws are strengthened by stricter placement mandates and enforcement mechanisms. Overall, these results suggest that parties prioritize equality after a quota regardless of whether it increases the number of women members. Quotas as a gendered institution therefore affect party behavior independently of their influence on party demographics.

I take several steps to ensure that these findings are not the result of model misspecification. Robustness checks include estimating models with no controls and models that drop political parties responsible for proposing quota laws (strengthening the case that this law was exogenously imposed on anti-quota parties). My findings are robust to these alternative specifications (presented in Weeks 2019). My findings are also robust to specifications that exclude one country at a time to ensure the results are not being driven by a single country (results available on request).

I also test the robustness of the difference-in-differences identification. First, I estimate a model with party-specific time trends. When these trends are included, the identification relies on there being a sharp change in the outcome on treatment rather than an effect that grows gradually (Pischke 2005). In this model, the coefficient on quota law is positive but does not reach standard levels of statistical significance ($p = 0.2$; see Appendix Table A4.5 Model 4). As another test of the

---

[8] To estimate the mediated effects of women MPs in the party on equality policy priorities, I use the mediation package in R (results available on request) (Tingley et al. 2014).

parallel-trends assumption, I estimate a dynamic panel model that estimates the treatment effect on positive attention to equality before and after quota implementation (lags and leads). The results show increasing effects over time, and importantly, no "placebo" effect in the years before the law was implemented. The results of these tests are thus somewhat mixed, but the lack of pretrends shown in the dynamic panel model strengthens the plausibility of the parallel-trends assumption and a causal interpretation of the results (see Appendix A4.5 Model 3).

In the next section, I narrow the focus to party attention to work–family policies in order to test the argument about quotas and women's cross-cutting preferences for maternal employment.

4.4   GENDER QUOTAS AND PARTY ATTENTION TO WORK–FAMILY POLICIES

So far, this chapter has shown that gender quotas increase party attention to equality issues (including gender equality), but not welfare state expansion – an issue that lies squarely on the main left–right dimension of politics. This provides some evidence in line with the main argument that quotas lead to policy shifts on issues that women prefer which are off the main left–right dimension. However, the MARPOR categories are broad and do not measure attention to specific issues relevant to women's preferences. Chapter 3 establishes that women's preferences for maternal employment are strong, and cut across parties. The best way to test whether parties increase attention to this issue in their agendas is to consider their approach to work–family policies. Some such policies encourage maternal employment (shared parental leave, paternity and other father-specific leave, child care) while some do not (family allowances). The MARPOR policy category of "Equality: Positive" sometimes includes work–family policies (as a mechanism to increase gender equality) but they are also sometimes coded in other categories. There is no one category in which work–family policies are coded in the MARPOR data, and because work–family policies impact maternal employment in different ways, it is important not to lump them together in any case.

To supplement the MARPOR analysis, in this section I take a closer look at party attention to work–family policies, manually coding manifestos based on their level of attention to various such policies. To code work–family policies, I followed the basic approach of the Manifesto Project Database's Manifesto Coding Instructions (5th revised ed., 2015),

which entails coding sentences and quasi-sentences into separate policy categories.[9] The coding process involved first translating manifestos
into English, and then extracting sentences and quasi-sentences related to
work–family policies. I then aggregated the number of mentions of each
policy per party-year, and merged this party-level data with the MARPOR
data to calculate the percentage of sentences devoted to different work–
family policies.[10] Sentences and quasi-sentences were only coded if they
mention a specific policy. For example, if the manifesto expresses a general need to support women's work–life balance, or a general statement
that mothers are the best source of care for children, these sentences were
not included. Such statements are typically followed by more detailed policy proposals, which I did code. The coding process resulted in over 2,000
observations of work–family policies within manifestos, which aggregate
to percentages for twenty-three parties in the four countries from 1990
to 2018 (N = 156 at the party-year level).

4.4.1 Work–Family Policies

I focus on three main types of work–family policies expected to impact
maternal employment: child care, family allowances, and gender-equality-
promoting leave.[11] Past research has consistently found that child care
policies boost maternal employment, especially among mothers with
young children (Attanasio, Low, & Sanchez-Marcos 2008; Boeckmann,
Misra, & Budig 2015; Erhel & Guergoat-Larivière 2013; Lewis 1992).
Experimental evidence suggests that when child care is available, women
are not only more likely to be employed but more likely to compete for
senior management roles (Latura 2021). Family allowances or child benefits, conversely, are cash transfers to families that can enable women
to stay at home as full-time caregivers. Evidence suggests that family

---

[9] These guidelines include: Do not code chapter and section headings; Do not code
introductory remarks, tables of contents, or statistics; Each sentence is at least one quasi-
sentence (i.e., all sentences should be coded separately); Only if the natural sentence
contains more than one unique argument should this sentence be split; Examples, reason-
ing, explanations, and so forth are not unique arguments and therefore are not separate
quasi-sentences.

[10] Manifestos were translated using Google Translate. While this is not perfect, I found it
more than adequate for identifying attention to different work–family policies. Coding
was carried out by myself and a research assistant between 2017 and 2019. I checked
every line of the coding personally.

[11] For a more detailed description of how work–family policies affect maternal employment, see Chapter 5, Section 2.

allowances and similar types of financial support policies decrease the likelihood of a mother being employed (Nieuwenhuis, Need, & Van Der Kolk 2012; Schwarz 2012). To measure the level of attention devoted to child care in manifestos, I code for any mention of publicly subsidized or private child care (such as corporate daycare), service vouchers specifically for child care, and any tax deductions/benefits for child care costs specifically. To measure attention to family allowances, I code any mention of monetary allowances distributed to families for children, including tax write-offs (deductions), cash benefits, birth allowances or bonuses (one-time grants for parents), and adoption premiums.

Leave policies impact maternal employment differently depending on the specific policy configuration (parental, maternity, or paternity leave), the length of leave, and whether/how well it is paid. The consensus is that long maternity-only leave periods break mothers' ties to the labor market, especially if they are not well paid (Blau & Kahn 2013; Boeckmann, Misra, & Budig 2015; Hideg et al. 2018). Well-paid shared parental leave and father-specific (paternity) policies have been shown to increase women's employment as well as fathers' time at home (Bartel et al. 2018; Boeckmann, Misra, & Budig 2015; Patnaik 2019). To measure gender-equality-promoting leave in manifestos, I sum the share of sentences related to parental and paternity leave (job-protected leave from work for parents or fathers specifically, which can be paid or unpaid), and then subtract the share of sentences related to maternity-only leave (job-protected leave from work for mothers only, which can be paid or unpaid). This variable, which I call *Gender Equality Leave*, measures the extent to which leave policy configurations prioritize parental and father-specific leave over maternity-only leave.[12]

I use the hand-coded work–family manifesto data to conduct two different types of analysis. First, I replicate the baseline regression specification from the quantitative analysis using the new hand-coded sample of party attention to different types of work–family policies. If my theory is correct, I should see parties shift attention toward policies that promote work–family equality (child care, gender equality leave) and away from those that do not (family allowances). In the second type of analysis, I use a close reading of the entire corpus of the work–family dataset and any observed changes in attention to work–family policies among these parties to conduct a global assessment of the trends over time in parties that

---

[12] Appendix Table A4.2 reports the summary statistics for the hand-coded data, and lists the parties included for each country.

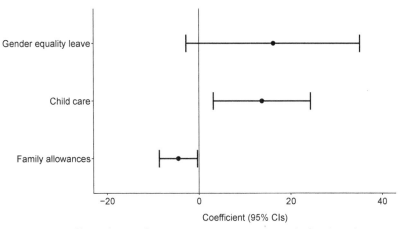

FIGURE 4.2 Effect of quota law on party attention to work–family policies in four countries

The figure displays the regression results shown in Appendix Table A4.4, including three models regressing party attention to work–family policies on quota implementation. Models include controls, party and year fixed effects, and robust standard errors clustered around election. The countries included in analysis are Belgium, Austria, Portugal, and Italy.

are subject to a gender quota law versus those that are not. This second analysis uses the matched pairs of Belgium and Austria, and Portugal and Italy to structure the discussion. The control cases that did not adopt a quota during this period (Austria and Italy) provide a mutual counterfactual to explore how party attention to work–family issues might have evolved in the quota countries (Belgium and Portugal), absent a quota (Tarrow 2010).

Figure 4.2 shows that gender quota laws affect attention to work–family policies in the expected direction. The figure uses regression results from three models regressing work–family policies on quota implementation, including controls and party and year fixed effects.[13] Gender quotas reduce attention to family allowances by 4.5-percentage points, and increase attention to child care by 13.7-percentage points. Quotas

---

[13] Controls include the same potential confounders used in other models of party attention to issues (party quotas, women's labor force participation, and economic development measured as the log of GDP per capita), as well as fertility rate and EU membership, which are potential confounders of the relationship between quota laws and work–family policy attention in particular. Chapter 5, Section 3 discusses these latter two control variables, which are also included in models of spending and policy outcomes related to work–family policies. All control variables are lagged because manifestos are written before the election.

are also associated with a 16.1-percentage-point increase in attention to gender equality leave (significant at the 0.1 level).

The results are confirmed for child care and gender equality leave in models dropping all control variables. Quotas are positively associated with attention to these policies, and the results are significant at the 0.01 level for both models, although the size of the effects is smaller. In a model with no controls, the negative link between quotas and family allowances is no longer statistically significant (see Appendix A4.6). Overall, the results from these four countries provide initial evidence that quotas shift party attention to family policies in the direction of women's preferences for maternal employment. Parties pay more attention to child care and gender equality leave after a quota law has been implemented. How exactly do parties change their emphasis on work–family policies after a quota law? In the next section, I use qualitative evidence from a close reading of manifestos in the four countries (Belgium, Austria, Portugal, and Italy) over time to shed light on this question. I focus on mainstream parties because their agendas are more relevant to policy outcomes than smaller parties.

4.4.2   Case Study Comparisons

Belgium and Austria

Taking the matched pair of Belgium and Austria first, both countries had strong social democratic and Christian democratic parties during the study period (1990–2018). Belgium's parties are also divided linguistically, with French and Flemish versions of most parties. Both Austria and Belgium had nationalist or far-right parties during this period – the New Flemish Alliance (Nieuw-Vlaamse Alliantie, N-VA) and the Flemish Block/Flemish Importance (Vlaams Blok/Vlaams Belang, VB) in Belgium and the Freedom Party (Freiheitliche Partei Österreichs, FPÖ) in Austria.

Before the quota law was implemented in Belgium in 1999, there was no consensus across the country's political parties on the need for gender-neutral parental leave or paternity leave. The green parties (Ecolo and Green), the French social democrats, and the Flemish Christian democrats (CD&V) all included parental leave in their proposals in the pre-quota period (1990–1998). For example, in its 1995 manifesto the CD&V called for "the extension of parental leave for men and women" in order to "optimize the combination of work and family life." The French Christian democrats, the liberal Open Flemish Liberals and Democrats (PVV/VLD/Open VLD), and the far-right VB did not propose parental leave or paternity leave before the quota came into effect. These parties focused on other proposals, including part-time and flexible working (Open VLD) and family allowances and tax breaks for large families (VB). For example, in 1991 the VB stated that it, "considers the family built upon marriage in principle open to children, as the firmest basis of a balanced society." To help families combat the threat of "individualism and materialism, and the utter absence of a principled vision of the traditional political parties," the VB proposed tax breaks for large families and wages paid to parents who work at home.

After Belgium implemented its quota law, parties across the political spectrum began to converge on parental leave and the need for father-specific leave. For example, the VB's 1999 manifesto says that, "The right to parental leave should be available to all professionally active parents," and four out of five of the party's post-quota manifestos reiterate the need for parental leave. The Liberal Party also included parental leave in its proposals after the quota was implemented, for example in 2007: "Parents should have the right to additional parental leave, provided that care is equally divided between the two partners." In 2010 the liberals suggested that, "Men do not fully use their potential paternity leave. Therefore, we must make it possible to take parental leave as flexibly as possible." The nationalist, conservative N-VA, which only gained seats after the quota law was implemented in Belgium, followed suit. The party's 2010 manifesto called for both mothers and fathers to have at least two months' leave during the first six months of infancy, "so that fathers and mothers have the opportunity to take care of their young children."

This evolution in how political parties discuss leave (from maternal to parental, including father-specific leave) is the most noticeable change to work–family policy proposals in manifestos after the quota law was implemented in Belgium. Many parties consistently discussed child care both before and after the quota law (the Christian democrats, the social democrats, the green parties). However, both the VB and Liberal Party mentioned the need for child care only after the quota was implemented. For example, the Liberal Party (Open VLD) stated in its 2007 manifesto that, "Open VLD considers child care a basic condition that contributes to a higher employment rate, which supports a better combination of work and care, which increases the economic independence of women." The far-right VB also begin to call for more affordable and accessible child care. This represents a big shift from its pre-quota rhetoric, which suggested that the best care for children was within the family (in 1995: "no kindergarten can replace the nurturing, protective and educational role of the family"; see Chapter 6 for a further discussion of this shift in VB's rhetoric).

Left-leaning parties in Austria also shifted their focus from maternity-only leave to parental and father-specific leave over time. For example, the social democratic party (Sozialdemokratische Arbeiterpartei Österreichs, SPÖ) mentioned fathers in the context of leave for the first time in 2008, saying, "We focus on strengthening the father's participation and the further development of childcare." This statement foreshadowed the concrete proposal of *Papamonat* (a father's month of leave upon the birth of a child) for the private sector in the 2013 manifesto. However, the parties on the right – the Christian democratic Österreichische Volkspartei (ÖVP) and far-right FPÖ – did not shift toward a gender-neutral conception of parental leave or encourage fathers specifically to take it. Neither party ever mentioned any paternity or father-specific leave in their manifestos during the study period. Instead, the FPÖ proposed to extend maternity leave to three years and give benefits to all mothers rather than only those who previously worked outside the home (a policy mix between an allowance and leave). This policy was implemented in 2002 while the FPÖ was in a coalition government with the ÖVP, as discussed in Chapter 6. In its 2002 manifesto, the FPÖ claimed that the policy gives women, "for the first time a real freedom of choice between family and occupation." Yet, the extension of maternity leave to three years was widely viewed as a step backwards for women's labor force participation and gender equality in Austria.

Portugal and Italy
Portuguese political parties also increasingly converged on policies that promote shared parental leave and encourage fathers to take up leave. The social democrats (PS) were behind the major policy change in this area, which replaced maternity leave with gender-neutral parental leave in 2009. The parental leave policy was first mentioned in the 2005 manifesto, which stated the need "To assume, in the State's discourse, the importance of sharing responsibilities between men and women, namely by giving equal value to maternity and paternity, as an essential condition for economic development and social and the quality of life of our society." After the quota law was implemented in 2009, the party continued to focus on encouraging gender equality in leave and proposed significant investment in child care (400 new daycare centers were pledged in 2009, and universal access to preschool for children aged three to five in 2015).

The main conservative party, Partido Social Democrata (PSD), and Christian democratic party, Centro Democrático e Social-Partido Popular (CDS-PP), included proposals for tax breaks and transfers for families (which do not encourage maternal employment) in their manifestos during the study period. Yet notably, they also shifted toward promoting shared parental leave over maternity-only leave and made important proposals to expand child care. For example, in 2009 the Christian democrats highlighted the need for "equality of sharing of parental responsibilities between father and mother." In their 2015 joint manifesto, the PSD and CDS-PP called for "a more balanced sharing of parental leave for the father and the mother."[14] They also proposed to lower the age of universal preschool from four to three, which would have a large impact on public child care provision.

Did trends in political party attention in Italy also move toward promoting gender equality in leave over time? The only mention of paternity leave by Italian political parties I found was from 2018 (when the country's most recent gender quota law was implemented),[15] when both the Democratic Party and the Five Star Movement called for extended paternity leave. During the non-quota period in Italy (1996–2017), party proposals focused a great deal on cash transfers (family allowances, baby bonuses, tax breaks for families), although also on child care. For example, in 2008 the conservative party People of Freedom called for the "reintroduction of the 'baby bonus' to support the birth rate." Similarly, in 2008 the far right Northern League said that, "We need to support family incomes with birth support policies." Both of these parties also called to expand child care, as did parties on the left. Yet in contrast to Portugal, proposals for parental leave, especially policies that actively encourage fathers to take leave, were notably absent during this period in Italy.

In summary, the cases of Belgium and Austria, and Portugal and Italy offer initial insights into how parties alter their policy agendas after the implementation of a quota law. In both quota countries (Belgium and Portugal), parties across the political spectrum converged on promoting shared parental leave over maternity-only leave after the quota law – and specifically mentioned the need for fathers to participate. Even parties that previously praised women's traditional role within the family, like the Belgian far-right VB, did so. In the non-quota countries, this transition

---

[14] For the 2015 election, the PSD and CDS-PP formed an electoral alliance called "Portugal Ahead," which was dissolved after the election.
[15] Italy's first quota law was in place from 1994 to 1995.

occurred among some parties on the left (Austria's social democratic SPÖ) but not on the right. In both Austria and Italy, the main center-right and far-right parties instead focused primarily on cash transfers that support family care at home rather than maternal employment, although they often mentioned child care as well. Nor did Italy's center-left party move toward encouraging gender-neutral parental leave. These agenda shifts (or lack thereof) are important. In Chapter 6, I show that these party agendas are connected to real policy changes in the expected directions in all four countries, and explore the mechanisms that link quotas to these important changes.

4.5 CONCLUSION

This chapter examines the impact of quota laws on party priorities in high-income OECD democracies. It finds that parties in countries with gender quota laws increased the positive attention they devoted to equality issues, but not to issues related to welfare state expansion. The findings suggest that the effects are not driven by associated increases in the share of women in parties after a quota law is implemented. I interpret this finding as evidence of the salience mechanism: the quota itself cues parties to increase their attention to equality via a path not directly related to the gender composition of the parties. By elevating gender equality to the national stage, quota laws might increase the salience of equality concerns more broadly among the public and elites. These results should not imply that women's presence in office is unimportant. Chapters 5 and 6 provide additional evidence that women play pivotal roles as factions within parties, and when elevated to government roles (ministers), in bringing about work–family policy outcomes.

The analysis of four country cases (Belgium, Austria, Portugal, and Italy) complements the comparative manifesto findings by providing an in-depth study of trends in party attention to different work–family policies over time. Quantitative analysis of these four countries confirms that quotas shift party attention in the direction of women's preferences for maternal employment: the results show they pay more attention to child care and gender equality leave after a quota law has come into effect. My qualitative reading of manifestos suggests that the biggest agenda shift in work–family policies after a quota law relates to the configuration and framing of leave policies. In the two countries that adopted a quota law (Belgium, Portugal), parties across the political spectrum strengthened their emphasis on gender equality in leave (promoting parental leave and father-specific leave). In the two countries that did not have a quota law in place during the study period (Austria, Italy), I did not observe a similar consensus on gender equality emerging. In both countries, parties on the center-right and right in particular are more likely to propose cash transfers that tend to support women staying at home.

Quotas are one mechanism that can lead to the greater substantive representation of women's interests within political parties, particularly if these interests are orthogonal to the standard class-based issue dimension. I find no evidence that quotas lead to changes on important, "sticky" issues at the core of a party's identity, such as welfare policy. A key implication of these findings is that, in line with theoretical expectations, the translation of women's policy demands into outcomes depends on how those demands map onto traditional political cleavages.

Agenda setting is an important stage of the policymaking process. These results suggest that quotas can expand the scope of decision-making beyond standard issues of importance to dominant groups. Quotas are one way of shifting the distribution of power in politics. Yet it is unclear whether party positions translate into national-level policy outcomes. The quotation from Viviane Teitelbaum at the start of this chapter – the gender equality chapter goes in the party program, but no one in the party reads it – leaves room for doubt. Particularly in parliamentary democracies with strong party discipline, individual legislators may have less influence over the later stages of the policymaking process. The next two chapters examine this question, exploring the effects of gender quotas on work–family policies.

5

The Effects of Gender Quota Laws on Work–Family Policies

Now the people that should be talking about it [work–family issues] are talking about it. That is what I meant, it is not credible to have a debate about child care, which is in my view the promotion of the free choice of women, with this kind of society we have now, just amongst men.

—Gerolf Annemans, Belgian politician (Vlaams Belang, VB)[1]

There is an association I think, a statistical association, between for instance the approval of the quota rules and its practical consequences on the one hand, and on the other hand measures approved by the Socialist government or the parliament such as the extension of maternity leave and the reconceptualization and re-framing of these maternity leaves as parental (mother and father). This is an obvious effect for me.

—Augusto Santos Silva, Portuguese politician (Partido Socialista, PS)[2]

Do political gender quota laws change work–family policies in the direction of women's preferences? Chapter 4 provides evidence that quotas lead to shifts in policy priorities within parties: political parties in countries that have implemented a quota pay more attention to equality concerns and work–family policies that encourage maternal employment. But do gender quota laws shift actual policy outcomes that impact men and women's ability to combine work and family life? This question is important because ultimately most people consider political representation to be about policy outcomes. There are many different theories of what constitutes "good" representation, but the vast majority of representatives are judged by their concrete actions in the policymaking process (Mansbridge 2003).

[1] Personal interview, October 9, 2013, Brussels, Belgium.
[2] Personal interview, November 12, 2013, Lisbon, Portugal.

The previously mentioned quotations from politicians in countries that have passed a quota law suggest that policymakers across the left (Silva) and right (Annemans) think quotas have resulted in policy changes on work–family issues in particular. This chapter provides the first cross-country evidence that gender quotas shift work–family policies in the direction of women's preferences. I analyze both public spending on work–family policies and the duration of leave policies that promote gender equality for twenty-three countries from 1980 to 2016. I find that implementing a quota law leads to a shift in the composition of leave policies toward more paid, shared parental leave and father-specific leave, which encourage mothers' employment. Such laws also lead to less spending on family allowances, which tend to discourage women from returning to paid work (but do not change overall family policy spending levels). I find no change to spending in areas in which men and women tend to have similar policy preferences (such as old age benefits and education), or areas characterized by a gender gap on issues that align with the main left–right dimension (health and overall social spending). The results suggest that quota laws are an effective tool to increase the substantive representation of women's interests, particularly those that are relatively "uncrystallized" (Mansbridge 1999) and thus otherwise easily ignored.

The chapter proceeds as follows. After reviewing the literature on gender, quotas, and work–family policies, I develop the implications of the theory proposed in Chapter 2 for national-level policy change. The main argument is that quotas will lead to policy changes in work–family issues because they are characterized by a gender gap in preferences and are orthogonal to the mainstream policy dimension. This chapter focuses on identifying the effects of quota laws, while Chapter 6 assesses qualitative data to provide an in-depth analysis of the mechanisms driving these effects. After presenting the empirical results, the chapter concludes by discussing the implications and potential extensions of this work.

5.1 PREVIOUS LITERATURE: CAN WOMEN, OR QUOTAS, SHIFT SOCIAL POLICIES?

The political economy literature on redistribution and social policy outcomes does not typically include gender as a category of analysis. Prior studies in the field instead highlight the importance of several key determinants, including inequality (Benabou 1996; Lindert 1996; Milanovic 2000; Moene & Wallerstein 2001), electoral institutions (Austen-Smith

2000; Edwards & Thames 2007; Iversen & Soskice 2006; Milesi-Ferretti, Perotti, & Rostagno 2002; Persson & Tabellini 2005), partisanship (Esping-Andersen 1990; Huber & Stephens 2001; Klingemann et al. 1994; Korpi 1983; Korpi & Palme 2003), and skill specificity (Estevez-Abe, Iversen, & Soskice 2001; Iversen & Soskice 2001). Identity is considered insomuch as it relates to *voters* and their preferences, but not the identity of politicians. For example, ethnic and other forms of identity-based cleavages have been explored as potentially important determinants of policy choice (Alesina & Glaeser 2004; Anesi & Donder 2009; Austen-Smith & Wallerstein 2006; Roemer 1998; Scheve & Stasavage 2006). Huber and Stephens (2000) show that women's labor force participation is an important determinant of the expansion of social welfare services, which they argue is because women's employment generates new demand for services such as caregiving. According to Roemer's (1998) model, voters who care deeply about a noneconomic issue (like integration or religion) may not necessarily support the party that proposes the most economically rational policy for them. However, these studies do not apply the same logic to *policymakers* themselves.

Prior studies from the gender and politics literature, which carefully considers women's descriptive and substantive representation, find a relationship between women's representation and spending levels, from overall spending (Bolzendahl 2009; Bolzendahl & Brooks 2007; Holman 2014) to, for example, spending on child care (Bonoli & Reber 2010; Ennser-Jedenastik 2017; Profeta 2020; Svaleryd 2009) and defense (Koch & Fulton 2011). Looking at other types of policy outcomes besides spending, O'Regan (2000) finds that higher shares of women in office are associated with stronger employment and wage protection and equal wage policies. Kittilson (2008) shows that women in parliament significantly influence the adoption and scope of maternity and child care leave policies. Although it is not their main focus, Skorge and Rasmussen (2021) demonstrate that the percentage of women parliamentarians is significantly positively related to parental leave generosity in eighteen OECD countries. Likewise, greater shares of women in cabinet have been linked to child care policy and job-protected leave (Atchison 2015; Atchison & Down 2009, 2019) and government attention to gender equality and violence against women (Annesley, Engeli, & Gains 2015). These examples show that women in politics and government are linked to social policy spending and outcomes in the direction of women's preferences, even if cause and effect are difficult to establish with observational data.

Moving beyond gender to the effect of adopting quotas, evidence found in previous studies suggests that quotas have had a causal effect on policy outcomes in India, where political reservations for women were implemented across the country randomly from 1993. These studies find that women leaders are more likely to adopt laws and invest in resources that women favor – for example, clean drinking water (Beaman et al. 2011; Chattopadhyay & Duflo 2003, 2004, but see Ban & Rao 2008; Bardhan, Mookherjee, & Torrado 2010, who fail to replicate these results in South India and West Bengal over time, and Jensenius 2017, who fails to find similar effects for reserved seats for Scheduled Castes). Considering how quotas affect the enforcement of rights in India, Brulé (2020) finds that women leaders increase the likelihood that women will inherit ancestral land on marriage, but can also lead to backlash. Two studies also find that quotas affect public expenditures in a global context, specifically increasing spending on social welfare and health (Chen 2010; Clayton & Zetterberg 2018). Yet, research on the effects of quotas on spending within OECD democracies such as Spain and Italy sometimes returns null findings (Bagues & Campa 2021; Rigon & Tanzi 2012). Notably, the reservations in India require women to be elected in executive roles, which is not true of quotas in rich OECD democracies. The latter require women to be nominated but not elected, in a context where the norm is parliamentary democracies with strong party discipline. Individual legislators in high-income OECD democracies have fewer opportunities to impact policymaking, which makes my dataset a more difficult case for testing the effects of quotas.

This chapter investigates whether gender quota laws affect work–family policies. It reports the results of one of the first studies to examine how quotas affect public policy outcomes. Its main contribution to the identity politics literature is to provide a comparative study of the effects of the same type of measure (national quota laws) within similar units (high-income democracies). Comparative analysis allows us to explore whether the effects of quota laws apply to a variety of political contexts, and how social and structural differences in different societies mediate these effects. The theory of quotas and policy change outlined in Chapter 2 suggests that quotas will generate policy change on issues characterized by a gender gap in preferences, especially if these issues cut across the main left–right party dimension. This is the main relationship I test in the quantitative analysis. I explore the relative importance of the three mechanisms that I suggest link quotas to policy change (factions, ministers, and salience) in Chapter 6.

Men and women agree on many policies, and on these I do not expect a quota law to have any effect. Nor do I expect quota laws to change policies that are characterized by a gender gap, but are well embedded within traditional left–right politics. Because maternal employment is both characterized by a large gender gap and orthogonal to traditional party lines, I expect quotas to change policies that either help or hinder mothers returning to paid work. In the next section, I build on the discussion of work–family policies in Chapter 4, elaborating on how work–family policy configurations can encourage or hinder women's employment.

5.2 HOW DO WORK–FAMILY POLICIES RELATE TO GENDER EQUALITY?

This chapter focuses on two main "work–family" policies: (1) family allowances or child benefits, which tend to discourage maternal employment and (2) leave policies, which can facilitate or hinder maternal employment depending on the policy configuration. Other work–family policies of interest are child care and measures that enable part-time work. Child care policies have been found to increase maternal employment (Attanasio, Low, & Sanchez-Marcos 2008; Lewis 1992). Part-time work is more attractive than full-time work for many mothers of young children (Morgan 2006, p. 169), but it does not encourage the equal distribution of paid and unpaid work. Because reliable comparative data on child care or part-time working policies are not currently available, they are not included in this analysis. In this section, I discuss the implications of family allowances and leave policies for working mothers and related expectations for how gender quotas will affect these policies. The main expectation is that quota laws will increase work–family policies that encourage women to return to paid work, and decrease work–family policies that discourage or do not prioritize women's paid employment.

Family allowances were the first type of work–family policy to emerge, as early as the late nineteenth century in some countries. Such allowances, also known as child benefits, are cash transfers to families with children; in some countries the payment level is based on the age of the child. These programs were often designed to encourage women to have children to combat declining fertility rates, and to protect the earnings of a single male breadwinner (Gornick, Meyers, & Ross 1997; Gottfried & O'Reilly 2002). They enable mothers to stay at home as full-time caregivers; such policies do not support their involvement in paid work. For example, Belgium's *allocations familiales* are monthly payments to a child's primary caregiver (typically mothers) until he or she turns eighteen. Some allowances, such as Italy's *assegni familiari*, are targeted at low-income families, which tends to foster "single-earner"/male breadwinner family patterns (Naldini 2004).

Leave policies enable women and men to remain employed while temporarily giving priority to care responsibilities. They vary in length, payment (paid or unpaid, and if paid at what level), and entitlement (who can take it up). There are three main types of leave policies: maternity, parental, and paternity. Historically, paid leave policies have mainly applied to mothers, as *maternity leave*. Leave policies for mothers can be a double-edged sword: if it is too short, it may not provide women enough incentive to return to paid work, while if it is too long, it may break women's ties to the labor market (Baker & Milligan 2008; Dustmann & Schönberg 2012). Prior studies have found that well-paid maternity and parental leave policies are correlated with women's employment, particularly if the leave period is not very long – for example, up to twelve months (Baker & Milligan 2008; Bergemann & Riphahn 2011; Rønsen & Sundström 1996). A relatively short period of well-paid maternity leave is thought to be most effective at encouraging women's return to the labor market; the International Labour Organization's Maternity Protection Convention, 2000 recommends no less than fourteen weeks. Long maternity-only leaves (usually defined as one year or more), conversely, tend to discourage mothers of young children from working and are linked to discrimination in the labor market. Beyond the mechanical effect, whereby if long leaves are available only to mothers, some will take them but fathers cannot (Blau & Kahn 2013; Boeckmann, Misra, & Budig 2014); research suggests that women who have taken leaves of twelve months or more are viewed negatively as job candidates and seen as less suited for leadership roles (Hideg et al. 2018).

Scholars and politicians have recently stressed the need to shift from maternity-only leave to *parental leave* that can be taken by either parent, and to include some leave that is specific to fathers. Parental leave can be set up either as a nontransferable individual entitlement or a family entitlement. When it is structured as a family entitlement that can be shared between the parents, mothers are much more likely than fathers to take it up. This can be detrimental to mothers' employment. When father-specific parental leave cannot be transferred to mothers (what is sometimes referred to as "use it or lose it"), fathers have more incentives to take it because the family will lose this funding if they do not.

The third type of leave policy, *paternity leave*, is designed to explicitly promote fathers' participation in child care responsibilities. Paternity leave is typically taken around the time of a child's birth. Research shows that shared parental and paternity leave can increase both the time fathers spend at home and in household labor, and the time mothers spend in the workplace (Bartel et al. 2018; Patnaik 2019). It also helps to normalize gender roles in society more broadly. As Collins (2019) describes in her qualitative study of working mothers, when government policies promote gender-equal parental leave policies, men's involvement in caring for children is visible every day. In Sweden, it is normal to see "latte dads" out with their children without mothers.

As the discussion so far indicates, work–family policies shape whether (and how) mothers return to work, and they are not gender neutral. They tend to either support women's integration into the labor market or reinforce the traditional gender division of labor – men at work, women at home. The consensus is that the best way to promote gender equality through work–family policies is to focus on child care provision and well-paid leave entitlements that encourage the father to participate (Jaumotte 2003; Moss & Deven 2019). For example, the European Commission recommends, "gender-balanced family related leaves" with a balanced use of leave between women and men and, "accessible, affordable, and quality formal care services" to address women's underrepresentation in the labor market (?). Long maternity-only leave periods and cash transfers to families with children are likely to encourage women to stay home. I therefore expect quota laws to lead to increases in policies that help mothers return to paid work – namely, well-paid parental leave policies that encourage fathers to take leave (over long, maternity-only leave policies). Quota laws should also lead to a decrease in spending on family allowances, which discourage mothers from returning to paid work.

5.3   DATA AND METHODS

The discussion so far suggests that we should see a relationship between quota laws and women's policy preferences, especially those that lie off the main left–right dimension (maternal employment and associated work–family policies). Ideally, in order to make causal inferences about the effect of quota laws on policy outcomes, such laws would be randomly assigned to countries. Since this is not possible, a concern is that the effect is not causal and that another factor (such as culture or attitudes toward women) is determining both the adoption of a quota law and policy outcomes.

I cannot fully resolve this problem, but I take three steps to allevi-
ate such concerns. First, I estimate models that include country and year
fixed effects. Country fixed effects control for any country-specific omitted variables (observable and unobservable) that are constant over time,
which constitute a potentially large source of omitted variable bias. Year
fixed effects deal with group-invariant trends over time, such as global
economic conditions. The two-way fixed effects design is a generalization of the difference-in-differences approach in which countries that have
implemented a quota law are "treated" and those that have not are the
"controls." The specification compares average policy outcomes post-
quota minus policy outcomes pre-quota in the treated countries to the
change in policy outcomes in the control countries over the same period.
The results should be interpreted as within-unit changes, that is, the link
between quotas and policy change in quota countries. The difference-in-
differences approach thus helps address endogeneity concerns, given that
the parallel-trends assumption holds – that is, that trends in policy priorities would have been the same across countries in the absence of a quota
law.

Second, I carefully identify and control for potential confounding variables, factors that could affect both the probability of quota adoption and
policy outcomes. The critical identifying assumption in this approach is
that there are no potential time-varying confounders that have not been
accounted for in the analysis. Conditioning on these observed characteristics helps ensure that the groups being compared are indeed comparable,
and strengthens support for a causal interpretation of the results. Third,
I also test the parallel-trends assumption – that trends in policies would
have been the same across countries in the absence of a quota law. I test
for the validity of this assumption by including unit-specific time trends
in robustness checks.

The baseline model with country and year fixed effects can be written
as:

$$Y_{it} = \beta_1 \, Quota \, Law_{it-1} + \beta_2 Z_{it-2} + \alpha_i + \eta_t + \mu_{it}$$

where Y_{it}, the outcome of interest, measures work–family policy spending, or leave policy duration, in country i in year t; *Quota Law* is a
dummy variable equal to 1 after the implementation of a quota law and 0
otherwise, and β_1 is the coefficient for this main independent variable; Z_{it}
represents a vector of covariates, and β_2 the coefficients for these covariates; α_i and η_t are country and year fixed effects, respectively; and μ_{it} is the
error term. *Quota Law* is lagged by one year to acknowledge the time it

takes to influence outcomes, and the other right-hand-side variables are lagged by two years because they can be affected by the treatment and may induce posttreatment bias (King & Zeng 2006). Standard errors are clustered by country.

5.3.1 Dependent Variables

The main dependent variables are social expenditures on work–family policies and the duration of gender equality promoting maternity, paternity, and parental leave. I use time-series cross-sectional data for twenty-three high-income OECD democracies between 1980 and 2016, from two main datasets: OECD Social Expenditures (for spending outcomes), and OECD Employment (for leave policy duration).[3] The OECD Social Expenditure Database measures government expenditures on many types of social spending, including family allowances and maternity, paternity, and parental leave policies, and it runs from 1980 to 2013. Spending on family allowances refers to child-related cash transfers to families with children; in some countries payment levels are means tested and/or vary with the age of the child.[4] Spending on leave refers to public income support payments during periods of maternity, paternity, and parental leave. Maternity and paternity leave are defined as employment-protected leave of absence for employed mothers and fathers, respectively, at or around the time of childbirth (or adoption, in some countries). Parental leave is employment-protected leave of absence for employed parents, which is often supplementary to specific maternity and paternity leave periods.[5] While I would like to include spending on child care, unfortunately the OECD data on child care spending are not reliable because of a change in definition in 1998 and many countries are missing data (as others have noted; see Bonoli & Reber 2010). The Social Expenditure data also includes measures of overall social expenditure, education spending, health spending, and old age spending, which I use to test my argument that quotas should not affect these other outcomes, which do fall along the left–right spectrum. Data are measured as percent of GDP.[6]

---

[3] The countries are: Australia, Austria, Belgium, Canada, Denmark, Finland, France, Germany, Greece, Iceland, Ireland, Italy, Japan, Luxembourg, Netherlands, New Zealand, Norway, Portugal, Spain, Sweden, Switzerland, United Kingdom, United States.

[4] "PF1.3: Family cash benefits," OECD Family Database.

[5] "PF2.1: Key characteristics of parental leave systems," OECD Family Database.

[6] The OECD calculates spending-to-GDP ratios using their *National Accounts* data (where GDP is recorded for the calendar year). The recording period for social expenditure data is typically the calendar year; where the financial year recorded differs from the

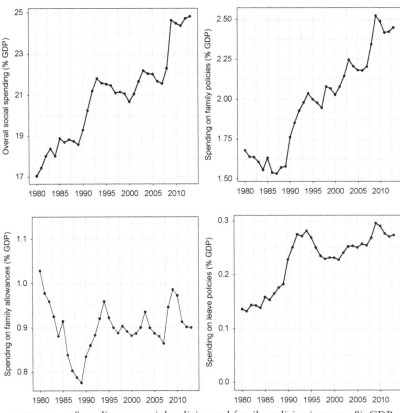

FIGURE 5.1 Spending on social policies and family policies (average % GDP, 1980–2013)

Figure 5.1 displays the average spending (% GDP), for overall social spending and different types of family policies, for all of the countries in this study. The mean family policy spending overall in the sample is 2 percent, with family allowances constituting most of this (mean = 0.9 percent), compared to leave policies at 0.23 percent. The rest of the spending on family policies is on early education and child care, as well as home help. Average spending on allowances (bottom left panel) has decreased slightly from 1 percent in 1980 to 0.9 percent in 2013, although the average has not fallen linearly over time. Spending on leave policies, by contrast (bottom right panel), has nearly doubled from 0.14 to 0.27 percent during the same period; its trajectory has followed a similar linear

calendar year, special adjustments for GDP are made. For full details, see Adema, Fron, & Ladaique 2011, p. 100.

pattern to that of overall social spending and family spending (top left and right panels).

I supplement the spending data with OECD Employment data on the duration (in weeks) of different kinds of leave policies from 1990 to 2016.[7] Spending data is not the best way to measure leave policies, because they can take many different forms (which have different implications for gender equality) but cost the same amount. For example, a short, well-paid leave may cost the state the same as a longer leave that is paid at a lower rate, but the former more effectively encourages women to maintain ties to the labor market (Baker & Milligan 2008; Dustmann & Schönberg 2012). The leave duration data thus allow me to assess whether the composition of leave policies has shifted to encourage greater gender equality over time. It offers more observations over time compared to the manifesto data (which ends in 2011) or the spending data (ends in 2013), giving useful leverage to assess the impacts of quota over the medium and long term.

The OECD Employment data measures the duration of: (1) maternity leave, (2) total paid maternity and parental leave available to mothers, and (3) paid father-specific leave.[8] I use the OECD leave policy duration data to create a new measurement of gender-equality-promoting leave policies, which builds on the extensive research linking leave policy configurations to gender equality discussed earlier. The consensus in this literature is that well-paid parental leave and father-specific leave promote gender equality at home and at work, and long maternity-only leave does not. A 2019 review of leave policies summarizes:

"long periods of maternity leave, such as in the UK, implicitly express a maternalist view about the care of young children, a gendered assumption that young children are the primary responsibility of mothers (Moss & O'Brien 2019); while substantial periods of well-paid, father-only leave, such as in Sweden, are based

---

[7] OECD   Employment   database: www.oecd.org/employment/labour-stats/onlineoecdemploymentdatabase.htm

[8] The OECD Employment data are measured as follows. Maternity leave refers to the number of weeks of job-protected leave available to mothers before and after childbirth. Total duration of paid maternity and parental leave refers to the total number of weeks that a woman can be on paid leave after the birth of a child, combining both maternity and parental leave. Finally, paid father-specific leave refers to the number of paid weeks reserved for the exclusive use of fathers, including entitlements to paid paternity leave or periods of paid parental leave that cannot be transferred to the mother, and any weeks of paid shareable leave that must be taken by the father in order for the family to qualify for "bonus" weeks of parental leave.

on a strong commitment to promoting gender equality in child care" (Moss & Deven 2019, p. 434).

To measure gender-equality-promoting leave using the OECD Employment data, I sum the total weeks of paid maternity and parental leave available to mothers and the total number of paid weeks reserved for the exclusive use of fathers. Then, I subtract the total number of weeks of leave (paid or unpaid) available to mothers only (maternity-only leave).[9] The new indicator, which I call *Gender Equality Leave*, measures the extent to which leave policy configurations prioritize paid parental and father-specific leave over maternity-only leave. It is consistent with the indicator used in Chapter 4 to measure party attention to gender equality leave in their manifestos (constructed as the share of manifesto sentences related to parental and paternity leave minus the share of sentences related to maternity-only leave). This is the primary dependent variable I use to analyze the impact of quotas on leave policies that promote gender equality. I also include an analysis of how gender quota laws affect each separate leave duration included in this indicator (maternity, paid maternity and parental, and paid father-specific) in the Appendix.

Figure 5.2 displays the average total number of weeks of gender equality leave for all countries in this study. The average weeks of gender-equality-promoting leave during the study period across countries is twenty-nine. The average duration of leave policies promoting gender equality has increased significantly over time, from fifteen in 1990 to thirty-four in 2016. This indicator can be negative – the minimum in the data is −24 (United Kingdom from 2003 to 2006) – if more weeks of (paid or unpaid) maternity-only leave are provided than paid maternity, parental, and father-specific leave combined. This type of leave policy configuration is very likely to discourage maternal employment. The highest values of gender equality leave are achieved when paid maternity, parental, and father-specific leave far exceed the number of weeks of maternity-only leave offered. This is the case for Finland, which achieves the maximum value in the data of 152.5 weeks of gender equality leave from 2013 onward (it was also the first country to introduce paternity leave in 1978). Maternal employment rates are indeed higher in Finland

---

[9] These variables are not strongly correlated. The Pearson correlation coefficients are: maternity leave and paid maternity and parental leave (0.11), maternity leave and father-specific leave (−0.06), and paid maternity and parental leave and father-specific leave (0.23).

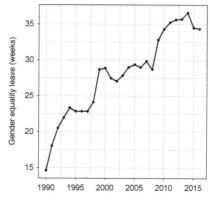

FIGURE 5.2 Duration of gender equality leave policies (average weeks)

than in the United Kingdom, and the difference between mothers of children zero to fourteen years working full time in the two countries is particularly striking (66 percent in Finland vs. 40 percent in the United Kingdom, 2019 data).[10] The new gender equality leave indicator thus seems to provide an accurate measure of the extent to which leave policies promote gender equality.

5.3.2 Independent Variables

The key independent variable is *Quota Law*, a binary variable coded 1 after a quota law is implemented (including and after the first election in which the quota was in operation), and 0 otherwise. Five of the twenty-three countries included in the analysis implemented a quota law during the study period – Italy (from 1994 to 1996), Belgium (from 1999), France (from 2002), Spain (from 2008), and Portugal (from 2009). Appendix Table A5.1 shows summary statistics for all parameters used in the analysis, and provides details about the data sources. To specify the covariates to be used as controls, I consider how the adoption of quotas is related to established determinants of work–family policies. The key issue is whether adopting a quota causes parties and governments to change their policy priorities, or whether something else contributes to a quota being adopted *and* causes a shift in spending outcomes, such as an underlying cultural norm shift in favor of women. I focus only on time-varying confounders here, because all models include fixed effects that account for any (observable or unobservable) time-invariant confounders. The

---

[10] Data on maternal employment come from the OECD Family Database.

fixed effects control for important potential confounders such as electoral rules (which are mostly stable over time), history of Catholicism, and the relative size of gender gaps in preferences for maternal employment (i.e., the fact that gender gaps are on average highest in liberal and social democratic welfare states, and lowest in Mediterranean welfare states).

5.3.3 Control Variables

I control for four variables that are potentially linked to both adopting quotas and family policy outcomes: *GDP per capita*, *Women's Labor Force Participation*, *Left Government*, and *Party Quota*. Economic development (measured as *GDP per capita*) and *Women's Labor Force Participation* (measured as the ratio of female-to-male labor force participation) are both considered important determinants of changing sex roles and attitudes toward women (Inglehart & Norris 2000). As the service sector grows and education for women improves, women are better able to compete with men for jobs. And as women gain entry into previously men-dominated labor markets, they obtain the experience necessary to run for political office; voters thus become more receptive to women candidates, and potentially, quota laws. Both variables are also related to policy outcomes. For example, as incomes and government revenues increase, the demand for public expenditure should also rise (Wagner's Law). Workforce participation entitles some women to benefits that they would otherwise not be eligible for and increases their need for services to help balance work and family.

The variable *Left Government* controls for the possibility that left-wing parties and governments push through both quota laws and women's policy agendas. Left-leaning parties are often the ones that introduce and support national quota legislation (as they have done recently in Spain and Portugal, for example). Commitment to gender equality has been a longstanding element of socialist (and many other left parties') ideology (Duverger 1955), while conservative parties tend to favor laissez-faire policies over concrete affirmative action measures. Leftist parties have also been linked to a range of feminist policy outcomes (Huber & Stephens 2000; Mazur 2002; O'Connor 1999). Left power is operationalized as the share of left cabinet seats rather than parliament seats, because previous research identifies government partisanship as particularly important for social policy outcomes (e.g., Huber & Stephens 2000).

I include the share of relevant parties with voluntary gender quotas (*Party Quota*) to control for concerns that internal party quotas are driving changes to both national quota legislation and policy outcomes for women. Previous research posits a "contagion effect" between party and national-level quotas, whereby the existence of party-level legislation paves the way for the law (Meier 2004). Parties also gain experience implementing the law and are able to see that it is effective, which might increase their support. I expect that voluntary party quotas could be linked to policy outcomes mainly through the indirect mechanism of increased women's representation.

I also control for two variables from the literature on the determinants of family policy spending that are not known to affect quota laws, but are included to increase the accuracy of the model estimates. *Fertility Rate* is included because many family policies are only granted in connection with the birth of a child. Higher fertility rates suggest a greater need for family spending; alternatively, countries with lower fertility rates might implement family policies to encourage women to have more children. *EU Membership* may lead to convergence on higher family policy spending levels. The European Union (EU) has issued directives on maternity and parental leave, which continue to be monitored by the European Commission.[11]

5.4 RESULTS

Figure 5.3 presents the main results of the effects of quota laws on work–family spending (full regression tables are reported in Appendix Table A5.2). All figures are derived from models including country and year fixed effects and (observable) time-varying potential confounders. Recall that a fixed-effects regression of this form estimates the effect of changes *within* countries over time, while also partialing out any time-based shocks and trends common to all countries.

The results suggest that after a quota is adopted, governments spend less on family allowances, which can discourage maternal employment. No significant association is found between quotas and overall family spending, or spending on parental leave policies. Within countries, adopting a quota law leads to a 0.33-percentage-point decrease in spending on family allowances. For example, a country that spent 1 percent of its GDP

---

[11] See Council Directive 1992/85/EEC on maternity leave; Council Directive 1996/34/EC on parental leave; Council Directive 2010/18/EU on parental leave; and outside of my data Directive (EU) 2019/1158 on work-life balance.

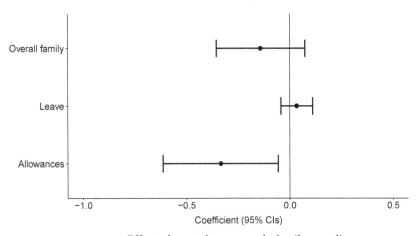

FIGURE 5.3 Effect of quota law on work–family spending

Notes: The figure displays the regression results shown in Appendix Table A5.2, including three models regressing spending outcomes on quota implementation. The models include controls, country and year fixed effects, and robust standard errors clustered by country.

on family allowances before a quota law would be expected to spend 0.67 percent of its GDP on family allowances after such a law is implemented.

Quotas do not shift the amount of leave policy spending, but what about the composition? Figure 5.4 shows the results of the effects of quota laws on gender equality leave policy. It shows that quotas significantly shift the composition of leave policies toward more equality-promoting leave. All else equal, quotas lead to nineteen more weeks of leave that promotes gender equality. Appendix Table A5.4 reports the results of models regressing the duration of maternity-only, paid maternity and parental, and father-specific leave on quota laws. In line with the results in the main text, I find that quotas decrease the number of weeks of maternity-only leave while increasing the weeks of paid maternity and parental leave and father-specific leave (all significant at the 0.1 level). Specifically, quotas are linked to 14.6 more weeks of paid parental and paternity leave (9 more weeks of paid shared parental leave plus 5.6 weeks of paternity leave), which is offset by 4.6 fewer weeks of maternity-only leave. This suggests that relative spending priorities favor investing in paid shared parental and paternal leave over maternity-only leave after a quota law.

My theory maintains that quota laws should only affect policies characterized by a gender gap in preferences. To test this argument, I estimate regressions on spending for two areas not characterized by a significant gender gap in preferences (and for which data are available): *Old Age*

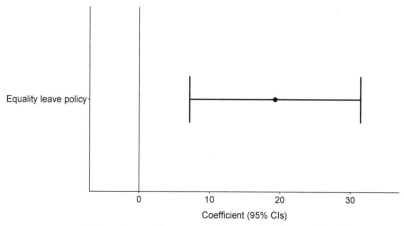

FIGURE 5.4 Effect of quota law on gender equality leave policy duration
Notes: The figure displays the regression results shown in Model 1 of Appendix Table
A5.3, where the model regresses gender equality promoting leave policy duration on quota
implementation. Models include controls, country and year fixed effects, and robust
standard errors clustered by country.

Benefits and *Education*.[12] The majority of both men and women support spending on these issues, and gender differences are typically small or nonexistent. Figure 5.5 presents the results from models that regress public spending on old age benefits and education on quota laws. The results show no significant association between quotas and spending in these areas, which provides support for the main argument. When men and women's political preferences are virtually indistinguishable, as in old age benefits or spending on education, quota laws do not affect spending outcomes.

I also suggest that quota laws should be especially important for shifting orthogonal policies, those not aligned with the main left–right dimension in politics. To test whether this is the case, I run a set of regressions on spending in areas that are characterized by a gender gap in preferences, but also fall along the main left–right policy dimension. The dependent variables are public spending on *Overall Social Policies* and *Health Care*.[13] These policy areas are characterized by some of the

[12] Both variables measure public expenditure as a percentage of GDP. *Old Age Benefits* includes standard and early retirement pensions, and in-kind benefits including residential care and home-help services, while *Education* includes public expenditure on all levels except preprimary education. The data come from the OECD's Comparative Welfare States Dataset 2014 (Brady, Huber, & Stephens 2014).

[13] Both variables measure public expenditure as a percentage of GDP. *Overall Social Policies* measures total public social expenditure, while *Health Care* includes public

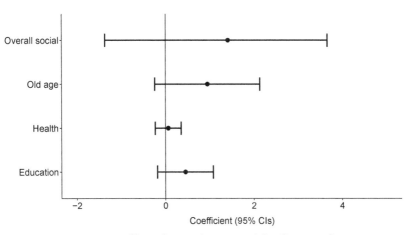

FIGURE 5.5 Effect of quota law on social policy spending

Notes: The figure displays the regression results from Appendix Table A5.4, including four models regressing social policy spending on quota implementation. Models include controls, country and year fixed effects, and robust standard errors clustered by country.

largest gender gaps in preferences, after maternal employment (see Figure 3.1).

Figure 5.5 shows no significant link between quotas and spending in these areas, which provides additional evidence to support the credibility of the proposed theoretical framework. In line with my main argument, quotas seem to be most effective at shifting orthogonal issues, on which parties have not yet staked a distinct claim. I also note that left party government is not a significant determinant in models of family policy spending or leave policy duration, as we might expect if it were a left–right issue (see Appendix Tables A5.2 and A5.3 for regression models).

5.4.1 Quota Shocks: Do Increases in the Number of Women MPs Condition the Effects of Quota Laws?

Previous work emphasizes the strong role of women descriptive representatives (in parliament and government) on work–family policy change. In Chapter 2, I suggest that quotas lead to policy changes through the mechanisms of factions, ministers, and salience. I explore these mechanisms in depth in Chapter 6 using qualitative data, but I can also test this argument

expenditure on health care, both cash and in-kind benefits. These data come from the OECD's Comparative Welfare States Dataset 2014 (Brady, Huber, & Stephens 2014).

using the quantitative data by evaluating whether quotas are more effective at shifting policy if they bring in more women MPs. I expect quota laws to have a larger effect on work–family policies in countries with greater "shocks" of incoming women after their implementation.

I test this expectation by fitting models including the variable *Quota Shock*, defined as the change in women's descriptive representation following quota implementation (rather than a binary variable; O'Brien & Rickne 2016). The mean quota shock is 6-percentage points, while the minimum is 0.3 (Spain) and the maximum is 11.3 (Belgium). No country decreased the share of women elected after a quota law was implemented. The coefficient on *Quota Shock* is significant for both spending on allowances and the composition of leave policies (see Appendix Table A5.5 for the regression table). For spending on family allowances, a small 3 percent quota shock is linked to a reduction in spending of 0.15 percent GDP, while a larger 8 percent shock is linked to a reduction of 0.4 percent of GDP. While a relatively small 3 percent quota shock is linked to an increase in gender equality leave of 6.5 weeks, a larger 8 percent quota shock is linked to a more sizeable increase of 17.5 weeks. In contrast to the findings on quotas and party priorities discussed in Chapter 4, the results reported here suggest that the effect of quotas on real policy changes is at least partially driven by the size of the increase in the number of women in office. In Chapter 6, I provide evidence from case studies suggesting that women's increased leverage within parties (factions) and ascending to leadership roles in parties and government are both important drivers of change.

Quotas shift the composition, but not the overall size, of work–family policy spending. This suggests that insofar as the total budget is fixed, relative spending priorities favor investing in shared leave arrangements and father-specific over maternity-only leave and family allowances after a quota law. It can be very unpopular and difficult to take away benefits once they have been introduced (e.g., Pierson 2000). So why would women politicians want to decrease funding for family allowances? One explanation is that the goal is to prioritize new models of shared leave rather than reduce allowances. When faced with limited funding or spending cuts, women politicians might push to expand paid parental and paternity leave, as well as child care, even if this requires cuts to family allowances, which constitute the majority of the work–family policy budget for most countries.

For example, in 2013 France announced cuts to its generous system of family allowances along with a reformed parental leave scheme that effectively reserved six months of leave for men, and a goal of 100,000 new public child care places for children under three by 2017. The socialist Minister for Social Affairs Marisol Touraine spearheaded the policy changes, which were often discussed together as a trade-off. She said in an interview, "A strong family policy today is one that creates child care places. It can not be limited only to benefits."[14] She also claimed that the new parental leave would "put in the discussion the idea of fair sharing" between men and women.[15]

5.4.2   Robustness Checks

To ensure that these findings are not the result of model misspecification, I conduct a series of checks. I reestimate the significant results from the main models (family allowances and gender equality leave) excluding all control variables (Appendix Table A5.6). I also estimate models that exclude one country at a time to ensure the results are not driven by a single country (results available upon request). The findings for both dependent variables are robust to these additional specifications.

I also estimate models that include country-specific time trends to test the parallel-trends assumption – that trends in policy outcomes would have been the same across countries in the absence of a quota law. This specification relies on the assumption of a sharp change at implementation. While the results still hold for gender equality leave, the coefficient on quota law for the model of family allowance spending is no longer significant at conventional levels (see Appendix Table A5.6, Models 3 and 4). This suggests that, for family allowances, changes might be more gradual, occurring as the numbers of women and the salience of the law increases. The results also indicate that it is difficult to fully disentangle underlying country-level trends in family allowance spending from the causal effect of quotas.

Taken together, these results suggest that quota laws can be an important way to facilitate congruence between women's policy preferences and outcomes. The implementation of a quota law is a statistically significant determinant of shifts in the composition of leave policies, and less spending on family allowances. The results are not driven by some broader

[14] "Touraine : 'Une politique familiale ne peut se limiter qu'à des allocations'," *Le JDD*, October 28, 2014, translated by Google Translate.
[15] "Parental leave: According to Marisol Touraine 'We will put in the discussion the idea of fair sharing'," *Public Senat*, 2014.

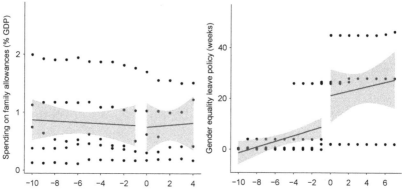

FIGURE 5.6 Event history graphs, family allowances and gender equality leave

process that influences both spending and adopting quotas simultaneously. Indeed, Figure 5.5 shows that there were no significant changes to education, health, or overall social spending in these countries, which we might expect if some underlying trend was driving a move toward gender equality in politics. The analysis also shows that the strength of a quota law is influenced by the size of quota "shocks" to the number of women in office. Greater rates of policy change are found where the quota increased the share of women in parliament more.

5.5 A CLOSER LOOK AT CHANGES WITHIN THE FIVE QUOTA COUNTRIES

This section compares real spending and parental leave policy changes from before versus after a quota law in the five countries in the sample that implemented such a law during the study period – Italy, Belgium, France, Spain, and Portugal. Figure 5.6 displays event study graphs in which the x-axis is centered on the year of quota implementation as "0." The left panel shows spending on family allowances (% GDP), and the right panel indicates the duration of gender equality promoting leave (in weeks). Note that because Portugal implemented a quota in 2009, four years of post-quota data are included for family allowances (this data ends in 2013) and seven years for gender equality leave policy (these data end in 2016).

Figure 5.6 shows no change in the four post-quota years for family allowances, but a large increase in the duration of gender equality leave policies. Part of the reason that no change is seen for family allowances is that the figure does not include the longer time-series data for countries

TABLE 5.1 *Real policy changes in quota countries, before and after quota law*

	Italy	Belgium	France	Spain	Portugal
△ Allowances (spending, % GDP)	−0.01	−0.24	0.09	0.04	−0.09
△ Gender equality leave (weeks)	0	10	54	0	42.4
Composite parts of gender equality leave					
△ Maternity leave (weeks)	0	0	0	0	−11.1
△ Paid maternity and parental leave (weeks)	0	4.3	26	0	13
△ Paid father-specific leave (weeks)	0	5.7	28	0	18.3

Notes: Change is calculated by subtracting the value of each policy from the first year before the quota law was implemented from the value in the most recent year for which data are available (2013 for family allowances, and 2016 for all leave policies). The year before quota implementation for each country is: Italy (1993), Belgium (1998), France (2001), Spain (2007), Portugal (2008).

that have had a quota for more than four years. Table 5.1 reports the pre- to post-quota changes using all data available for each country; it shows that spending on family allowances decreased for three of the five quota countries. Spending on family allowances increased in some non-quota countries (e.g., Ireland, Japan) during the same period.

The large jump in the length of gender equality promoting leave is due to significant increases in paid parental and father-specific leave in three of the five quota countries, as well as a large drop in the weeks of maternity-only leave in one country, Portugal. Table 5.1 breaks down these changes in leave policy duration. Recall that Italy had a quota law in place for only two years in the data analyzed here (1994–1995), and so the lack of change within that country is not surprising. Spain also seems to be a laggard; however, it has been increasing paid parental and father-specific leave continually just after the study period. In 2017, it doubled paternity leave from two to four weeks, and in 2018 it increased again to five weeks. In 2019, Spain passed a law that significantly raised paternity leave to equalize paid maternity and paternity leave. The law progressively increased paternity leave to eight weeks in 2019, twelve weeks in 2020, and sixteen weeks in 2021 (increasing the original father-specific leave offering by fourteen weeks). In short, the country is very much following the overall trend observed here, despite having a relatively small gender gap in preferences on the issue of working mothers.[16] Taking Spain's recent changes into account, every country that implemented a quota law except Italy (which only had one in place for two years) made large and significant changes to the composition of its leave policies. The table also shows that greater policy changes are seen in countries with larger gender gaps in attitudes toward working mothers (Belgium and France) compared to those with smaller gender gaps (especially Italy and Spain).

While Portugal began changing parental leave policies in the first year of quota law implementation (2009), other countries saw changes more gradually over time. In addition to the example of Spain, which shifted the leave policy configuration significantly ten years after quota law implementation, Belgium made significant changes to father-specific leave in 2005 and 2012 (seven and fourteen years after quota law implementation). This suggests that the effects of quota laws on parental leave policies are not limited to the short term, but increase over time. In Chapter 6 I explain how these changes are linked to women within the parliament and in key cabinet roles. The increased salience of gender inequality among male political leaders also plays a role, especially in Portugal where political experience in parliament is not a route to cabinet positions.

What role did the EU play in these policy changes? Recall that EU membership is included as a control variable in the main analysis because the EU has issued directives on maternity and parental leave. However, as Moss and Devan note, the directives, "usually create a floor below which countries cannot go, rather than a ceiling that they must strive to reach" (Moss & Deven 2019, p. 431). The European Council passed three main directives related to maternity and parental leave during the study period. The 1992 Directive on maternity leave (92/85/EEC) requires countries to grant fourteen weeks of maternity leave, but four of the five quotas countries in my data already offered more than this, and so were unaffected. Portugal increased its maternity leave by 1.1 weeks to adhere to the directive, but it was well before the quota law was passed.

---

[16] Royal Decree-Law 6/2019, of March 1, on urgent measures to guarantee equal treatment and opportunities for women and men in employment and occupation. www.boe.es/buscar/act.php?id=BOE-A-2019-3244

The two other directives concern parental leave. The 1996 Directive on parental leave (1996/34/EC) requires a right to parental leave of at least three months, and the 2010 Directive on parental leave (2010/18/EU) increases the length to four months, at least one of which is non-transferable for each parent. These also have little impact on my analysis because they do not require member states to offer paid leave. This is very important, because "in some countries parental leave is unpaid, while in others it is paid only for a certain period and these differences are identified by experts as a justification for the practical take-up of the leave or for its effective duration" (Ramalho, Foubert, & Burri 2015, p. 8). Recall that the measures of both paid maternity and parental leave and father-specific leave collected by the OECD Employment data and used to create the Gender Equality Leave indicator use only paid leave.[17]

Notably, EU directives did not require any paid paternity or father-specific leave at all during the study period. The European Council adopted a new directive on work/life balance in June 2019 (Directive (EU) 2019/1158) that does require member states to have paid father-specific leave by August 2022: ten days of paid paternity leave, and two of the four months of parental leave are to be paid and non-transferable. In summary, the considerable leave policy changes within quota countries that I observe cannot be attributed to compliance with EU directives.

What about the role of women's movements in driving quota adoption or work–family policy change? It is very difficult to measure the presence or strength of women's movements across countries over time. The best data available come from Htun and Weldon (2012), who compile measures of the strength and autonomy of feminist movements over time in seventy countries. Their data show that there was no change in the strength or autonomy of women's movements in Belgium, France, or Portugal before a quota law was passed. In the remaining two countries that have adopted a quota, Italy and Spain, the strength of feminist women's movements declined before the quota law passed (autonomy remained the same). I find little evidence from previous research that popular women's movements were behind the push for quota laws in Belgium and Portugal (Weeks 2018). The exception is France, where a popular parity movement

---

[17] In analysis not shown here but available from the author, I also look at the impact of gender quota laws on the total weeks of parental leave with job protection, also collected by OECD Employment. This refers to the number of weeks after maternity leave which a woman can take as parental leave with her job protected, *disregarding payment conditions*. No association is found between quota law implementation and the overall period of job protection provided in a leave.

was influential in coercing political actors to address the issue (Murray 2012).

While popular feminist movements have often pushed for change on issues like child care, previous studies do not find a strong link between women's movements and policy change on work–family issues (Htun & Weldon 2018; Katzenstein & Mueller 1987; Morgan 2006). As Morgan (2006) comments, "The United States has one of the most significant feminist movements in the Western world, yet it has failed to produce a national child care policy or paid parental leave" (p. 20). Looking at family leave generosity and child care in a global context, Htun and Weldon (2018) find that strong, autonomous feminist movements are negatively associated with leave generosity, but positively linked to national child care policies (significant at the 0.1 level). They conclude that while feminist movements are especially important for status issues (such as violence against women), for work–family policies other factors such as economic conditions matter more. Nor does my qualitative analysis of policy evolution in four countries (Chapter 6) suggest women's movements play a strong role in driving work–family policy change after a quota law is implemented.

5.6   CONCLUSION

This chapter examines the impact of newly popular quota laws on work–family policies in high-income OECD democracies. It finds that quota laws are an effective tool for increasing the substantive representation of women's interests. Quota laws shift the composition of leave policies toward leave that promotes gender equality (adding nineteen more weeks of gender equality leave), and decrease spending on family allowances. These changes are in line with women's greater support for working mothers compared to men.

These findings contrast with those from previous studies which find that quotas increase spending on social welfare and health in a global context (Chen 2010; Clayton & Zetterberg 2018). The disparity in these findings is likely due to two important differences between the global context and that of rich democracies. First, the level of spending on social policy is much higher in rich democracies, but since 2000 the growth in social expenditures has been most pronounced in Asia and Latin America. Rich democracies, and Western European countries in particular, lead social expenditure tables, whereas global levels of welfare and health spending are on average far lower. For example, in 2010 average social protection spending (measured as % GDP) by region was 33 percent for Western Europe, compared to 27 percent for North America, 9.6 percent for Asia and the Pacific, 7.7 percent for Latin America and the Caribbean, 7.4 percent in Central and Eastern Europe, 1.7 percent for Middle East North Africa, and 0.9 percent for sub-Saharan Africa (Adema 2014). Social expenditures have been rising around the world since 2000, but the most pronounced increases have been observed the Asia/Pacific region, followed by Latin America (Adema 2014). Outside of Western Europe and North America, then there is arguably more room to significantly increase levels of social spending according to women's priorities.

The second important difference is that party competition in rich democracies centers on a left–right cleavage over redistribution and spending. My argument is that in this context, we should expect quotas to lead to change especially on issues that do not neatly align with the left–right cleavage and thus are not subject to intense preexisting party competition. The structure of party competition is very different in other regions of the world, and many democracies do not have the same left–right differences over social spending, or strong parties at all. In these countries, quotas and an increasing number of women in office could have more power to shift welfare policies that are not already clearly crystallized, with parties organized in opposite positions around them.

Work–family policy changes are important in their own right, but also have implications for broader social welfare outcomes. Future research should explore related micro-level outcomes to search for trade-offs. For example, are lower-income women better off, given that quotas reduce spending on family allowances? Could quotas lead to a trade-off that benefits educated, professional women at the expense of lower-income women? What about children? Maternal employment has been shown to be one of the main safeguards against child poverty (Lichter & Eggebeen 1994), but this assumes that public investment yields high-quality care.

Quota laws are often viewed with derision as artificial, and even undemocratic, mechanisms of altering the composition of policymaking bodies. The results presented here suggest that quotas cannot be dismissed so easily. Even in the "most difficult" institutional context of parliamentary democracies, quota laws lead to changes in the direction of women's aggregate preferences – and thus increase democratic responsiveness. The findings also point to fruitful new directions for models of the policy process and welfare state development. The theory presented here suggests that mechanisms designed to facilitate more equal representation, such as quotas, are especially likely to shift outcomes on issues that are:

(1) characterized by a gap in preferences and (2) orthogonal to the main left–right party dimension. This framework can be used to identify and test other potential outcomes of interest for women as well as for other identity groups. One such promising issue area is violence against women, which is both relatively new to the political agenda and characterized by a gender gap in preferences (more women than men view it as a problem and prefer tougher laws).[18]

Finally, the analysis presented here suggests that quotas lead to change in the composition of work–family policy policies in the direction of women's preferences, but it cannot tell us why. An important puzzle is thus how do quotas shift policies, if the mechanism is not purely the number of women in parliament? In the next chapter, I use qualitative evidence from countries that are otherwise similar but differ on passing a quota law to shed light on this question.

---

[18] Eurobarometer 73.2: Humanitarian Aid, Domestic Violence against Women, and Mental Well-Being, February–March 2010.

6

How Gender Quota Laws Change Work–Family Policies

Women [candidates] go in, they are put on a list by usually men who are president of the party at the provincial level. They look for women very well known in media, and she is interesting for four years, but then they look for another newer one to get more votes… so our task now when the lists are being formed, we say what we already have we want to keep. What makes a woman a minister, is being already in parliament.

–Els van Hoof, Belgian politician (Christian Democrat and Flemish party, CD&V)[1]

Why should women be more concerned about it [work–family issues] than men? Children are both from the father and the mother, why should it be a female concern? [Laughs] Then we always… we talk ourselves into it. Why should it be, this sort of reconciliation between family life and working life, why should it be a woman's concern? It is, and I'm leaving here and have to get my son and feed him and give him a bath.

–Teresa Caeiro, Portuguese politician (Centro Democrático e Social party, CDS)[2]

The previous chapters established that quota laws lead to policy change on work–family issues in the direction of women's preferences – including reduced spending on family allowances and shifting leave policies toward more shared parental and fathers-only leave, with less maternity-only leave. This chapter investigates *how* such changes come about. Understanding the mechanisms linking quotas to policy change makes the quantitative findings more plausible and deepens our understanding of quotas' political influence. I focus on three such mechanisms: women

[1] Personal interview, October 16, 2013, Brussels, Belgium.
[2] Personal interview, November 5, 2013, Lisbon, Portugal.

in parties (factions), women in government (ministers), and increased salience of gender equality among men party leaders. I argue that electoral quota laws uniquely amplify all of these mechanisms: they increase the number of women across the political spectrum and often especially on the right, where parties have not already embraced other affirmative action measures. This opens up more opportunities for change – and men from all parties must grapple with this.

To explore how quotas lead to change, I use qualitative evidence from two matched-pair case studies – countries that are similar to each other in most respects except for quota adoption. The "most similar" cases provide a framework for thinking about what would have happened, all else equal, if a quota had not been adopted, and vice versa. Detailed narratives of work–family policy evolution in the quota countries of Belgium and Portugal, compared to the counterfactual, non-quota countries of Austria and Italy, provide new insights into the mechanisms that link quota laws to policy change. I draw on over sixty personal interviews with politicians and activists in all four countries conducted in 2013 and 2014, and supplement this data with party and government documents, parliamentary proceedings, and newspaper coverage of leave policy debates (see the Appendix to Chapter 1 for details on interview methods). I focus primarily on the evolution of leave policies (1990–2019) and the major conceptual change between policies that incentivize mothers to stay home (long maternity leaves) versus those that encourage gender equality in the labor market and household (shared parental leave, father-specific leave). I also discuss family allowances and child care policy when relevant. These dependent variables reflect the large gender gap in preferences for maternal employment demonstrated in Chapter 3, on which women are much more progressive than men.

The quotations at the start of the chapter indicate the key ways in which quota laws are linked to policy outcomes in the four countries I studied. Belgium's quota law led to more women in parliament and in government, particularly in the labor and social affairs portfolio, which is responsible for leave policies. The first above-mentioned quote from van Hoof, a Flemish Christian democrat politician and former leader of the women's section of the party, illustrates a keen awareness among women politicians that gender quotas for parliament were not enough. After the quota law was passed, women actively campaigned for more women in the government, including an action in 2010, supported by women across parties, that disrupted the parliament chambers by unfurling banners reading "More Women in Government!" As the van Hoof quote illustrates, part of the strategy involved pressuring party leaders to keep the experienced women in their parties in winnable positions on the ballot, because these women had the potential to become government ministers. As a result, nearly every minister of labor and social affairs since the gender quota was introduced in Belgium has been a woman, and they have made policy changes consistent with women's preferences to support working mothers.

In Portugal, the quota law has been in place for a shorter period of time, but women have found new ways to legislate from the backbench. This includes a new working group on parenting and gender equality that is composed of nearly 90 percent women across political parties. The quotation from Christian democrat Teresa Caeiro demonstrates a sentiment from women across parties in Portugal, and indeed in all four countries I studied, that women are driving this agenda. Passing a quota law increases the share of women in office, which gives them more power to negotiate as factions within and across parties for change. Quotas did not increase the number of women in key ministerial posts, most likely because ministers are not promoted from within parliament in Portugal.

In both quota countries, it is also clear that the salience of women's policy concerns has increased. Men party leaders often act as key supporters and protagonists of policy change in the direction of gender equality. The biggest changes are observed within parties on the right and far right, where the number of women increased the most after a quota law. The counterfactual cases instead offer evidence of backsliding (Austria) or the absence of significant policy change (Italy), particularly when parties on the far right with few women in their ranks gain government power.

This chapter first details the logic of three potential mechanisms through which quotas could shift national-level policies for women (factions, ministers, and salience), and then examines evidence from the four cases. I then compare the evolution of key leave policies across countries, tracing the origins and motivations of reforms and their links to quota laws.

6.1   QUOTAS AND LEAVE POLICIES: FACTIONS, MINISTERS, AND SALIENCE

This section briefly reviews leave policies and how they relate to maternal employment. Leave policies historically applied only to women (*maternity leave*). Maternity leave is intended to offer job protection for working mothers as they prepare for and recover from childbirth. For example, some countries require mandatory maternity leave for a certain number of weeks before and after birth. Maternity leave is typically paid in high-income OECD democracies, although the rates of pay differ.

Parental leave can be taken up by either parent, and is typically longer than maternity leave because it is intended to be used for caring responsibilities rather than medical or health reasons. Parental leave can be unpaid, or paid at different rates; it is typically not as well paid as maternity leave. It can be set up as either a family entitlement (where theoretically the leave can be split by mothers and fathers, but in practice it is mostly taken by mothers) or an individual entitlement that is non-transferable. The consensus is that short, well-paid maternity leave is better at encouraging women to maintain ties to the labor market than longer leave paid at low rates (Baker & Milligan 2008; Dustmann & Schönberg 2012). Because mothers are much more likely than fathers to take parental leave, many countries have legislated special incentives in the form of extra months of parental leave or extra cash if fathers use a certain amount of it. For example, Austria's 2016 Family Time Bonus Act pays families a bonus if fathers take at least twenty-eight days of leave (see Table 6.1).

Paternity leave is job-protected leave for fathers only. Paternity (or "daddy") leave is typically allocated for days or weeks rather than months, and is often fully paid. Research shows that well-paid, shared parental and daddy leave can increase both the time fathers spend at home and in household labor, and the time mothers spend in the workplace (Bartel et al. 2018; Patnaik 2019). Few fathers take leave that is low paid or set up as a family entitlement. If gender equality in the workplace and shared caring at home are the goal, the direction for leave policy is clear: shared parental leave with more well-paid, fathers-only leave to encourage men's active involvement in caring (Moss & Deven 2015).

Chapter 2 proposes three mechanisms that could link gender quota laws to leave policy change. First, more women in parties and parliament (a "critical mass") might shift policy priorities, particularly early on in the policymaking process as agendas are set. Critical mass theory suggests that as women's descriptive representation increases, they will increasingly be able to work together to promote legislation related to their shared political interests (Childs & Krook 2009; Kanter 1977). In a more gender-balanced environment, women may feel more comfortable expressing "gendered" preferences, and men may be more likely to be receptive to their views. Mendelberg, Karpowitz, and Goedert (2013) find that as the number of women increases, so does their authority, and that with a critical mass, women begin discussing different issues (specifically, caring responsibilities).

All four countries under consideration here are parliamentary democracies with strong party discipline, where individual legislators are assumed to have only a minimal role in policymaking. Yet, even in this context backbenchers can exert influence within the party as factions (e.g., Lovenduski 2001; Morgan 2006) and in their work on parliamentary committees, which often have legislating power (Pansardi & Vercesi 2017; Strøm 1998). Political parties decide on the distribution of committee positions, typically taking individual preferences into account (Hazan 2001). Prior studies have shown that committee assignments correspond well to women's preferences (Bækgaard & Kjaer 2012; Espírito-Santo & Sanches 2019; Zetterberg 2008). Thus, I expect quotas to lead to more women in parliamentary parties, which will increase the strength of women's sections or informal groups ("factions") within parties, and women's voices on parliamentary committees.

Although MPs can play a role, policy in parliamentary democracies typically originates in the party leadership and the government rather than the legislature (Laver & Shepsle 1996; Martin 2004; Strøm 2000). Government ministers play a crucial role in shaping the policy agenda by determining the form and content of draft legislation within their portfolio area. However, it is notoriously difficult to assess individual ministers' relative contributions to policy development (Blondel & Müller-Rommel 1993). This is partly because individual ministers differ in their ability and desire to shape policy beyond their party leaders' preferences (Dewan & Hortala-Vallve 2011; Indridason & Kam 2005). Alexiadou (2015) finds that certain types of cabinet ministers ("partisans" and "ideologues") are more influential than others ("loyalists") in changing social welfare policy. Thus, the background of women ministers (are they feminists? are they working mothers?) and which portfolios they are allocated is likely to be especially important for this mechanism. Leave policy typically falls under the purview of labor or employment, social affairs, and/or equality portfolios.

There are at least three reasons why gender quota laws might lead to more women in the cabinet. First, a large and consistent body of work demonstrates that: (1) quotas increase the share of women in office (Hughes 2011; Paxton & Hughes 2015; Paxton, Hughes, & Painter 2010; Schwindt-Bayer 2009; Tripp & Kang 2008) and that (2) the share of women in parliament and cabinet are highly correlated (Arriola & Johnson 2014; Barnes & O'Brien 2018; Bego 2014; Claveria 2014; Krook &

O'Brien 2012). The logic behind this link is that as women gain seats and experience in parliament, the pool of potential women cabinet ministers grows. Second, Claveria (2014) finds that governing parties that have adopted party quotas are more likely to promote women. The same logic ought to apply to the link between quota laws and cabinet seats, particularly over time as women gain experience and leadership roles in parliament. In addition, increased numbers of women in parliament may form "strategic coalitions" to influence men party leaders' decisions on cabinet selection (Childs & Krook 2009; Claveria 2014). The third reason why gender quota laws might increase the number of women in the cabinet is that such laws commit parties and countries to gender equality. The quota law sets an important precedent that could lead to the expectation that not just parliaments but also governments should incorporate relatively equal shares of women.

A wealth of research suggests that women are more likely to be appointed to certain types of portfolios, like welfare, education, health, and equality, than to what are often considered the more prestigious posts of budget, finance, foreign affairs, or defense (Escobar-Lemmon & Taylor-Robinson 2005; Krook & O'Brien 2012; Reynolds 1999; Siaroff 2000). Increased shares of women in cabinet are linked to the passage of women-friendly social policy, including child care, job-protected leave, and the environment (Atchison 2015; Atchison & Down 2009, 2019). Atchison and Down (2009) show that it is not just more women in cabinet that leads to policy change on leave policies, but specifically women in social welfare portfolios. After all, they (rather than women in defense or foreign affairs ministries) are in a position to directly influence these policies. I therefore expect that quotas will lead to more women in key ministries for leave policies (such as social issues, labor, employment), who then shift leave policy in the direction of women's preferences.

Finally, the quota law itself might increase the salience of equality, leading men party leaders across the political spectrum to prioritize related issues. The literature on policy feedback, the idea that past policies significantly affect future policy outcomes, suggests that policies send certain messages to the electorate and can shape attitudes and behavior (Campbell 2003, 2012). In this case, by raising the importance of gender equality to the national stage, quota laws can lead the public to take this as the new norm and even expect greater attention to women in politics. For example, in France the concept of parity was once deemed unconstitutional and became the subject of a long, acrimonious debate. Over time, as media coverage and public awareness of the concept grew, parity became normalized. When the quota law eventually passed, it enjoyed high levels of support in opinion polls (Murray, Krook, & Opello 2012). The discussion of public debates about quota laws in the introduction to this book establishes that quotas are often linked to women's broader political interests, including work–family issues.

Men elites are likely to interpret growing support for women in politics after a quota law (Beaman et al. 2009; Burnet 2011) as a cue to better represent women's interests in order to claim credit with women constituents (Mayhew 1974). If they do not, they risk losing voter support – even if they did not support the quota law in the first place. Parties that were openly opposed to the quota might feel an added incentive to highlight and/or develop their policies related to women's interests to avoid appearing outdated. Less cynically, party elites may internalize changing norms. Over time, they may come to accept the notion that a more balanced representation of gendered policy concerns is normatively appropriate, and shift their parties' positions accordingly. Recent experimental evidence demonstrates that gender quotas can increase men's generosity, potentially because quotas could "make the idea of equity more salient" (Czibor & Dominguez Martinez 2019, p. 24).

In short, quotas can put women's political issues on the radar of men elites. Political salience in the context of parties typically refers to which issues receive the bulk of a given party's attention (Budge, Robertson, & Hearl 1987). Following this definition, I interpret salience here as increased attention to maternal employment, and the policies that support it, from party leaders across political parties. I look for two main observable implications of salience in the following cases. First, if increased salience among party elites after a quota law drives policy change, I expect to find that policies are proposed by the government, or hammered out in coalition agreements, rather than influenced by individual ministers or women in parliament. Second, I expect to see an emerging consensus across the political spectrum on policies to promote working mothers' and fathers' roles in the household (as opposed to policies that mainly support women's caregiving roles). In other words, if increased salience is driving policy change, we should start to see party leaders across the left and right prioritize the issue of how dual-income families can combine care and work, even if they have different specific policy proposals. If, alternatively, women as factions or ministers drive policy change, I would expect individual women ministers or women in parliament to influence policy change more directly.

An important attribute of gender quota laws compared to the growth of women's descriptive representation in rich OECD democracies absent a quota is that such laws lead to increases in the number of women across political parties – not just on the left. If quotas lead to greater changes in party demographics on the right, the implication is that all three mechanisms are potentially heightened more among parties on the right compared to those the left. Women might reach "critical mass" numbers for the first time within right-leaning parties, giving them more leverage to draw party leaders' attention to their priorities. Over time, parties on the right might elevate women to leadership roles within the party or government for the first time – especially if the party now perceives that gender equality throughout the party is important. Because parties on the right often did not support quota legislation, they might feel an added incentive to develop their credentials on gender equality and women's interests to compensate for past opposition. In other words, if quotas cue increased salience of gender equality to men party leaders, this ought to affect parties on the right especially.

The remainder of this chapter tests the relative strength of these mechanisms by tracing the evolution of leave policies in two countries that passed a quota law, Belgium and Portugal, and two that did not, Austria and Italy.

6.2 BELGIUM AND AUSTRIA: "MORE WOMEN IN THE GOVERNMENT!"

Belgium and Austria are similar across many dimensions that are relevant to gender-related policies: they are both conservative welfare states that have historically supported a "male breadwinner" model by conditioning relatively generous benefits on strong ties to the labor market (Esping-Andersen 1990; Orloff 1996). Both countries had similar levels of women's labor force participation when Belgium adopted a quota, and similar levels of economic development (see Appendix Table A1.1). About 90 percent of the population in each country historically identifies as Catholic. Finally, the gender gap in preferences regarding maternal employment is moderately large in both countries (5–10 percent; see Figure 3.2 in Chapter 3), making it more likely that these issues will be prioritized after a quota law.

The share of women increased dramatically in Belgium after the quota law was implemented in 1999 (Figure 6.1). The 1999 election resulted in 23 percent women in parliament, nearly doubling the previous 13 percent. Women's representation increased again in Belgium when the

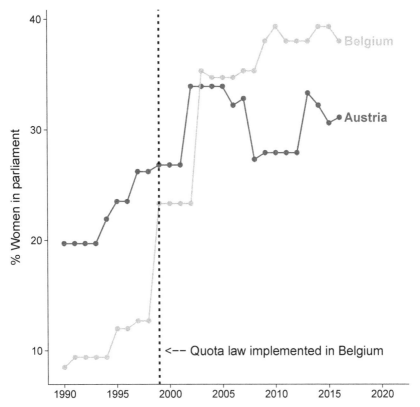

FIGURE 6.1 Share of women in parliament, Belgium and Austria
Note: Data from the comparative political dataset (Armingeon et al. 2016).

quota law was strengthened in 2002: the quota threshold was raised to 50 percent, the first two positions on the list were required to alternate by gender, and compliance was required for the list to be accepted. The share of women in parliament reached 35 percent the following year, after the election in 2003. Since then, levels of women in parliament have typically remained in the range of 35–40 percent in Belgium. Austria has experienced a more gradual increase in women's representation in recent years, typically electing around 30 percent women. The jump in women's representation in 2002 was driven by a bad result for the male-dominated far-right party FPÖ, which lost thirty-four seats in the election, as well as moderate gains from the Greens and social democrats (SPÖ) (Muller 2004).

Belgium and Austria are parliamentary democracies with proportional systems of representation, so coalition governments are the norm in both. Austria has typically been governed by a coalition of social

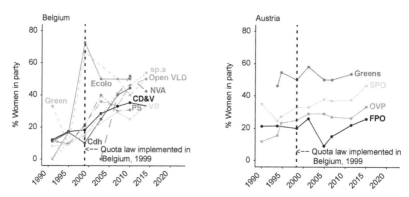

FIGURE 6.2 Share of women in parties, Belgium and Austria
Belgian parties: Ecolo (French greens), N-VA (nationalist, right), sp.a (Flemish social
democrats), Open VLD (Flemish liberals), Cdh (French Christian democrats), Groen
(Flemish greens), CD&V (Flemish Christian democrats), PS (French social democrats), VB
(far right).
Austrian parties: Die Grunen (greens), SPÖ (social democrats), ÖVP (Christian
democrats), FPÖ (far right).

democrats (SPÖ) and Christian democrats (ÖVP), although the far-right
FPÖ has occasionally been in government. In Belgium, parties are divided
both ideologically and linguistically; there are French and Flemish versions of most major parties (such as the Christian democrats, social
democrats, and greens), as well as some far-right and nationalist parties
like the Vlaams Belang (VB) and New Flemish Alliance (N-VA). Belgium's
consociational design requires an equal number of Flemish- and French-
speaking ministers in government. This means that in both countries,
many policies (including parental leave and child care) are negotiated in
written coalition agreements before governments take office. However,
both countries are also known for relatively high levels of ministerial independence (?Timmermans 1994). Decisions on policy design and
implementation are often made by individual cabinet ministers who have
considerable autonomy, particularly on issues that are not formally on the
cabinet agenda. Parliamentary committees associated with cabinet portfolios can also play important roles in the policymaking process (Strøm
1998).

Figure 6.2 takes a more detailed look at how the quota law changed
women's representation within parties in Belgium (left), and trends in the
counterfactual case of Austria (right). The dotted vertical line indicates the
year that the quota law was first implemented in Belgium (1999). With so
many parties in Belgium individual party trends are hard to discern – but
the important point to notice about the figure is that all parties in Belgium

vastly increased the share of women in their ranks after the quota. Some parties did so in the first election after implementation (the green parties), and some after the quota threshold increased to 50 percent in 2002 (the Flemish and French Christian democrats, the CD&V and Cdh, as well as the far-right VB, the French social democrats (PS), and so on). The average party increase in women's representation after the quota's introduction is 27-percentage points for center-right and right parties (CD&V, Cdh, VB) and 34-percentage points for those on the center-left and left (sp.a, PS, Ecolo, and Green).[3] Austria did not experience a large jump around this time period. The share of women in parties slowly increased for all parties except the far-right FPÖ, for which the share of women ebbed and then increased again. In summary, the figure shows that Belgium's quota increased the share of women within parties across the political spectrum, while Austria exhibited much more variation in women's representation across parties (most were affiliated with the Greens, and the fewest with the far right).

Table 6.1 summarizes the major changes to leave policy in both countries since Belgium's gender quota law was implemented (1999). Table 6.1 shows that, in line with the findings reported in Chapter 5, all of the leave policy changes in Belgium after the implementation of the quota law relate to strengthening shared parental leave and paternity leave.

Before the quota law, the Belgian state provided fifteen weeks of job-protected maternity leave, three days of fully paid paternity leave, and an individual, nontransferable right to parental leave of three months. In 2005, after the law's passage, the pay for parental leave was increased, and the policy was made more flexible to allow parents to take the leave part time. In 2009, the time in which parents can take parental leave was extended (up to the child's twelfth birthday), in 2012 the leave was extended from three to four months, and in 2018 another law was passed to allow parents to take half days. The 2012 provision reflects an EU directive that requires four months of (paid or unpaid) parental leave; this extension to leave is paid in Belgium.

The major change to paternity leave occurred in 2001, when fathers were given the right to ten days total – three mandatory and fully paid and the rest paid at 82 percent of current wages (Hartlapp 2009; Vandeweyer & Glorieux 2008). After the quota law, there was no change to

---

[3] The post-quota increase in women's representation within parties is calculated by subtracting women's representation as MPs before quotas (1995) from the most recent post-quota year (2014).

TABLE 6.1 *Summary of leave policy changes 1999–2019, Belgium and Austria*

	Belgium	Austria
Maternity leave	No change	No change
Paternity leave	2001: First introduced: right to ten days, three days mandatory and paid *Min. Labor Onkelinx* **(F, PS),** *Min. Social Affairs Vandebroucke (M, sp.a),* *Min. Enterprises Daems (M, VLD)*	2016: Fathers "bonus payment" of 700 euros if they take leave of twenty-eight to thirty-one days; employers must agree (not legal right) *Min. Family Karmasin* **(F, ÖVP)** 2019: Right to leave from work for a period of one month *Min. Social Affairs Hartinger-Klein (F, FPÖ)*
Parental leave	2005: Introduces more flexibility in how leave can be taken (full time, half time, 1/5 options); increases the level of benefits paid *Min.Employment Van den Bossche (F, sp.a)* 2009: Extends time limit during which leave can be taken (up to age twelve) *Min. Labor Milquet (F, Cdh)* 2012: Right to parental leave increases from three to four months *Min. Labor De Coninck (F, sp.a)* 2018: Introduces more flexibility (1/10 option) *Min. Social Affairs De Block (F, Open VLD),* *Min. Labor Peeters (M, CD&V),* *Min. Justice Greens (M, CD&V)*	2002: Extends cash benefits for care from two to three years; benefits no longer require that the parent previously worked *PM, Schussel (M, ÖVP),* *Min.Social Affairs Haupt (M, FPÖ)* 2007: Introduces more flexibility in cash benefit options for care (short-term, mid-range, and long-term options) *Coalition agreement (SPÖ, ÖVP)* 2010: Introduces more flexibility (two more options), including a well-paid short-term option based on income. *Min. Family Marek (F, ÖVP)*

Notes: Table shows changes in leave policies after Belgium (but not Austria) implemented a gender quota law in 1999. Key actors in italics; women in bold.

the duration of leave available solely for mothers. Additionally, the right to paid breastfeeding breaks to express milk at work was passed in 2002. In summary, both parental leave and paternity leave were extended and made more flexible and generous in Belgium after the quota came into effect, while maternity-only leave remained the same. Notably, Belgium has no extended, low-paid parental leave option encouraging women to stay at home. Overall, Belgium has relatively short maternity and parental leave (maternity leave is fairly well compensated but parental leave is not),[4] and relatively long leave available to fathers, given the paternity leave and the right to individual and nontransferable parental leave. Policy can thus be characterized as moving in the direction of greater support for working mothers after the law, although it is far from the "ideal" of well-paid shared parental leaves found in Scandinavia.[5]

Before 1999, Austria offered extended parental leave of up to two years, with six mandatory prenatal and ten postnatal weeks for the mother. The sixteen maternity-only weeks are fully paid, and the extended parental leave is paid at a lower rate. Technically, fathers are allowed to share the leave after the mother's sixteen weeks. In 1996, a sharing rule was introduced that prohibits one parent from taking more than eighteen months of the two-year leave period; an additional six-month leave is only available if the other parent takes it. In practice, fathers rarely took any extended parental leave.

What happened after a quota law was implemented in Belgium but not in Austria? In 2002 Austria's parental leave was again extended, this time to three years. This law also extended benefits to all parents rather than only those who previously worked outside the home – making it a policy mix between parental leave and family allowance. The job protection remained at two years, while three years of leave/child care benefits became available (a mismatch that would hurt parents trying to return to paid work after the two-year period). This law was controversial and widely interpreted as a step backwards that would discourage women's

---

[4] Current rates of parental leave entitle parents to 721 euros per month net of taxes (Merla, Mortelmans, & Fusulier 2018).
[5] Another unique aspect of the Belgian leave system is the system of "time credits," which existed since 1985 but was revised and made more flexible in 2001. The time credit system exists alongside parental leave, and allows employees the right to take a paid leave (right to up to one year full-time equivalent) over their entire career, during which a state allowance is paid. The purpose of the scheme is increasing the quality of life by facilitating a better combination of work and private life, and it is used disproportionately by younger women to perform care work (Devisscher & Sanders 2007; Morel 2007).

employment in Austria; employee and women's organizations and the social democrats denounced it (Blum 2014).

More parental leave options were introduced in 2010, including a well-paid short-term option based on income (guarantees a share of the individual's salary) that would benefit working mothers. This option was modeled on the German policy shift from long, low-paid leave to a shorter, income-based leave in 2007, except the Austrian policy retained the option to take leave for up to three years (Blum 2010, 2014). In 2016, the Family Time Bonus Act established a bonus payment for fathers who take at least twenty-eight days of leave, but this leave is not a right and must be agreed by employers. Statutory paternity leave was extensively debated for years, with the legal right to one month's paternity leave (referred to as *Papamonat*) finally passing in 2019.

Summarizing the changes in Austrian leave policy since 1999 (when Belgium implemented a quota law but Austria did not), the state extended parental leave to very long periods (the extension to three years in 2002 was seen as particularly damaging), although it has more recently made changes to leave policy to enable working mothers to take advantage of shorter, well-paid leaves and to encourage fathers to participate. It stands out for having one of the longest parental leaves in the world and for having adopted statutory paternity leave only very recently.

How do these policy changes affect the take-up of leave within families? Parental leave in Belgium is an individual, nontransferable entitlement, while in Austria it is a family entitlement with an incentive for fathers. As a result, a much greater share of fathers take leave in Belgium than in Austria. In Belgium, the vast majority (93 percent) of fathers take paternity leave (an average length of 9.8 days), and about one-third of fathers go on to take parental leave as well.[6] In Austria, 8 percent of fathers have taken the new "bonus time" month,[7] and fewer than 3 percent are estimated to take parental leave (Rille-Pfeiffer, Dearing, & Schmidt 2018).

The comparison of Belgium and Austria shows that after the quota law, Belgium shifted toward policies that help women combine work and family, and in the absence of a quota law Austria did not. Belgium

---

[6] "Bijelke geboorte info ouderschapsverlof voor vaders," Press release, *Office of Minister Kris Peeters*, January 14, 2019, www.krispeeters.be/sites/default/files/20190114_PB_campagne_ouderschapsverlof_vaders.pdf.

[7] "Pressure grows in Austria for paternity leave for all," *France 24*, February 13, 2019, www.france24.com/en/20190213-pressure-grows-austria-paternity-leave-all.

extended paternity leave and made it mandatory, kept moderate-length periods of leave available for women, and made parental leave more generous and flexible. Table 6.1 shows that women ministers were involved in every major reform. Austria followed a different trajectory over this period, instead implementing policy that was widely regarded to support women's traditional roles in the household rather than working mothers.

What can explain these countries' different trajectories, and what role did the gender quota law play in policy development in Belgium? Considering the mechanism of a critical mass of women first, while the number of women did increase significantly in Belgium, this did not directly contribute to the evolution of the country's leave policy. Individual MPs can table legislation in Belgium, but (as in most parliamentary democracies) the government initiates most laws, including all of the leave policies considered here (Bergman et al. 2003; Vliegenthart & Walgrave 2011). All of the relevant legislation originated from government offices – especially the ministries of Labor/Employment and Social Affairs.

Women in the executive were involved in every leave policy change after the quota's adoption. Women have held the portfolio for Labor/Employment for fourteen of the twenty years since then; four of the six ministers have been women (66 percent), up from 25 percent during the twenty years before the quota was introduced.[8] From 1999 (the period after the quota law): Onkelinkx (F), Van den Bossche (F), Piette (M), Milquet (F), De Coninck (F), and Peeters (M). Thus after 1999, women were more than twice as likely to hold the labor portfolio. This suggests support for the minister mechanism: in Belgium, the quota increased the number of women holding cabinet positions with influence over leave policies.

MP and former leader of the Flemish Christian democrats' women's section, Els van Hoof, explained that this was no accident; women in parties have been keenly involved in making sure the quota translates into not only more women in parliament but also in government:

What we see here is a "revolving door" for women, they go in politics but then are replaced quicker than men. Women go in and then they go out, they are replaced by other women. Here it's a problem because women are in the parliament, but then they are replaced in the next election and then men still have the power. Women go in, they are put on a list by usually men who are president of the

[8] The Labor/Employment ministers from 1978 to 1999 (the period before the quota law) are: Spitaels (M), Hansenne (M), Van den Brande (M), and Smet (F; i.e., 25 percent were women).

party at the provincial level. They look for women very well known in media, and she is interesting for four years, but then they look for another newer one to get more votes. The woman with experience, she will be on the list but not the most important place, because when she gets more power she can also get in government. So our task now when the lists are being formed, we say what we already have we want to keep. You see when you are in parliament, and I have experienced this myself, you need experience to know the system… and what makes a woman a minister, is being already in parliament.[9]

This quote illustrates that after the passage of Belgium's quota law, women legislators actively pushed their parties not only to comply with the law and include more women, but to keep experienced women on lists so that they had a chance to obtain government roles. The push for more women in the cabinet came not only from the Flemish Christian democrats, but from women across parties. In June 1997, after the quota law was adopted but before it was first implemented, a cross-party group of women senators tabled a bill that would have required equal gender representation in the federal cabinet.[10] The bill argued that unequal representation leaves Belgium "faced with a democratic deficit that is particularly evident at the level of the federal government." Similar proposals were tabled in 2000 and 2001, in both the House and Senate.[11] Women made up the vast majority of co-signatories on these bills, and they came from across the political spectrum: the French and Flemish greens, social democrats, liberals, and Christian democrats.

   None of these bills made significant progress (the debate focused on, among other issues, the added logistical problems of forming a government, given the linguistic quotas), but they show concerted action by women across parties to increase attention to the issue (Marques-Pereira & Gigante 2001). This continued, more visibly, in the 2000s when women across parties (nationalist/conservative, Christian democrats, liberals, social democrats, and greens) protested in front of parliament, with chants and colorful banners reading, for example, "More aunts in government!", "More mothers in government!", "More grandmothers in government!". They called again for equal representation in the cabinet. They unfurled banners from the balcony of the House, to cheers and clapping across parties.[12] Women MPs also wore black arm bands in parliament as a sign of protest.

---

[9] Els van Hoof, personal interview, October 16, 2013, Brussels, Belgium.
[10] Senate, Doc. parl., 1-657/1 (1996–1997).
[11] Senate, Doc. speaking, 2-250/1 (1999–2000); House, Doc. parl., 624/001 (1999–2000).
[12] A video of the action is available at: www.youtube.com/watch?v=wfUQNOkGO40.

The additional women brought in by quotas added strength and plausibility to actions to increase the number of women in government. After all, it would be hard to argue for parity in the cabinet with only 13 percent women in parliament. While the quota law did not drastically increase the overall share of women in the cabinet, it did increase the share of women in certain portfolios. As mentioned earlier, the majority of employment ministers have been women since 1999, but they have also been frequently promoted to the social affairs, justice, and especially equality portfolios. Women have been less visible in ministries like defense or finance (in line with cross-national trends). In an interview, Liberal MP Viviane Teitelbaum suggested (with frustration) that women do have more experience in certain fields than others, but that stereotypes also play a role: "that's what women do, they deal with children's issues, social issues, maybe health issues, culture, education, but never never the other issues, never. And that's something that is changing but very slowly."[13]

Women in parliamentary parties pressed for experienced women to get good list positions and coordinated across parties to undertake actions within and outside parliament. The result is that women were appointed to at least some cabinet portfolios, although these typically fell within stereotypically "feminine" areas. Quotas enabled and encouraged the coordinated action of women in parties (*factions*), which also helped to ensure their representation in government roles, albeit on only some types of portfolios (*ministers*).

The salience of gender equality likely increased among men party leaders during this time. Interviews in Belgium conducted for this study often suggested that some of the most important changes after the quota law was introduced were observed among (strategic) men: "those men who were conscious of the fact of these [work–family] issues and who started to promote and give attention to these issues, they found themselves in a favorable position toward women."[14] However, women ministers (not men party leaders) were the key protagonists of leave policy change. Many of these policy changes were not included in formal coalition government agreements; for example, the government agreement of 1999 does not mention any change to paternity leave or the right to paid breastfeeding breaks.[15] Instead, such agreements tend to offer broad indications of priorities, as in the 2003 agreement: "The Government will actively

---

[13] Viviane Teitelbaum, personal interview, October 23, 2013, Brussels, Belgium.
[14] Vera Claes, personal interview, October 10, 2013, Brussels, Belgium.
[15] Déclaration du Gouvernmement Fédéral, July 14,1999, 20/1 - 1999 (S.E.).

promote the reconciliation of family and professional life by extending parental leave."[16] Changes went beyond this in 2005: leave was made more flexible (by making different part-time options available) and the level of benefits increased, with funding focused on helping single parents. This suggests that relatively independent women ministers were shaping policy in their preferred direction.

Minister of Employment Freya Van den Bossche was behind these changes in 2005. She was the youngest minister in Belgian history (she became Minister of the Environment at age twenty-eight, before moving to Employment), and her rapid promotion was openly attributed to gender quotas. *Time* magazine wrote of her: "by the time she ran for national parliament as a Flemish Socialist (sp.a) candidate in 2003, the law required that both sexes be represented in the top three slots on every party list – so her name was placed in a vote-getting position no novice male would have enjoyed" (she agreed that the parity law helped, while pointing out that she hoped to be remembered for her policies; Ripley 2005). She was a single mother herself, with her second child due around the time the new legislation she proposed to improve parental leave kicked in (one journalist called this a "nice coincidence," see Vaes 2005). She spoke openly about her experience as a working mother motivating her to seek policy changes (e.g., calling for more nurseries near rail stations: "Run to the nursery, to the station, then to work, and vice versa at night: what a mess!" Vaes 2007).

Van den Bossche is perhaps the clearest example of the link between quotas, ministers, and leave policies: most of the women ministers behind leave policy changes were first elected to parliament before the quota law was implemented. The quota law made it more likely that they would continue to be selected and promoted by their parties. Other politicians and ministers openly attribute their success to the quota; Liberal (Open VLD) Minister of Justice Annemie Turtelboom said in an interview with the media in 2013, "I am the product of quota, and I feel good about that. Without quotas in politics, women would never have been able to break through certain limits" (Van Roe 2013). Like Van den Bossche, women ministers often speak from personal experience when discussing leave policies. For example, in an interview in 2004, Laurette Onkelinx (who passed legislation on paternity leave, time credits, and the right to breastfeeding breaks in 2002) said, "We must investigate how parental

---

[16] "Texte de l'Accord de gouvernement Fédéral du July 8, 2003 (Verhofstadt II)," Réf. GRIP DATA: G2064. http://archive2.grip.org/bdg/g2064.html.

leave can be extended. Is your head completely at work when your child is in bed with a high fever? Oh no" (Albers & Otte 2004).

In my interviews with Belgian politicians, the dominant sentiment across parties was that women are driving the agenda on work–life reconciliation issues. Christian democratic Senator Sabine de Bethune explained, "Men, especially open and intelligent men, support it – but women drive this agenda."[17] The former leader of far-right party VB, Gerolf Annemans, went further to suggest that women *should* be the ones to lead the way because they are the most affected:

Not as a measure of credibility but a measure of truth, you must not as a man try to explain things that women can better explain. What should we do with children while Mama is going to work?… what is a man to do in a debate like that? I don't mean he should not say anything, but if we promote better child care, it is about whether women will have the free choice between a career or not, so it is not a big issue for men. You might say that this is conservative, because it could be an issue for men too. . . for the moment it is not and in my view it is a promotion of women's free choice. For a society of free choice, free speech, opportunities, should care about child care because otherwise women in society as it is now do not have this free choice.[18]

This quotation is surprising because it is progressive – Annemans is saying that child care is important because it gives women career choices – yet it comes from the then-leader of a far-right party (VB) that has historically espoused more traditional views of the family. The VB's position on work–family policies fundamentally changed after the quota law. Before the quota, the party advocated increases in family allowances and child benefits to promote care for children within the family. The party emphatically stresses the role of mothers as primary carers. Its 1995 manifesto ostracized working women: "Feminism has led to a one-sided, selfish and socially destructive mentality, in which the female nature is grossly misunderstood, and that leaves no place for children. . . homemakers play a valuable role. No school, no kindergarten can replace the nurturing, protective and educational role of the family" (p. 20).

Since the quota law was first implemented in 1999, women have risen to top positions in the VB, and have emphasized social policies that help women combine work and family. Barbara Pas was first elected in 2007 and became parliamentary party leader in 2013, the first woman in her party to do so. When she took power, she told the party it could expect

---

[17] Sabine de Bethune, personal interview, September 5, 2013, Brussels, Belgium.
[18] Gerolf Annemans, personal interview, October 9, 2013, Brussels, Belgium.

new issues on the agenda, in addition to the classic Flemish independence themes.[19] She stressed the need for affordable child care, linking it to women's labor force participation: "Vlaams Belang wants to create a sufficient number of child care places in Flanders."[20] Anke Van dermeersch is another VB woman party leader who is outspoken on work–family issues. Van dermeersch was first elected to the Senate in 2003 and went on to become group leader in the Senate from 2011 to 2014 – again, the first woman in her party to hold this position. Both women have sponsored bills on parental leave and to better protect pregnant workers against discrimination. In a speech to a party conference in Antwerp in 2012, Van dermeersch drew on her own experiences to advocate for child care:

As a wife and mother of two young children, child care in my home town is very close to my heart. Far too few Antwerp families find a place in child care. The number of child care places in our city is well below the Flemish average. . . The Vlaams Belang would like more, cheaper and quality child care because your children are our future.[21]

In summary, the VB's position on whether mothers of young children should stay at home shifted dramatically after the quota law, when more women came into the party and ascended to leadership roles. Attitudes on the far right in countries that did not pass a quota – like Austria – did not change. The case of Belgium thus demonstrates the importance of both women ministers and increasing the salience of gender equality issues across parties – especially on the right.

In the absence of a gender quota law in Austria, leave policies regressed, particularly under far-right Minister of Social Affairs Herbert Haupt. Haupt was behind the 2002 policy change that extended parental leave to three low-paid years, which he explained was designed to stop the erosion of the traditional family. He claimed that public child care institutions contributed to increases in drug abuse and violence in society. According to Haupt, mothers should stay home with children and only after several years take on at most a part-time job (FPÖ Minister Herbert Haupt, Nationalrat 2001, as cited in Haussman & Sauer 2007, p. 28). The FPÖ's position would likely have been different if the party included more women. Unlike Belgium's far-right VB, which was forced to include women, Austria's FPÖ has consistently had low numbers of

---

[19] "Kennismaking met Barbara Pas," *Golfbrekers*, May 31, 2013.
[20] "Vlaams Belang: Sociale Volkspartij," *Congresteksten*, September 2013, pp. 55–56. www.vlaamsbelang.org/files/sociaalprogramma.pdf.
[21] "Toespraak Anke Van dermeersch op programmacongres in Antwerpen," May 27, 2012. www.vlaamsbelangantwerpen.be/4/428.

women MPs (see Figure 6.2) – 23 percent in 2019, the lowest of any party in the Austrian parliament.

Former FPÖ member Martina Schenk said in an interview that the negative atmosphere for women within the party contributed to her decision to leave and join another party on the right (she then became an MP and spokeswoman for gender equality for another far right party, Team Stronach). She told me, "Some people in the party were treating women in a way that was not equal to men. So this is one of the reasons I left."[22] In the same interview, Schenk explained that her goals to help women achieve equality are focused on work–family policies: "The best recipe [for equality] would be to generally improve conditions for women concerning how to manage job and family." She went on to express her desire to move toward a Scandinavian system in which mothers have a better work–life balance, including more high-quality and flexible child care.

Before we began speaking, Schenk told me that one of her advisers in the room would need to leave midway through the interview to pick up her child from school, and that this was part of her regular flexible working schedule. This example shows that in both their stated views and everyday lives, at least some women on the far right in Austria support policies to enable mothers to work. The right to paternity leave, *"Papa-monat,"* was finally passed in 2019 (some eighteen years after a legal right to paternity leave was established in Belgium) due to the intervention of FPÖ Minister of Social Affairs and mother of two, Beate Hartinger-Klein. Hartinger-Klein pushed through the legislation, overcoming significant challenges from coalition partner ÖVP and the Austrian Chamber of Commerce. FPÖ party leader and then-Vice-Chancellor Heinz-Christian Strache himself took one month's paternity leave early in 2019, but Hartinger-Klein made clear that this did not inspire her proposal: "As a mother of two, I had already considered that beforehand."[23]

Of course, there are also women on the far right who support women's traditional roles in the household. For example, former deputy head of the FPÖ, Barbara Rosenkranz, has asserted in the media that the best care for children in their early years is within the family.[24] However, survey data suggests that even within Austria's far right, women are less likely

---

[22] Martina Schenk, personal interview, May 7, 2014, Vienna, Austria. Translation assistance from Denise Aichelburg, present at the interview.

[23] "Recht auf Papamonat? ÖVP Bremst," *Die Presse*, February 3, 2019.

[24] "Kinderbetreuung: Rosenkranz für echte Wahlfreiheit," *Austria Press Agency*, February 27, 2007. www.ots.at/presseaussendung/OTS_20070227_OTS0225/kinderbetreuung-rosenkranz-fuer-echte-wahlfreiheit.

to hold these views than men: the 2012 wave of the International Social Survey Programme detected a 6-point gender gap on attitudes toward maternal employment within FPÖ voters. Yet, because the FPÖ remains men dominated, it has not shifted to accommodate women's views on working mothers.

As in the other countries studied here, when women did obtain relevant leadership roles in Austria, they made a difference. In addition to Minister Hartinger-Klein, Christian democrat Christine Marek is credited with reformulating Austria's parental leave system with better options for working mothers by introducing a shorter-term, income-based leave option in 2010. Marek is a single mother, who like the other mothers previously discussed in the context of Belgium (Van den Bossche, Onkelinx) often talks about how her experiences shape her political goals. In an interview she gives a personal example of her philosophy of combining work and care: "If we want women to be in top positions, family should not be a problem. Just a small example: I remember how my son called during a recent meeting of the government. I looked at President Prammer, and she said, 'No problem, get out of here.' A man would have rolled his eyes" (von SM Steinitz 2010).

Chamber of Labor Representative Ingrid Moritz recalls, "She [Marek] was very important. She brought up also the income-related child care benefit, and we were very surprised because we always wanted to get this, and we were very surprised that it was coming from her." She was known to have a certain awareness of these problems because of her background as a single mother.[25] The director of a nonprofit women's organization, Manuella Vollman, commented of Marek,

> "I knew her before she was in politics, when she was in a big company. And I knew this about her, that she as a person always said we need this [policy]. But my party doesn't want it. And then she came into the job and had the opportunity and the power to do it, with the other party. But in my opinion it was not really the conservatives. It was Christine Marek, but not the conservatives."[26]

As in the case of Belgium, then, in Austria women ministers drove change in the direction of policies to benefit working mothers – but there were fewer women ministers with this portfolio in Austria.

Without women pushing the agenda on the right, parties have little appetite to make changes to benefit working mothers. A clear example is the slow progress toward statutory paternity leave. Julia Valsky,

---

[25] Ingrid Moritz, personal interview, April 30, 2014, Vienna, Austria.
[26] Manuela Vollman, personal interview, April 30, 2014, Vienna, Austria.

TABLE 6.2 *Summary of mechanisms driving leave policy change, Belgium and Austria*

	Belgium	Austria
Factions	✓ Share of women increases across parties; Women across parties coordinate on legislative proposals and action to push for more women in federal government	X Share of women on right remains low, feeling of inequality among women on far right
Ministers	✓ Women appointed to majority of labor portfolio positions (responsible for leave policy); Key actors in all major changes	X Man minister responsible for backwards step in 2002 (long, poorly paid child care leave); ✓ Women ministers responsible for moves forward in 2010 (shorter, well-paid leave option) and 2016, 2019 (paternity leave)
Salience	X Perception that quota increased the salience of gendered issues, but major policy changes driven by ministers rather than formal coalition government agreements	X Lack of consensus on some major policies (no statutory paternity leave); no appetite for change on right

Spokesperson for Minister for Women Gabriele Heinisch-Hosek, said that, "The problem is that our coalition partner [the ÖVP] and especially the representatives of the economy, companies, they are not really fond of this idea. They don't really like it, so we don't have it in the private sector."[27] Despite being debated for years, there was no consensus on paternity leave in Austria until very recently. This demonstrates the issue's historical lack of political salience: for years, parties across the spectrum did not agree that it was a priority. In September 2019, the legal right to paternity leave was finally passed (some eighteen years after it was adopted in Belgium).

Table 6.2 summarizes evidence across the two cases, focusing on mechanisms that drive leave policy change in the direction of women's preferences (i.e., to support working mothers). The Belgian case suggests that quotas led to more women in parliament and in key positions in

[27] Julia Valsky, personal interview, May 5, 2014, Vienna, Austria.

government, at least on the relevant portfolios. This was due in part to the increased leverage that added numbers gave women to push their parties to include them, as they worked together across parties to promote the issue of gender equality in the cabinet. They proposed legislation and took action to the streets. Successive women ministers were promoted to portfolios in employment and social affairs, and they often connected their policy decisions to their own experiences as working mothers. Without a quota law in Austria, policy took a step backwards under a far-right (man) minister before moving forward again under women ministers from right-wing parties. As in Belgium, these ministers' personal experiences seem crucial to their policy priorities. If Austria had implemented a quota, would its policies have been different? My interviews suggest that women on the right in Austria tend to hold more progressive views about work–family policies than men. The dramatic shift on family policy within the far right in Belgium after a quota law – from supporting stay-at-home mothers to pushing for high-quality child care and parental leave – suggests the same. Both cases highlight the strong role of ministers in driving policy change, the key mechanism linking quotas to women-friendly leave in Belgium.

6.3   PORTUGAL AND ITALY: "WOMEN HAVE BEEN PUSHING CERTAIN AREAS"

Portugal and Italy are Southern European economies, which are often considered a distinct cluster of welfare states due in no small part to the central role of the family in social policy (Ferrera 2005). Historically Catholic, and with similar experiences of authoritarian and dictatorial rule, these countries tend to be characterized by a moral conviction that the family provides better care and services than the state (Moreno 2006). Accordingly, both countries have relatively conservative views on maternal employment, and a relatively small gender gap in preferences on the issue (see Figure 3.2 in Chapter 3). Both countries faced severe effects of the global economic crisis from 2008 onward (right before the quota law took effect in Portugal), including mandatory spending cuts in social policies. In addition, Portugal's quota law has been in place for a relatively short period of time. These factors (small gender gap in preferences, budget constraints, and a shorter time period since quota adoption) make it a "most difficult" test of my argument about the link between quotas and policy outcomes (Gerring 2007).

Portugal's political context involves two main parties that alternated in power during the study period (2009–2019) – the center-right social democratic party (Partido Social Democrata, PSD) and the center-left Socialist Party (Partido Socialista, PS). Smaller Christian democrat (Centro Democrático e Social CDS), far left (Left Bloc; Bloco de Esquerda, BE), and communist (Partido Comunista Português, PCP) parties are also represented in parliament. In Italy, the party system is more fragmented and coalitions are the norm, but the main parties in power during this period included Silvio Berlusconi's center-right Go Italy (Forza Italia, later renamed Il Popolo della Libertà, PdL), the center-left Democratic Party (Partito Democratico, PD; formerly called Democratici di Sinistra, DS), the far-right Northern League (Lega Nord, LN), and more recently the populist Five Star Movement (Movimento 5 Stelle, M5S). Cabinet ministers are considered to be relatively autonomous in Italy, while in Portugal they are thought to be more constrained by the prime minister and his inner cabinet of senior party members (Criscitiello 1994; Neto & Lobo 2009). In both countries, individual MPs can sponsor and cosponsor legislation (in Portugal, MPs have only had this right since 2007, Leston-Bandeira & Tibúrcio 2012).

Since Portugal's quota law was passed, the share of women in parliament has increased from 21 percent (2006 election) to 27 percent in the first election after its implementation (2009) and to 35 percent in 2015 (see Figure 6.3). Portugal's quota law requires one-third of candidates to be women, and parties are fined if their lists do not comply; it is thus weaker than Belgium's law, which from 2002 has required 50 percent women and lists rejected for noncompliance.[28] Figure 6.3 shows that the share of women in Italy's parliament also increased during the same period (from 17 percent in 2006 to 31 percent in 2015), without a gender quota law in place. The difference is that in Portugal, the shares of women increased due to parties on the right including more women (percentages of women on the left, the PS and BE, were relatively high before the quota, and stayed the same after the law), whereas in Italy the bump seen in 2013 was due to the election of a center-left alliance. In 2015, Italy passed a gender quota law as part of an electoral reform. This applied for the first time in the 2018 election.

Figure 6.4 examines how the quota law affected parties across the political spectrum in Portugal (left), and trends in the counterfactual case of Italy (right). It shows that Portugal's quota brought about large changes to two parties in particular – the center-right PSD and Christian

---

[28] In 2019 the Portuguese parliament voted to increase the quota to 40 percent, and lists will now be rejected for noncompliance; these changes took effect in the federal election of 2019.

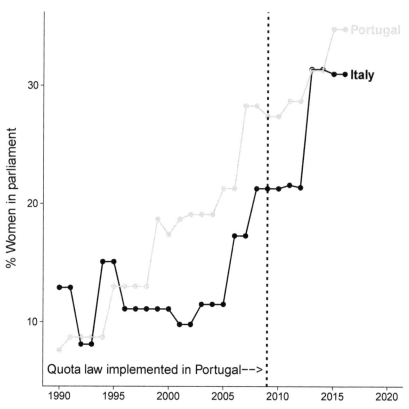

FIGURE 6.3 Share of women in parliament, Portugal and Italy
Note: Data from the comparative political dataset (Armingeon et al. 2016).

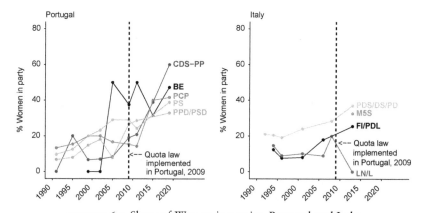

FIGURE 6.4 Share of Women in parties, Portugal and Italy
Portuguese parties: BE (new left), PSD (center-right), PS (social democrats), CDS-PP
(Christian democrats), PCP (communist).
Italian parties: PD (social democrats), M5S (populist), FI/PdL (right), LN (far right), AN
(far right).

democratic CDS-PP – in its first year of implementation (2009). The center-left Socialist Party (PS) and new Left Bloc (BE) did not experience major changes in the number of women after the law, perhaps because they already came close to or surpassed the 33 percent threshold beforehand. The average increase in women's representation post-quota was 28-percentage points on the right (PSD and CDS-PP) and 11-percentage points on the left (PS, BE, and PCP). Note that the rise in women's representation on the left is driven mainly by the Communist PCP party's large 25-percentage-point increase. Excluding the PCP, the average increase in women's representation in left-leaning parties after the quota is 4 points.[29]

In Italy, both the center-left (PD) and center-right (FI/PdL) increased the number of women in their ranks during the same period. The increase of women seen in 2013 (Figure 6.3) is explained both by major gains on the left (over 130 seats) and the rise of the new M5S. The M5S was originally characterized as left populist, but has since moved to the right. When it emerged in 2013, it was seen to be "stealing" votes from the center left, appealing to voters on both gender and youth (Bordignon 2014, p. 5). The share of women in the far-right Lega Nord, however, has declined over time – as in the case of Austria's far right.

What happened to leave policies during this time period, which was characterized by recession and extreme pressure to cut social spending? Before its quota law was implemented in 2009, Portugal offered four months of fully paid maternity leave (with an option to take five months at 80 percent pay instead), five days of fully paid, mandatory paternity leave, and an individual entitlement to an unpaid parental leave of three months for each parent. After the quota law, leave policy in Portugal became a benchmark model of encouraging both mothers and fathers to take on caring responsibilities, to support women's position in the labor market (ILO 2016).

In 2009, the year the quota was first implemented, the *Lei da Parentalidade* replaced maternity leave with an initial parental leave policy (*Licença parental inicial*) which can be taken by either parent (of this, there is a mandatory mothers-only parental leave of six weeks after birth; the rest can be shared equally). Paternity leave was replaced by fathers-only parental leave, and was extended to twenty days, ten of

---

[29] The increase in women's representation within parties after a quota law is calculated by subtracting women's representation before quotas (2005) from the most recent post-quota year (2019).

which were made mandatory. Additional parental leave (*Licença parental complementar*) gave an individual entitlement to leave of another three months per parent, paid at 25 percent. The mandatory fathers-only leave increased to fifteen days in 2015, and then to twenty days in 2019, with another five days optional. In 2019, legislation also clarified that same-sex couples are eligible to claim shared parental leave, and extended the period of leave for parents with premature babies or children with chronic illness (Wall & Escobedo 2009; Wall & Leitão 2018). Portugal also reformed family allowances (cash benefits not connected to leave) in 2010, eliminating all family allowances for the top two income categories – roughly 30 percent of beneficiaries. These cuts were in response to the economic crisis and estimated to save 250 million euros per year.[30] In short, Portugal shifted away from cash benefits for families toward a model of leave that encourages parents to share caring responsibilities.

As of 2008 (before the quota law in Portugal but not Italy), Italy offered five compulsory, job-protected months of maternity leave (two before and three after birth), paid at 80 percent. Parental leave was an individual entitlement of up to six months, paid at 30 percent, with an additional bonus month for the family if fathers use at least three months of leave. No paternity leave was available. As Table 6.3 shows, in 2012 one day of mandatory, paid paternity leave was introduced, with an additional optional day (this policy was temporary, stipulated to run until 2016). Mothers could give two of their maternity days to fathers, giving fathers access to four days in total. A "babysitter bonus" was also passed to let working women who do not take up optional parental leave receive child care subsidies instead (up to 600 euros per month for six months).

In 2015, parental leave was made more flexible, and in 2016 the mandatory paternity leave was renewed and extended from two to four days. The "babysitter bonus" was cancelled. In 2019, the mandatory paternity leave was increased to five days. Unlike Portugal, Italy increased family allowances during this period and extended them to self-employed individuals, provided a one-time lump sum bonus of up to 1,000 euros for low-income families, and provided a lump sum birth grant to help with the cost of diapers and formula (all from 2009).[31]

---

[30] "Cortes no abono de família atingem 1,4 milhões de beneficiários," *Economico*, October 1, 2010.
[31] "Renzi accelera sul taglio dell'Irpef 'E non toccheremo assegni familiari'," *La Stampa*, April 14, 2014.

TABLE 6.3 *Summary of leave policy changes 2009–2019, Portugal and Italy*

	Portugal	Italy
Maternity leave	2009: Maternity-specific leave reduced from seventeen to six weeks; replaced by (shared) initial parental leave *Government (PS)*	No change
Paternity leave	2009: Mandatory paternity leave extended from five to ten days; Right to optional additional ten days *Government (PS)*	2012: First introduced: one day mandatory and paid, plus one day optional (temporary, from 2012 to 2015) ***Min. Labor Fornero (F, Ind.)***
	2015: Mandatory paternity leave extended from ten to fifteen days *Min. Employment Mota Soares (M, CDS)*	2016: Extends paternity leave policy and increases mandatory leave to four days from 2018 *Min. Family Fontana (M, LN)*
	2019: Extends mandatory paternity leave to twenty days with another five days optional ***Working Group on Parenting and Gender Equality (88 percent women)***	2019: Extends mandatory paternity leave to five days ***MP Boschi (F, Pd)***
Parental leave	2009: Major reform of leave policy replaced maternity with initial parental leave that can be taken by either parent; additional parental leave now paid at 25 percent; sharing bonus of one month introduced *Government (PS)*	2015: Introduces more flexibility (can be taken by the hour); Extends limit during which leave can be taken *Min. Labor Poletti (M, Ind.)*
	2019: Clarifies that same-sex couples are eligible to claim shared parental leave; extends leave for parents of premature babies and children with chronic illness ***Working Group on Parenting Gender Equality (88 percent women)***	

Notes: Table shows changes in leave policies since Portugal (but not Italy) implemented a gender quota law in 2009. Note that Italy implemented a quota law in 2018. Key actors in italics; women in bold.

In line with the quantitative findings discussed in Chapter 5, Portugal has moved toward more progressive policies for working mothers since its quota law was implemented. It enacted a major shift toward shared parental leave when the quota came into effect, and instituted increasingly long mandatory, paid paternity leave. Italy is also slowly moving toward promoting fathers' leave, but little has changed since 1990. At the same time, Italy also promotes policies that are more targeted at increasing fertility than work-life balance, such as increased cash benefits for families. As a result, take-up of paternity leave (taking at least fifteen days) has increased in Portugal from 26 percent in 2002 to 71 percent in 2017 (Wall & Leitão 2018), while in Italy as of 2016 fewer than half of fathers claimed their compulsory four days of paternity leave (Addabbo et al. 2016). What explains these two countries' different approaches to work–family policies in the context of major budgetary constraints?

The first point to note is that the timing of the major 2009 reform to parental leave suggests that it was not a result of the quota law. Instead, it is likely that the two reforms (the quota law and parental leave) were intended to appeal to women voters, since the main left-wing party (PS) had been losing them to the emerging challenger on the left, the Left Bloc (Weeks 2018). The proposals were only prioritized after the growth of this competitor that was widely perceived to be stealing young, urban voters away (Baum & Espírito-Santo 2012; Lobo 2001). Both policies originated in the women's section of the PS, which campaigned on three issues in 2005: (1) a gender quota (parity) law; (2) a law to change maternity to shared parental leave; and (3) instituting gender mainstreaming analysis for all legislation. Former leader of the PS women's section Sónia Fertuzinhos explained that "we did change it [maternity leave] to parental leave, and we have now one of the most innovative and progressive examples of how you can promote conciliation between men and women in family and private life."[32] Their proposal, which was developed through consultations within and outside the party with academic experts, first entered the PS party platform in 2005. It was prioritized by the party and implemented in 2009 by Minister of Labor Jose Antonio Vieira da Silva.

Since the 2009 parental leave reform, significant extensions to paternity leave have been made, and these were driven by men and women actors from parties across the left and right (see Table 6.3). The 2015 reform that increased mandatory fathers' leave from ten to fifteen days was proposed by a man Christian democrat, Minister of Solidarity,

---

[32] Sónia Fertuzinhos, personal interview, November 22, 2013, Lisbon, Portugal.

Employment and Social Security Pedro Mota Soares. This aligns with expert views that the direction of leave policy has recently become a "transversal subject crossing different parties."[33] In other words, leave policy is on the agendas (salient) of parties across the spectrum, which agree on the general direction of the policy. While many interview subjects in Portugal suggest that women have been the drivers of attention to this policy, they were the key actors directly influencing legislation in only the most recent 2019 reforms.

The mechanism of factions suggests that the quota law increases the number of women in parliament, who then have more leverage to advocate their preferences either within the party or in parliamentary committees. Previous research by Fernandes, Lopes da Fonseca, and Won (2021) shows that the quota law in Portugal significantly decreased the gender gap in legislative debates, although not necessarily in the debates considered most important. My interviews confirm the perception that gender quotas increased the inclusion of women in Portugal's legislature, and offer additional insights into the effects of quotas in another aspect of legislative work, committees. PSD MP Monica Ferro confirms, "Now you actually have women in parliament, and you have women pushing for certain number of public policies that I wouldn't call a gender agenda, but women have been pushing certain areas that I think you wouldn't have the same momentum if you didn't have them."[34]

One example that provides evidence of the increased role of women in committees is the post-quota Parliamentary Working Group on Parenting and Gender Equality. Working groups are increasingly common in Portugal's parliament, and they are dedicated to a time-restricted study of specific topics, with the goal of providing specialized input to the committee (Fernandes 2016). Formed in 2017 under the Committee on Labor and Social Security, the working group is composed of eight members from all major parties, seven of whom (88 percent) are women, and it has legislative powers. It has approved proposals to extend paternity leave to a mandatory twenty days with another five days optional (approved unanimously), clarified that same-sex couples are eligible to claim shared parental leave, and extended parental leave for parents of children with health problems.

---

[33] Mafalda Leitão, Institute of Social Sciences of the University of Lisbon, email correspondence, May 2, 2019.

[34] Monica Ferro, personal interview, December 5, 2013, Lisbon, Portugal.

Would this working group have played a similar role in policymaking without a gender quota and increased numbers of women? Most of the women on the subcommittee (six out of seven) were first elected to the national parliament after the gender quota law, including all three of the women from the center-right PSD and the chair, Clara Marques Mendes. The dominance of women in the group would have been very unlikely before the quota law because there were very few women on the right, and they would not all be assigned to the same committee. As parliamentary leader of the Communist Party António Filipe said in the context of legislative debates, "the mere presence of more women in the group empowers them to have more likelihood to intervene."[35] The same is true of committee assignments. The PSD and CDS only had 8 percent women MPs before the quota; in the third election after its implementation (2015), both parties elected the quota threshold of 33 percent women.

As in the previous country cases, this matters because women across parties tend to express similar (and often personal) attitudes toward the difficulties of combining work and family for women. These issues tend to be prioritized by women even if they are not always considered the most important issues by (mostly men) party leaders. For example, Christian democrat Teresa Caeiro, quoted at the start of this chapter, believes that, in theory, work–family issues should not be a "women's issue." Children have both mothers and fathers, and both parents should care about these issues equally. Yet in the next breath she contradicted herself, saying that for her personally this just is not true: "why should it be a woman's concern? It is, and I'm leaving here and have to get my son and feed him and give him a bath."[36] Caeiro's response illustrates how women across the left and right relate intimately to this policy issue: their shared experiences as working mothers often underline their support for policies to support other working mothers.

I find very little support for the mechanism of women in cabinet driving leave policy change in Portugal. Although the share of women in cabinet has increased, the key portfolios for leave policies have most often been filled by men (with the exception of Helena André as Minister of Labor and Social Solidarity from 2009 to 2011). Unlike the rest of the countries analyzed here, in Portugal, parliament is not a typical route to government. Ministers are often senior party members, but they cannot be MPs, and some have no political party experience (Pinto & de Almeida

---

[35] Quoted in Fernandes, Lopes da Fonseca and Won 2021, p. 15
[36] Teresa Caeiro, personal interview, November 5, 2013, Lisbon, Portugal.

2008). The theorized causal process whereby quotas lead to more experienced candidates (a pipeline) for ministerial portfolios thus does not fit the Portuguese institutional context.

The last mechanism, salience, suggests that men leaders of parties across the spectrum prioritize women's policy concerns more after a quota law is introduced, showing the increased salience of gender equality issues. The salience of parental leave was already high in Portugal when the quota law was first implemented, given the major reform that passed at the time. Gender equality remains on the agenda, and reconciliation policies are actively being reformed. Did the quota law have anything to do with this? Two-thirds of the politicians and activists I interviewed in Portugal believed that the quota law has influenced policy priorities, and many spoke of a new gender awareness rather than a direct effect of more women in parliament. PS Member of the European Parliament Ana Gomes explained that the law sent a signal to men who now feel "political pressure, the sense that they would be singled out by the media and by other politicians."[37] PSD Minister Teresa Morais reflects that, "we have a bigger sense now of human rights, gender equality, and domestic violence, and I think that this new sensibility is a result of the law at least partly."[38]

Within Portugal's parliament, the biggest increase to the salience of gender equality occurred within parties on the right, where the share of women has dramatically increased. These parties (the Christian democrat CDS-PP and center-right PSD) have traditionally supported more familialist views. The last time the center-right coalition was in power, from 2003 to 2005, the focus was on "pronatalist, pro-life and familialist objectives" like support for large families and more leave and work flexibility for mothers (much of this was not passed due to budgetary constraints; Wall & Escobedo 2009, p. 214). Yet, the center-right government that came to power after the quota, from 2011 to 2015, did not increase family allowances, despite having been against cuts at the time they were passed. Instead, the priority was "modernizing" the system by investing in child care (including a universal right to preschool from age four), even if it meant less spending on family allowances.

The increase in women's representation among parties on the right undoubtedly increased the salience of work–family issues. One important example is the agenda of the first woman leader of the Christian

[37] Ana Gomes, personal interview, December 6, 2013, Lisbon, Portugal.
[38] Teresa Morais, personal interview, December 2, 2013, Lisbon, Portugal.

democrats (CDS-PP), Assunção Cristas, who was elected party leader in 2016. Cristas was first elected to parliament in 2009, the first election after the quota law. She is a mother of four, and was the first minister in Portugal to be pregnant during her term in office in 2013. Her view of work–family policies is clearly focused on gender equality in the work-place and at home. In a speech to the party congress in 2018 she said, "It is time to change and I am convinced that a very substantial part of the issue has precisely to do with the work–family compatibility and the role of men in this equation."[39] Her colleague Sónia Fertuzinhos (PS) recalled a conversation with Cristas in which Cristas shared that she knew that her

"ideas about equality and the question of equality within family was not the main position within the majority of the [party] members... And she said that for her that was a really non-negotiable issue. So she said, as a leader of the party I have to present my gender approaches of policies and of legislation in a way that I can balance my positions with those positions that I know my party has. But still for me, it is not a question to give up my gender policy perspective."[40]

In summary, the evidence from Portugal suggests that the post-quota changes I observe were due to both the role of women in committees and the increased salience of reconciling work and family life across par-ties. This new consensus on policies to support working mothers was due in no small part to the increase in the number of women in the ranks of right-wing parties.

What role did these potential mechanisms play in the counterfactual case of Italy? First, despite having no quota law in place until 2018, there was a large increase in the number of women MPs during this period due to the election of a center-left alliance in 2013. As in the other cases, women ministers in Italy have influenced leave policy when they have been in power. In 2001, Minister of Social Affairs Livia Turco made parental leave an individual rather than a family entitlement, and introduced a bonus month to encourage fathers' participation. Only one woman served as Minister of Labor in Italy during the study period (Elsa Fornero, who served from 2011 to 2013).[41] Fornero, an economist, was

[39] "Cristas Assume Bandeira da Igualdade de Genero," *Jornal de Negocios*, March 11, 2018.
[40] Sónia Fertuzinhos, personal interview, June 2, 2019, phone call.
[41] During this time, thirteen different men served in this role, making the share of women labor ministers in recent years 9 percent). The share of women in charge of the social affairs/social solidarity portfolio is higher, at three out of seven (43 percent). The women were Rosa Russo Iervolino, Fernanda Contri, and Livia Turco.

appointed to Mario Monti's technocratic government in 2011, during the economic crisis. Her job was to implement a major labor market reform, but she was also given the equal opportunities portfolio. In an interview, Fornero noted that this latter portfolio was given to her unexpectedly, and there were low expectations about what she might do with regard to gender equality – but she was interested in working on it nonetheless. She explains, "we were the government to save the country from a financial collapse. They [political parties] recognized this role of the government. Not the role of for example trying to change society… But I said, it's only that you have to insert principles and do something and try to push it."[42]

When implementing the labor market reform, Fornero talked to women's groups and introduced the first paid paternity leave in Italy on an experimental basis (one day compulsory, with another day optional). Paternity leave was later extended by a far-right minister of family (Lorenzo Fontana of Lega Nord) and then an amendment proposed by a woman MP (Elena Boschi of the center-left PD). The "babysitter bonus" Fornero brought in also benefited working mothers, although it was not renewed under Minister Fontana. He instead announced an increase in birth grant incentives.[43] This illustrates the lack of consensus on the direction of leave policy in Italy. In Portugal, explanations of leave policy changes emphasize women's employment and the reconciliation of work and family responsibilities. In Italy, parties often stress the need to increase families' economic resources and combat declining birth rates instead.

For example, the Italian Ministry of Labor published a white paper in 2009 (the same year that Portugal passed its landmark parental leave policy) that places fertility, rather than women's employment, at the heart of family policies. It blames Italy's low birth rate for low productivity, but does not see supporting mothers' employment or child care as a solution to the problem:

The gap between the desire for motherhood and its realization is often attributed to the lack of child care or low rates of women's employment. This may be true only partially. If you look at the percentage of births in the regions with the largest number of high-quality child care centers, there is no significant difference in the number of births. Even women's employment does not seem a decisive element.[44]

---

[42] Elsa Fornero, personal interview, March 27, 2014, Rome, Italy.

[43] "Manovra, 40 milioni per i congedi dei neo padri. E torna il 'bonus bebe'," *Il Corrierre della Sera*, November 15, 2018.

[44] "La vita buona nella societa attivà," *Ministero del Lavoro, della Salute e della Politiche Sociali*, 2009, pp. 24–25.

Women MPs in Italy are frustrated by the lack of attention to these issues. Former Deputy Minister of Labor Cecilia Guerra (of the center-left PD party) served on a cross-party working group that was formed to address the issue of work–family conciliation in 2013. The working group was short lived; it did not survive the change in government in 2014. Guerra said, "The Renzi government has promised that not long from now there will be a proposal. We'll see. . . we are not done yet with this question. We must do more here."[45] Similarly, PD Senator Valeria Fedeli explained, "It is clear that women show a greater interest in concrete, daily-life concerns. This is mainly due to the unequal, stereotype-based burden-sharing in Italian households, in which women are the primary carers, which makes it all the more urgent to address the problem of services to families."[46] She goes on to lament that change is slow to come because "there is still in our parliament a male majority which tends to defend its privileges."

Italy's main center-left party has had a women's section since 1991 when the newly formed Democratic Party of the Left established this in its regulations. However, accounts of the women's section in the early 2000s report that "they have not obtained satisfactory influence in party policy-making" (Guadagnini 2005, p. 136). Little seemed to have changed by the mid-2010s. Several women I spoke to in Italy in 2014 noted that women's groups within parties are weak.[47] For example, MP Valeria Valente from the PD party expressed concern that the types of women being elected were loyalists rather than feminists. She said, "Men understand that they must comply with these principles of equal opportunities, but then they choose the women [candidates]. And they choose those women who will not necessarily fight battles for women. So these same women very often respond to the men, not women."[48]

Even the Minister of Labor, Elsa Fornero, was surprised by what she called an "anti-women attitude" that she had not been accustomed to in her previous academic career:

As for the presence of women in parliament, well, even in the previous parliament there were relatively high number of women but you had the impression that the decisions were still taken by men. Power was – all the secretaries of the political party were men, and in the key positions it's men that are there, not women... the

[45] Cecilia Guerra, personal interview, April 9, 2014, Rome, Italy.
[46] Valeria Fedeli, email correspondence, May 14, 2014.
[47] For example, Valeria Valente, personal interview, April 9, 2014, Rome, Italy; Ludovica Tranquilli Leali, personal interview, March 25, 2014, Rome, Italy.
[48] Valeria Valente, personal interview, April 9, 2014, Rome, Italy.

critical decisions were not taken by women but by men. I say this also because when there were meetings with for example Mario Monti and the leaders, almost invariably these people attending were men. All of them were men.

Fornero describes a context in which women lack access to the most powerful positions in politics, which causes their interests in issues like work–family policy to be sidelined – considered "women's things."[49]

Fornero's point about the negative attitude toward women in politics is exemplified by Forza Italia party leader Silvio Berlusconi's comment in 2016 that a pregnant candidate for the mayor of Rome should focus on being a mother instead: "It is clear to everyone that a mother cannot devote herself to a job."[50] Italy still frames much of its family policy as the need to support life (pro-life and familialist objectives) rather than working parents, particularly under right-wing governments. Yet women – even on the far right – often agree that more needs to be done to support working mothers. For example, Carolina Lussana, Lega Nord MP, said in a parliamentary debate in 2008, "we will have to reason seriously in order to carry out serious policies of equal opportunities and of reconciliation between working life and the role of a woman within the family. The directly proportional growth between the female employment rate and the birth rate shows that well-being and economic growth have a strong impact on population growth."[51] Yet not long after the time the far right in Italy was criticized for "disappearing" women; Lega Nord party leader Matteo Salvini promoted fewer women as candidates and in positions of power than his predecessors.[52]

The addition of more women legislators, including on the right, could well shift family policy toward a consensus on the need to support working mothers, over policies intended purely to support fertility. Italy is thus an important case to watch going forward: will its quota law implemented in 2018 spur such a consensus? Already in 2021, two paradigm-shifting bills to equalize paid parental leave have been proposed: one by Senators

---

[49] Elsa Fornero, personal interview, March 27, 2014, Rome, Italy.

[50] Isla Binnie, "Italy's Berlusconi says a woman cannot be a mother and a mayor," *Reuters*, March 15, 2016.

[51] Resoconto stenografico dell'Assemblea, XVI Legislatura, Seduta n. 36 di mercoledì July 16, 2008. http://briguglio.asgi.it/immigrazione-e-asilo/2008/luglio/ac-1366-16-7.html.

[52] Francesca Buonfiglioli, "Salvini e le donne scomparse dalla Lega Nord," *Lettera* 43, December 16, 2014.

TABLE 6.4 *Summary of mechanisms driving leave policy change, Portugal and Italy*

	Portugal	Italy
Factions	✓ Share of women increases across parties, especially on the right; Women are the majority of new cross-party working group on parenting and gender equality	X Share of women remains low on right, especially far right; Women say women's sections in parties are weak
Ministers	X Majority of labor ministers post-quota are men (parliament not a path to government)	X Majority of labor ministers have been men; the exception in this period (Fornero) passed paternity leave and babysitter bonus policies
Salience	✓ Consensus across parties on consistent direction of work–family policy; First woman leader of Christian democratic party shifts party agenda	X Lack of consensus on direction of work–family policy; Some parties stress cash benefits to combat declining fertility over supporting women's employment

Tommaso Nannicini and Valeria Fedeli and another by MP Giuditta Pini.[53]

Table 6.4 shows that the key mechanisms driving leave policy change in the direction of women's preferences in Portugal were factions and salience. As in Belgium, the quota led to increases in the number of women MPs across parties in Portugal. Women MPs are driving change through their active membership in parliamentary working groups and within their parties, which has generated a new consensus on the direction the country should be moving on work–family issues. The role of women *ministers* was not as important in Portugal as in Belgium, because in Portugal parliament is not a stepping stone to government since MPs cannot be ministers. The institutional context thus conditions the relative importance of different mechanisms across countries. Parties across the spectrum in Portugal now agree on the direction of work–family policies (the issue has increased salience and centrality on agendas across

[53] Anna Ditta, "Congedo di paternità, la proposta del Pd: 'Portarlo da 10 giorni a 3 mesi'," *The Post International*, June 23, 2021.

parties), due in no small part to more women entering parties on the right. The Christian democratic party's first woman leader was elected after the quota law came into effect. She is credited with moving her party toward policies that help women reconcile work and family over those that encourage more traditional gender roles or part-time working for women. In Italy, where a quota law did not go into effect until 2018, the share of women especially on the far right remained low, and only one woman (in a technocratic government) has been appointed to the labor portfolio since 1990. While work–family policies have often been salient in Italy, parties do not yet agree on the direction of policy. The focus is often on cash transfers to promote fertility, rather than reconciling work and family responsibilities.

6.4 CONCLUSION

This chapter has investigated how quotas have led to changes in leave policies in the four case countries. The key findings are that all three mechanisms – factions, ministers, and salience – matter, but the relative importance of each is determined by the country's institutional context. In both quota countries analyzed here, the law, and increases in the number of women across parties, helped women gain more leverage within parties and parliament to push for change. This finding was not expected, given the minor role that backbench MPs are expected to play in policy-making in parliamentary democracies. Yet, women across parties worked both within the parliamentary system (Portugal) and outside it, protesting for change (Belgium) to make their voices heard. Quotas also led to more women in portfolios responsible for leave policy in Belgium, partially due to women within parties publicly pushing for parity cabinets. These women ministers played a key role in leave policy reforms. In Portugal, parliament is not a clear pathway to government and so the minister mechanism did not play an important role; instead, an influx of women on the right was key to increasing the salience of maternal employment as the aim of work–family policy across parties.

The counterfactual cases of Austria and Italy also confirm that women are key protagonists in increasing support for maternal employment; there are just fewer of them. Across all four cases, women play an important role in moving leave policy toward gender equality at home and in the workplace. Without a quota law, women have less leverage within parties, particularly on the right and far right; in both Austria and Italy policies have regressed (supported working mothers less) when these parties are in government. Given that interviews with women on the right and far right suggest that they also favor policies to support working mothers, I expect that a quota in Austria and Italy, and the increasing number of women it would bring to right-leaning parties, could change these parties' positions and priorities.

An important finding from the qualitative evidence is that, across countries and parties, from the far left to the far right, women often sound the same when they talk about work–family issues. A social democrat from Portugal, for example, expressed essentially the same view ("We really tried to create the favorable conditions to approve changes to maternity and paternity leave at the time, with the objective of approving share of responsibilities between men and women, fathers and mothers")[54] as a representative of the far right in Austria ("We are talking about how to manage for men and women to spend together time as a family at the beginning").[55] This similarity in the way women talk about the optimal direction of policy reiterates that for women, this is not a partisan issue. Historically it was: the Christian democrats were built on a familialist agenda that valued fertility and the male breadwinner model. Yet, as the cases of Germany and Austria show, even without a quota law women in Christian democratic parties are changing their parties' positions to focus more on working mothers (Morgan 2013; Wiliarty 2010). For example, in Germany, then-Family Minister and mother of seven Ursula von der Leyen made parental leave her "prestige project" and took "enormous heat" from her own party for the bonus father months in particular (Wiliarty 2011, p. 456). The quota law makes it even more likely that women are elected across all parties (even on the right), and that the issue of maternal employment is prioritized over fertility alone.

The cases also provide little evidence to support two potential alternative explanations for the changes in leave policy I observe – party ideology and a general cultural shift in favor of gender equality. As discussed throughout the chapter, it is not the case that strong left-leaning parties are driving both quota laws and policy change. In fact, parties on the right experienced larger increases in the number of women MPs post-quota, and the salience of maternal employment increased by the largest margin within parties like the Flemish Christian democrats in Belgium, the far-right VB in Belgium, and the Christian democrats in Portugal. Reforms

---

[54] Sónia Fertuzinhos, personal interview, June 2, 2019, phone call.
[55] Martina Schenk, personal interview, May 7, 2014, Vienna, Austria. Translation assistance from Denise Aichelburg, present at interview.

are driven by women from parties across the spectrum in both Portugal and Belgium. The strong role of women within parties and as ministers also refutes the idea that a general attitudinal shift within Belgium and Portugal was driving both the quota law and leave policy change. If shifts in public opinion were the main cause of policy changes, we ought to see men and women equally involved in increasing attention to these issues within their parties and government. Instead, women – who were often mothers – played important roles as descriptive representatives.

These findings do not imply that quotas increase attention to all of women's policy concerns. Instead, they increase the number of women in office, especially on the right, and enhance the salience of women's political preferences. This is especially important for reform on orthogonal (cross-cutting) issues like maternal employment. Women across the political spectrum tend to agree on these issues, and can push parties to prioritize certain policies or shift agendas when otherwise the status quo would likely remain in place. The evidence here suggests that descriptive representation matters, and that men party leaders and members must adapt to new social norms – not on mainstream economic and fiscal issues, but on the growing relevance of reconciliation between work and family highlighted by women across parties.

7

Conclusion

Do gender quotas affect policy outcomes? In the Introduction I started by discussing stories about gender quota debates in four high-income OECD democracies: Belgium, France, Ireland, and Italy. These accounts illustrate that arguments linking identity to policymaking are common. Yet many scholars and politicians believe quotas will have only a limited impact on policy because party identity is often much stronger than gender identity. To explore the potential link between quotas and policy changes, this book develops a new theoretical approach, focusing on the conditions under which quotas ought to matter. My main argument is that quotas are likely to lead to policy change on issues that (1) are characterized by a gender gap in preferences (women prefer them more than men) and (2) cut across the main left–right dimension in politics (they are often ignored because they are not on mainstream political agendas).

I show that attitudes about whether mothers of young children should work, and associated work–family policies, fit this criteria well. I then provide quantitative and qualitative evidence that quotas shift party agendas and policy outcomes (the structure of parental leaves) to better match women's preferences. Quotas make gender more salient by giving women louder voices within parties and access to powerful ministerial roles, and encouraging men party leaders to compete on these now more normalized issues. In the rest of the chapter, I summarize the book's key findings and contributions, and discuss opportunities for future research.

7.1 THE CONDITIONS UNDER WHICH QUOTAS MATTER

Quota laws quickly increase the number of women in office. They also signal, on the national stage, that gender matters. How does this major change to electoral politics as usual affect the substantive representation of women's interests? The first step in answering this question is to clarify what we mean by women's interests. My approach focuses on gender gaps in preferences, and considers how these preferences fit into the structure of mainstream party competition.

Women face high barriers to entry into politics, due to an inability to access resources on an equal basis with men as well as bias in candidate selection procedures. Once elected, women may find it difficult to mobilize on behalf of a neatly defined set of gender-based issues since their preferences are heterogeneous in many areas. Women's numerical underrepresentation is especially detrimental to their substantive representation when their interests (e.g., work–family policies) cut across the main left–right (class-based) policy dimension. This is because existing parties have few incentives to advocate new policy concerns if they split core constituencies or detract from known ("owned") policy positions. In this scenario, women face a "political market failure": traditional parties will avoid addressing the cross-cutting issue, and forming a new party is not a feasible option.

My main argument is that quotas correct this market failure by increasing the number of women in politics, and thus the likelihood that women's preferences will be represented. After a quota law has been implemented, we should expect to see policy change in the direction of women's preferences, especially on orthogonal issues like work–family policies.

I propose three main mechanisms linking quotas to policy change. These mechanisms heavily weight the importance of intra-party decision-making, given the strong role of parties in most of these countries (largely parliamentary democracies). The first is *factions*: Quota laws increase the number of women, which in turn enhances their leverage to push the party toward their collective preferences. The second mechanism is *ministers*: The influx of women after a quota law comes into effect paves the way for more women in positions of power in government, who can directly impact policies related to women's preferences. Women are still more likely to be appointed to portfolios related to stereotypically gendered issues – for example, gender equality, health, and social affairs rather than defense, budget, and foreign affairs. While it is beyond the scope of this book to determine whether this approach to portfolio allocation is due to bias in the selection procedure or women's socialized preferences and professional experiences, I find that it does lead to change in work–family policies, which typically fall under the purview of ministers of labor or social affairs. Finally, quotas increase the *salience* of gender-related issues, which cues party leaders to better represent women's preferences – either to gain electoral advantage or because leaders shift their awareness of (and views about) the relevance of women's concerns.

My theory of quotas and policy change has two main implications for the study of identity politics, political parties, and public policy. First, the model of party incentives to address group-based demands highlights the need to disaggregate policy priorities based on whether the groups seeking change face *high barriers to entry* into politics, and whether the policy demand falls along *traditional lines of party competition*. This conceptual framework links recent scholarship on gender and identity politics to traditional political economy spatial models of party and voter behavior. Approaches from these distinct subfields yield different predictions that highlight the role of the key actors according to their worldview (i.e., individual politician identity vs. voters and parties). Spatial models predict that rational parties will respond to voter preferences (Adams et al. 2004, 2006; Ezrow 2007; McDonald & Budge 2005), as well as environmental factors such as economic conditions (Adams, Haupt, & Stoll 2009; Burgoon 2012; Haupt 2010) and party fortunes (Somer-Topcu 2009).

Existing political economy models often disregard politician identity. Yet the findings from the literatures on gender and politics, and identity more broadly, suggest that politician identity, including their gender and race, affects policy outcomes in favor of that group (Chattopadhyay & Duflo 2004; Funk & Gathmann 2008; Rehavi 2007; Svaleryd 2009; Ueda 2008; Washington 2008). This work typically uses the citizen–candidate framework, in which political actors have the autonomy to make certain policy choices (Besley & Coate 1997; Osborne & Slivinski 1996). However, this framework downplays the role of political parties, which play an essential role in helping voters choose between many complex political choices and helping politicians coordinate their policy preferences once in office (Aldrich 1995; Kitschelt 2000*a*). Neither spatial nor citizen–candidate models alone provide a satisfactory framework for understanding *when* politician identity and quotas are relevant to policy outcomes.

My approach acknowledges the dominant role of parties and highlights their strong incentives to downplay concerns that split their constituencies. The framework helps determine which issues quotas are likely to influence. I suggest that the interplay of *group status* (whether the group is historically marginalized, and thus more likely to be underrepresented in politics) and *issue type* determines whether (and how) identity influences policy outcomes. The theory predicts that a political market failure can occur in the promotion of issues that (1) cut across the main left–right dimension and (2) are primarily championed by disadvantaged groups that lack access to office. These issues are unlikely to make it onto the mainstream political agenda. This book focuses on one such issue: work–family balance.

I argue that it is especially important to have women in office as MPs and ministers, and that quotas can be an important vehicle for achieving both descriptive representation and policy change. The theory's general logic should apply to other contexts, such as whether the policy demands of ethnic minorities, immigrants, or labor market "outsiders" are addressed. It can also help explain why gender identity has been found to matter for some policy issues but not others, such as maternity leave policies (Kittilson 2008) but not education spending (Rehavi 2007).

This book's second main theoretical implication for the field is to provide new insights into *how* identity is linked to change in parliamentary democracies. The details of legislative structures are important for understanding policy change. In majoritarian systems, and in the government executive, individual politicians are likely to have more power to influence policies than they do as MPs in parliamentary democracies. I draw on the gender and politics, as well as party politics literatures, to argue that increased *numbers of women* in parliament and government and *issue salience* are likely to be important mechanisms for policy change in parliamentary democracies. In summary, this book offers a new theoretical framework that combines an inductive method of defining group-based interests with an emphasis on the structure of party competition. Future studies can fruitfully build on this approach to substantive representation to explore how it might apply to other groups, regions and systems of government.

7.2 KEY FINDINGS: HOW QUOTAS WORK FOR WOMEN

After showing that the gender gap on policy preferences related to maternal employment is large and cuts across partisan identities in Chapter 3, I examine how quotas affect policy outcomes. I look at two critical stages of the policymaking process: political party priorities and national-level policy outcomes. Chapter 4 finds that quotas increase party attention to women's preferences in party manifestos, which confirms my hypotheses. The comparative manifesto data allow an analysis of the short-term effects of quota laws (up to three election-years after implementation). My findings suggest that these short-term effects on party attention are driven directly by the quota law and the increased salience it brings to equality concerns, rather than channeled through increases in the number of women in the party. Quota laws cue parties to increase positive attention to equality issues, including gender equality, but do not affect the level of attention devoted to welfare state expansion. In other words, I find no evidence of change to issues that make up the main lines of party competition in high-income OECD democracies. The results hold up to several robustness checks, including removing parties that proposed quota laws from the sample to address endogeneity concerns.

While the comparative manifesto data provides initial evidence that party agendas shift in the direction of women's preferences after a gender quota comes into effect, the broad coding of this data does not allow me to assess work–family policies specifically. Thus, in order to understand the impact of quotas on this cross-cutting issue, the second part of Chapter 4 presents a new data set of party attention to various work–family policies in the four country cases (Belgium, Austria, Portugal, and Italy).

I find that quotas are linked to an increase in the amount of attention dedicated to policies that promote maternal employment (child care, equality-promoting leave) and a reduction in attention to policies that do not (cash transfers that encourage women to stay at home). My qualitative reading of party trends over time suggests that in countries that have implemented a quota law (Belgium and Portugal), parties across the political spectrum jointly promote parental leave and encourage fathers to participate. I do not observe the same trends in countries that do not adopt a quota, where parties on the center right and right tend to primarily focus on cash transfers, which support caregiving at home, rather than maternal employment.

In Chapter 5, I then demonstrate that quotas also shift government actions in the direction of women's interests. I examine data on public spending on family policies and the composition of leave policies. Work–family policies have evolved rapidly over time, and I look for evidence that quotas are linked to policies that support mothers of young children working outside the home, specifically paid leave which can be shared by parents, and paternity-only leave, as opposed to maternity-only leave and family allowances (both of which reinforce gender stereotypes of care, giving women incentives to stay home rather than return to work).

I find that quotas shift the configuration of leave policies toward gender equality – more paid parental and father-specific leave as opposed to maternity-only leave. Quota laws are linked to 19 additional weeks of leave that promotes gender equality – that is, 14.6 more weeks of paid parental and paternity leave, which is offset by 4.6 fewer weeks of maternity-only leave. Quotas also lead to a 0.33-percentage-point decrease in spending on family allowances. The size of these effects is influenced by how effectively the quota increased the number of women in office (the "quota shock"): the larger the quota shock, the greater the policy shifts observed. Unlike the findings on quotas and party priorities presented in Chapter 4, the results here suggest that when it comes to real policy changes, effects are driven at least partially by increases of women in office. I find no evidence of change to spending in areas in which men and women tend to have similar policy preferences (old age benefits and education) or where issues fall within the bounds of the mainstream, left–right policy dimension (overall social spending and health care). A key finding from Chapter 5 is that quota laws affect policy outcomes: They shift the spending and composition of work–family policies to better support women's preferences regarding maternal employment.

Chapter 6 compares evidence from qualitative case studies of similar countries that did and did not adopt a quota law, shedding light on the mechanisms linking quota laws to policy change, and the conditions under which they hold. One of the unique features of quota laws compared to increases in the number of women in parliaments without quotas is that quotas tend to increase the share of women on the right in particular. Quotas thus lead to more women from across the political spectrum entering parliament and, over time, taking on leadership roles. I find that the mechanism of factions (women's increased leverage within parties and parliament) played an important role in both Belgium and Portugal, as women pushed for greater gender equality in government and formed the majority of a new working group on parenting and gender equality.

While both quota cases highlight the role of women as factions within parties, I find that the importance of women as ministers depends on the institutional context of the country. Specifically, the process of cabinet formation differs across countries, and this has important impacts on women's access to government power. As Annesley, Beckwith, and Franceschet (2019) highlight, political experience is not always a qualifying criteria for cabinet appointments, and parties are also flexible about how they interpret such criteria. Thus, even when quotas increase women in parliaments, they might not increase women in governments. In Belgium, the quota led to more women in key portfolios for work–family policies (labor and social affairs), and these women were responsible for a consistent trajectory of reforms that supported working mothers. In Portugal, parliamentary experience is not a qualifying criteria for cabinet appointments (MPs cannot be ministers), and in this context more women were not appointed to relevant cabinet posts after the quota law.

Instead, the increased salience of gender equality issues proved more important in Portugal. A new consensus developed across the left and right on the direction of work–family policies. I argue that this new consensus was influenced by the influx of women in right-leaning parties, including the first woman leader of the Christian democrats, who played a significant role in shifting her party's position on work–family reconciliation. This initial evidence from Portugal suggests both that it can be difficult to disentangle salience from women's presence in parties and that the increased salience of equality concerns after a quota law is not just a short-term effect. The salience of equality issues can grow over time within parties in tandem with an influx of women in the party. In the counterfactual (non-quota) cases of Austria and Italy, women were often key protagonists in policy reform in the direction of maternal employment, but there are fewer of them, especially on the right and far right. This can result in policy stasis or backsliding.

This book's findings are important for three main reasons. First, gender quotas are increasingly popular. Until now, we knew very little about their policy effects within high-income OECD democracies. In line with quota advocates, such as those mentioned at the beginning of this book, this study confirms that quota laws can be an effective tool to increase the substantive representation of women's interests. Quotas therefore lead to a more inclusive democracy, and they are arguably more politically relevant than other "sticky" factors that might empower women like cultural norms or wholesale electoral system change. More broadly, the results add to mounting evidence suggesting that politician identity matters, even in parliamentary democracies, where party identity is often assumed to outweigh gender identity.

The book provides new insights into *when* identity is most likely to matter, and *how* women and other historically marginalized groups can influence policies. Descriptive representation is particularly important for issues that are off the main left–right dimension in politics, because parties have few incentives to address them and risk dividing their constituencies. Drawing on the literature on intra-party politics and gender and politics, I show that there are several ways that increased numbers of women can work within existing power structures to shift party priorities and influence government actions in parliamentary democracies. But this is not the whole story. Gendered institutions like quotas can also have important effects on political outcomes in their own right by enhancing the salience of gender-related issues and cueing party leaders to prioritize them.

The second reason is that adopting quota laws has practical policy implications that do not only affect women. For example, work–family policies are important for both men and women. While overall spending on family issues is now relatively low in wealthy OECD democracies, it is on the rise, unlike many other social policies that are receiving stagnating or declining spending (Morgan 2013). As attitudes toward gender roles in society are changing among younger generations, and more women enter the workforce in low- and middle-income countries, these policies will only become more critical. Maternal employment is also linked to other important outcomes, like children's well-being. Future work should explore the extent to which work–family policy changes associated with a quota law translate into improved welfare outcomes for women, men, and children. An important element of any such research agenda must involve understanding how these policy shifts impact lower-income and ethnic minority groups. Quotas tend to lead to the election of majority-group, highly educated women (Hughes 2011); therefore, it is important to recognize that there could be important "within-group" preferences for specific policies that majority-group women are not representing.

Third, my findings highlight the impact of quotas on work–family policies, but quotas likely impact other issue areas as well. This book's proposed theoretical model can serve as a framework for identifying other such issues. For instance, in Chapter 2, I mention violence against women and sexual harassment because they are likely characterized by a significant gender gap in preferences and have been relatively uncrystallized in party politics until recently. Another example is "pink" taxes – the surcharge women pay for everyday items over the amount men pay for equivalent products. Betz, Fortunato, and O'Brien (2021) find that women's descriptive representation is associated with decreased import taxes on women's goods, which they argue is not a salient dimension of left–right partisan competition. Finally, a third example is the further proliferation of gender quotas, whereby political gender quotas lead to quotas for corporate boards, public administration, and various levels of political office. I offer some initial, exploratory evidence of the impact of political quotas on further quota proliferation next.

Four of the five quota countries considered in this book (Belgium, Portugal, France, and Italy) went on to adopt a corporate board quota after a quota law had been passed for the national parliament (Espírito-Santo

2018; Meier 2013; Piscopo & Clark Muntean 2018; Teigen 2012).[1] Like maternal employment, support for corporate board gender quotas is typically characterized by a large gender gap in preferences, in both public opinion and within elite surveys of parliamentarians. For example, a 2011 Eurobarometer poll shows that 52 percent of women (but 38 percent of men) favor quotas of 50 percent women on corporate boards, a gender gap of 14 percent.[2] While quotas might be associated with the left (e.g., O'Brien (2018) finds that no conservative party has adopted a voluntary party quota for national elections), women's support for quotas often cuts across parties. In their analysis of candidates' political opinions, Espirito-Santo, Freire, and Serra-Silva (2020) show that there are significant gender differences in policy preferences for affirmative action (on the issue of whether women should receive preferential treatment for jobs and promotions) within different types of political parties. They also find that party family does not predict opinions on affirmative action for women, leading the authors to conclude that the issue is "not crystallized in any party family or ideological party position" (p. 234).

Within-party gender differences can also be observed in voting outcomes. For example, in Portugal the Christian democrats split their votes on the 2017 corporate board quota law: More women voted for the bill (including party leader Assunção Cristas) and more men voted against it.[3] After the law was passed, social democrat Elza Pais welcomed the position of Assunção Cristas, who "adhered early to the Government's proposal" and "brought with her many deputies."[4] In my interviews, I heard from women members of Christian democratic, liberal, and conservative parties who support quotas even though their party does not. For example, the former leader of the Open VLD (Flemish liberals) Gwendolyn Rutten supports gender quotas despite her party's opposition:

What is really remarkable is that when I talk to younger women [in the party], they almost in 100% of the cases say, "Oh I don't see the problem. I don't want to have some kind of advantage just because I'm a woman." And then I say, let's talk again in ten years. ... But over time, we've been arguing, we've been studying, and I've been telling them the way it works. So this legislation kind of pushes people to

[1] Spain also has a corporate board quota that was passed at the same time as the political gender quota law in 2007 (Verge & Lombardo 2015).
[2] Eurobarometer 76.1 (September 2011) Financial and Economic Crisis, Financial Services, Corruption, Development Aid, and Gender Equality.
[3] DAR I Series No. 101 / XIII / 2 2017.06.24 (pp. 46–47).
[4] Sofia Rodrigues and Maria Lopes, "Lei das quotas de genero aprovada no Parlamento," *Publico*, June 23, 2017.

look for diversity in a way. And then you see that after a while it becomes normal and it's kind of an advantage.[5]

The case of Portugal suggests that women as factions within parties (especially on the right) and the increased salience of gender equality link political gender quotas to further quota expansion. Parties across the political spectrum quickly accepted the quota. Even those who had previously opposed the quota soon came to agree with it ("We get along with it quite well. We're pacified," said a MP from the Christian democratic party).[6] This norm shift is hard to separate from the role of additional women in center-right parties who influence their colleagues, as in the case of Christian democrat Assunção Cristas. Other women on the right go further to support stronger quota laws. Conservative Party (PSD) MP Monica Ferro explains,

"I am totally in favor of a quota system ... but I would go further because we have a 33% quota in the parliament but what you see in the parliament is that if a woman steps out, because she is elected to government, goes to a municipality, or decides to leave, it's not mandatory that she's replaced by another woman. So this actually means that you don't have 33% women in parliament in Portugal."[7]

This initial evidence from Portugal suggests that quota laws can pave the way for additional equality measures that are in line with women's preferences.

7.3 FURTHER QUESTIONS AND EXTENSIONS

This book explains some important puzzles, but it also raises at least four further research questions yet to be answered in the field of identity and politics. How do gender quotas affect informal institutions and the process of political decision-making? Do gender quotas increase women's symbolic representation, their political engagement and participation? What types of effects have gender quotas facilitated in other social and political contexts, outside of wealthy OECD democracies? What effects would be generated by other types of quotas, for example, for ethnic minority groups?

Substantive representation is only one way of measuring the effects of quotas and politician identity in politics. The key outcome variables

---

[5] Gwendolyn Rutten, personal interview, October 10, 2013, Brussels, Belgium.
[6] Teresa Caeiro, personal interview, November 5, 2013, Lisbon, Portugal.
[7] Monica Ferro, personal interview, December 5, 2013, Lisbon, Portugal.

I use – party agendas and policy outcomes – focus on the content and priority of different policy issues. Another way of looking at substantive representation is to consider how women affect the style of political decision-making. Previous research has found that women take a more consensual approach to politics (Childs 2004; Kathlene 1994; Rosenthal 1998) and work more broadly (Eagly & Johnson 1990; McKinsey 2008; Niederle & Vesterlund 2008). For example, women in the US Senate were widely credited with finding a bipartisan compromise to end the 2013 government shutdown.[8] Studies have also suggested that increasing the number of women in a group makes not just women, but everyone in the group more inclusive and cooperative (Mendelberg, Karpowitz, & Goedert 2013), and that greater diversity can have positive effects on the group's stability and performance (Ararat, Aksu, & Tansel Cetin 2010; Cederman, Wimmer, & Min 2010; Erhardt, Werbel, & Shrader 2003; Wucherpfennig et al. 2012). Evidence from my interview data suggests that quotas might have an impact on gendered working routines and styles, which comprise some of the informal institutions of politics: "the words, the jokes, and the way they [men] use arguments."[9] More research is needed to understand how quotas, and the rapid entry of women, affect the style of political decision-making, and the stability and performance of parliaments.

A second promising line of research investigates the role of quotas in furthering women's *symbolic* representation. The presence of women in parliaments could increase public awareness of and attitudes related to gender equality, raise women's political engagement and participation, and encourage young women to aspire to political careers (a "role model" effect). It is hard to tease out the causal direction between attitudes and women in office, so the semi-exogenous implementation of a quota offers some useful leverage. Exploring the symbolic impacts of a gender quota in India, Beaman et al. (2009) show that quotas reduce discrimination against women leaders among men. Yet these results do not generalize to Southern Africa, where Clayton (2018) fails to find evidence that quotas reduce average levels of gender bias in Lesotho. At the same time, this study does suggest that the quota causes young women, in particular, to have more gender-egalitarian views.

The qualitative evidence I present here suggests that elites perceive public opinion shifts after a quota law: They observe that the public comes

---

[8] "Senate women lead in effort to find accord," *The New York Times*, October 14, 2013.
[9] Anne-Marie Lizin, personal interview, September 9, 2013, Brussels, Belgium.

to expect and value gender equality in politics. Further research could test whether this relationship can be measured and confirmed systematically. Survey evidence comparing attitudes toward women in politics, and women's political engagement and participation, before and after a quota law would help answer these questions. For example, Hinojosa and Kittilson's (2020) study of public opinion before and after a quota law was implemented in Uruguay finds that seeing women in office makes women citizens more politically engaged. Media analysis of attention to women in politics and women's political preferences would also shed interesting light on the question of how quotas shift norms.

We also know very little about whether quotas increase voter turnout, partially because most countries do not report turnout by gender.[10] Evidence from the local level in Italy suggests that quotas can increase both turnout (especially for women) (De Paola, Scoppa, & De Benedetto 2014) and the number of women running in future elections after a quota is repealed (De Paola, Scoppa, & Lombardo 2010). Research from India also finds that districts that previously had a quota in place elect more women than those that did not (Bhavnani 2009). Much of the effect observed in India appears to be driven by women who had benefited from the quota, whereas in Italy this does not appear to have been the case. Further studies using national-level and comparative data, if it is possible to collect, would help determine whether quotas can encourage women's political engagement and ambition.

A third critical area for future research raised by this book's findings is whether gender quotas outside of rich OECD democracies will generate similar policy effects. I focus on high-income OECD democracies primarily because my underlying theory is based on the existence of gender differences in policy preferences, which are well established in this set of democracies, where women have moved to the left. My work suggests that the largest gender gap in high-income OECD democracies is found on the issue of maternal employment: women are nearly 10 percentage points more supportive than men on average, across countries and over time. This gender gap is not observed in most low- or middle-income democracies. Figure 7.1 shows the gender gap in preferences for maternal employment in a selection of countries worldwide, using data from the 2012 International Social Survey Programme (ISSP) Family and Changing Gender Roles Survey. The figure displays gender

[10] See Inter-Parliamentary Union, *Voter turnout 1945 1999: A global survey, Appendix – Voter turnout by gender.* www.idea.int/vt/survey/

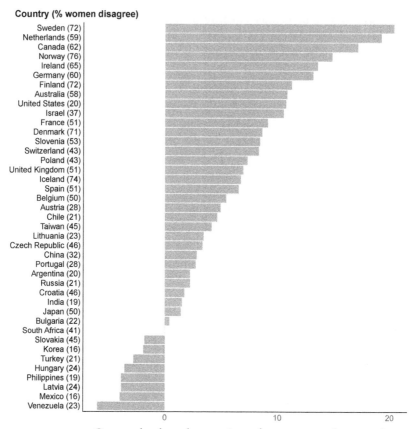

FIGURE 7.1 Country-level gender gaps in preferences toward maternal
employment worldwide (2012)

Notes: Values are the average share of women who disagree minus the share of men who
disagree with the following statement: "A pre-school child is likely to suffer if his or her
mother works." The figure in parentheses after the country name on the left is the average
share of women who disagree with the statement. Data come from the ISSP Changing
Gender Roles survey 2012. Survey weights are employed.

gaps of 15–20 points in some Western democracies (Ireland, Sweden),
but no gaps in countries like China, India, or across Latin America. In
some of these countries (Mexico and Venezuela), women are *less* likely
to support maternal employment than men. Of course, gender gaps may
be in the expected direction and larger among highly educated individuals in low- and middle-income democracies, but the data here suggest
that the issue of working mothers does not divide men and women
consistently across countries and regions worldwide. Quotas in low- or
middle-income democracies thus might not lead to the same types of

changes in work–family policies that I have identified in rich OECD democracies.

This raises the question, what issues *do* divide men and women in other regions of the world? There is a surprising lack of data on gender – and other social group – differences in preferences across countries and over time. Many cross-national surveys include questions about individual policy preferences, but analysis of gender gaps on specific policy issues is rare. One exception is Gottlieb, Grossman, and Robinson (2016), who analyze gender gaps in Africa. They find that gender differences in preferences are small but significant for poverty- and water-related issues in particular (see also Barnes & Cassese 2017; Chattopadhyay & Duflo 2004; Olken 2010). Clayton et al. (2019) find that these gender gaps in preferences are replicated among parliamentarians (in addition to a gender gap in preferences on gender equality), and further evidence suggests that these gender gaps ought to influence policy decisions. Recent work shows that Latin America still has a traditional gender gap in voting (women tend to vote to the right more than men) (Beall & Barnes 2020; Morgan 2015), but surveys of legislators indicate a gender gap on issues related to women's equality (women are more likely than men to prioritize this policy area; Schwindt-Bayer 2006). In short, we need better descriptive data on gender gaps across countries and over time, which also looks at whether such gaps persist across parties. Future research in this area could help us map the potential implications of quotas and other mechanisms that shape political selection worldwide.

The book's analysis hinges on the orthogonal nature of some issues, and thus the predominance of a left–right cleavage in politics. While this description of party competition and public preferences is useful in high-income OECD democracies, it might not be relevant or helpful in countries where the left–right dimension is weaker and other mechanisms (e.g., clientelism, personalized politics) play a more dominant role (Dix 1989; Levitsky 2003). For instance, Harbers, de Vries, and Steenbergen (2013) find that Latin American countries with programmatic party systems exhibit more stable left/right public attitudes. Scholars interested in using the approach developed here should thus take into account how gender gaps relate to a country's or region's structure of party competition, and might consider focusing on programmatic party systems.

It will also be important to consider how different political institutions could moderate the effects of quotas in other parts of the world. I examine quotas in parliamentary or semi-presidential systems with strong parties. Even within the set of mostly similar institutions considered here, different institutional norms (such as how ministers are selected) play an important role in conditioning the process through which quotas can lead to policy change. Looking at non-parliamentary democracies would help us determine whether quotas, and politician identity, lead to greater policy effects under other institutional conditions. Perhaps quota laws, and increased numbers of women, will be even *more* successful at changing outcomes in majoritarian systems with weak party discipline, since individual representatives from the governing party and the opposition have more power to propose bills and directly affect the agenda.

While this book focuses on women and their preferences in wealthy OECD democracies, for several reasons I believe the theory is broadly generalizable to other groups. Although they are less popular than gender quotas, at least twenty-eight countries have quotas for ethnic minority groups (Bird 2014). Looking beyond gender and ethnicity, there have been very few openly out lesbian, gay, bisexual, or transgender (LGBT) representatives in national parliaments, and voters still discriminate against them (Magni & Reynolds 2021). Reynolds (2013) counts only 151 in the past 35 years in a sample of 96 countries. Yet, evidence shows that LGBT representatives are more likely to make advances in gay rights in their countries, states, and towns (Haider-Markel 2010; Reynolds 2013). The first study of the representation of transgender candidates and elected officials found that there were only twenty transgender individuals in office worldwide as of 2015, and none of these at the national level (Casey & Reynolds 2015). The University of North Carolina at Chapel Hill report calls for an increased presence of transgender people in public office in order to "give the community an authentic voice in political decision-making" (p. 3). The increasing recognition of the political underrepresentation of identity groups underscores the importance of answering the central questions I have investigated in this book: *when* and *how* quotas, and politician identity, influence the policymaking process.

Future research should explore whether quotas and descriptive representation can have the same effect, for example, for ethnic minorities and their orthogonal preferences, such as racial equality. In this context, the group's political integration and institutional context both seem critical. A key difference between women, LGBT individuals, and ethnic minorities is that in many cases the latter group is more segregated within society (coinciding rather than cross-cutting). As Htun (2004) points out, this often leads ethnic groups to want their own parties, rather than to integrate with existing parties. Where this is not possible, such as in majoritarian two-party systems, ethnic groups might not be able to achieve change even with descriptive representation. Frymer (2010) makes a strong case that the US two-party system incentivizes parties to appeal to the median voter, who party leaders believe is white and hostile to specific Black interests (see also Gilens, Sniderman, & Kuklinski 1998). According to this logic, addressing racial equality – for instance by implementing policies strongly preferred by African Americans such as addressing discrimination in the criminal justice system, affirmative action, and reparations – would "disrupt the rest of the party's coalition" (Frymer 2010, p. 46) *and* potentially create an opening for the opposition to use race-based appeals as a divisive wedge. Wedge issues might be less powerful in proportional, multiparty systems since parties often have to work together in coalitions and do not want to jeopardize these relationships (Van de Wardt, De Vries, & Hobolt 2014). In this context of proportional, multiparty systems, descriptive representatives might be able to make progress even on controversial orthogonal issues. In summary, the logic that descriptive representation is likely to be important, especially for orthogonal issues, should hold across different groups, but it might be conditional on the group's nature (whether it is cross-cutting or coinciding) and institutional context.

7.4 QUOTAS AND THE SALIENCE OF GENDER EQUALITY

The pace of quota adoption is not slowing; if anything, it is speeding up. In recent years, gender quota laws have been proposed in the parliaments or electoral commissions of countries as diverse as Georgia, Luxembourg, Malawi, Malta, Scotland, and South Korea. In 2019, leading figures from parties across the political spectrum in Germany called for a 50–50 quota for the Bundestag.[11] An academic research report on gender inequality in the United Kingdom also called for a gender quota law, spurring some prominent women MPs to agree with the proposal, although it has not yet been debated in parliament.[12] And many countries that already have quota laws are making them stronger (Gatto 2017; Piscopo 2016). For

---

[11] Jochen Bittner, "Germany wants more women in politics: But quotas are a bad idea," *The New York Times*, February 1, 2019.
[12] "LSE study calls for gender quotas to place women in positions of power," *The Guardian*, October 12, 2015.

example, Portugal passed new legislation in 2019 to increase its quota threshold from 33 to 40 percent, and to make compliance with the quota mandatory for list submission (rather than simply fining non-compliant parties, as the legislation previously required). While only the social democratic party championed the initial quota legislation, all parties except the communist party supported tightening it. Quota laws are becoming more popular and considered more legitimate across parties and countries worldwide.

This book reveals important insights about the effects of political gender quota laws in high-income OECD democracies, and the process through which they can generate policy changes. Quotas are not a panacea; skeptics rightly assert that party is often more important than gender. On many issues, it is. Yet, on some issues, in some contexts (here, wealthy OECD democracies) women do share preferences that are distinct from those of men, even across parties. I make the case that in order to understand whether quotas lead to change for women we should focus on these issues, especially if they fall outside the traditional lines of left–right party competition. It should not be surprising that maternal employment is one example of such an orthogonal issue. The majority of women have children, and since the rise of the services sector (and for many groups of women before that) they have had to juggle primary responsibility for the home with work outside the home. Facilitating women's equality in the workplace requires men to become more involved in household and care responsibilities. Across parties, working women ought to have an interest in moving toward this shared goal. The survey data presented here confirms that they do.

Gender quotas help make the issues of work–family balance salient across parties. They amplify women's voices within their parties and parliamentary committees, and result in more women ministers with the power to change work–family policies. Quotas draw attention to gender equality in politics, as elites come to understand women's interests on these issues and their potential electoral value. Changes are particularly notable within parties on the right, which have experienced the largest increases to the number of women in their ranks in a number of countries. Quota laws give women more opportunities to push their parties to prioritize, or shift positions on, work–family policies that support working mothers. This is happening across high-income OECD democracies, even those without a quota law, but a quota speeds the process by quickly changing party demographics (especially those on the right and far right). Absent a quota, parties on the right in particular rarely prioritize maternal employment (often focusing instead on fertility), and often implement policies that discourage women's employment, like long, low-paid maternity leave and family allowances. Taken together, the analysis here illuminates the considerable work that women have undertaken across parties to change the status quo of women's inequality across the realms of home, work, and politics. Quotas help women make these changes, and create new allies as men begin to take on a greater share of the load.

Appendix

CHAPTER I

Details of Synthetic Control Methods

I construct synthetic control countries for Belgium and Portugal using the Synth package for R (Abadie, Diamond, & Hainmueller 2011). The synthetic control countries are constructed as a weighted average of potential control countries, with weights chosen so that the resulting synthetic control country best replicates the values of predictors of women's representation in the treated country before the quota law was passed. To produce the synthetic control countries I use predictor variables that are associated with women's representation and gender quota adoption. These are GDP (log of GDP per capita), women's labor force participation, and party quotas (Inglehart & Norris 2000; Iversen & Rosenbluth 2008; Kittilson 2006; Matland 1998; McAllister & Studlar 2002; Tripp & Kang 2008). These variables are augmented by including the average percentage of women in parliament over several pre-treatment time periods. Other countries that had a quota law during the same time period are dropped from the potential control donor pool. I also drop countries that are missing data during the relevant time period, as the method requires a balanced panel.

Note that because countries have elections at different times, time units are constructed using elections rather than years. For each treated country I identify the election immediately before a quota law was implemented (i.e., the quota law was passed by the government resulting from that election) and code it ($t = 5$), and then order the elections before and after $t = 1$, 2, etc. I follow the same procedure for all potential control countries, where the last election before a quota law was implemented in the treated country is coded $t = 5$ and previous and subsequent elections are ordered accordingly. I repeat this procedure using separate data sets for both Portugal and Italy. Synthetic Belgium is composed of 75 percent Japan, 14 percent Denmark, 4 percent Sweden and the United Kingdom, and small percentages of other countries. Synthetic Portugal is composed of 46 percent United Kingdom, 24 percent Japan, 20 percent Finland, 9 percent Greece, and small percentages of other countries.

A comparison of the pretreatment characteristics of both "treated" (quota) countries with their synthetic versions and the average of all potential controls in the donor pool for each country shows that the synthetic control country provides a more suitable control than the average of all potential control countries. Prior to adopting a quota law, the percentage of women in parliament was lower in the countries that passed a quota law than in the average of control countries, for both Belgium and Portugal. In the election prior to the quota law implementation, the share of women in parliament was 12 percent in Belgium; the share of women in parliament in the synthetic version matches nearly exactly 11.99 percent compared to 25.1 percent for the average of all potential control countries. Similarly, in Portugal the share of women in parliament before the quota was 21.3 percent, which the synthetic version matches almost exactly at 21.27 percent, compared to the average of all potential control countries at 29.7 percent. The same is true looking at the previous two elections before quota implementation. Compared to the average of all potential control countries, the synthetic control countries are able to better reproduce the values for the share of women in parliament prior to the passage of a quota law (for a table of these results, see Weeks 2016).

The synthetic control countries do not necessarily provide a closer fit to the real country for the other predictor variables included in matching (GDP per capita, party quotas, and women's labor force participation). In fact, this turns out not to matter in terms of predicting the share of women in parliament. The synthetic control method is implemented by choosing a value V among all positive definite and diagonal matrices to minimize the mean squared prediction error of the percentage of women in parliament in the "treated" country during the pre-quota period (Abadie, Diamond, & Hainmueller 2011). The resulting value of the diagonal element for all other variables except for the previous percentage of women in parliament variables turns out to be zero, or very close to zero, in most cases. This means that given the other variables included (lagged measures of the outcome variable), these other determinants have little substantial power predicting the percentage of women in parliament before a quota law is implemented.

In order to assess the robustness of the results (presented in the main text), I follow Abadie, Diamond, and Hainmueller (2010) and others in running placebo studies (Abadie, Diamond, & Hainmueller 2010; Abadie & Gardeazabal 2003; Bertrand, Duflo, & Mullainathan 2004). The placebo studies answer the question of how often I would obtain results of this magnitude if I had chosen a country at random for the analysis instead of the "treated" (quota) country. I apply the synthetic control method to countries that did not pass a quota law during the sample period, for each quota country and associated period studied.[1] If the placebo studies create increases in magnitude similar to the ones estimated in the countries that passed a quota law, then the analysis would not provide significant evidence of a positive effect of a quota law on the percentage of women in parliament. If the placebo studies show that the increased estimated is relatively large compared to the change in countries that did not pass a quota law, then conversely the analysis shows significant evidence of a positive effect of quota laws on the percentage of women in parliament.

Figure A1.1 shows the results of the placebo tests for each country. The gray lines represent the change associated with each of the control country placebo tests, that is, the difference in the percentage of women in parliament between each country in the donor pool and its synthetic version. The dark black line shows the increase in women in parliament estimated for the "treated" (quota) country. As the figures show, the estimated increase for the quota countries is unusually large relative to the distribution of change in women in parliament for the other countries in the donor pool in both cases, and especially for Belgium. The positive effect for Belgium is the highest of all countries in its sample, and because the figure includes sixteen countries, the probability of estimating an increase of this magnitude under a random permutation of the intervention is 7 percent (1/14) – close to the conventional level of

---

[1] The placebo tests are done by iteratively applying the synthetic control method to every other country in the control donor pool, for each "treated" (quota) country. For more, see Abadie, Diamond, and Hainmueller (2010).

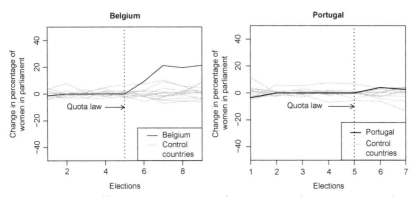

FIGURE A1.1 Differences in percentage of women in parliament in "treated"
(quota) countries and differences in placebo test countries
Notes: All analyses were carried out using Synth for R (Abadie, Diamond, & Hainmueller
2011).

statistical significance. Turning to Portugal, the positive effect observed
is higher than the majority of control countries, with the probability of
estimating an increase of this magnitude randomly 43 percent (6/14).

Case Study Matching Procedure

The following section provides further details about the statistical matching procedure used to select paired cases, including a discussion of
similarities and differences between the matched pair countries and tables
showing the data used. I focus on identifying the variables that might correlate with both quota adoption and policy outcomes related to women's
interests. A good understanding of potential confounders is critical
for addressing endogeneity concerns that inevitably arise with a cross-
national study of this type. I match on six variables identified as potential
confounders: percentage of women in parliament, proportional representation, economic development (income per capita), women's labor force
participation, percentage of parties with voluntary quotas (weighted by
seat share in parliament), and percentage of population Catholic (1980).[2]

Percentage of women in parliament is included because most countries
that pass a quota law have low levels of women in parliament before the
law is passed, as discussed in the main text. This makes an intervention

[2] Data on percentage of women in parliament, women's labor force participation, and proportional representation come from the Comparative Welfare States Data Set, February
2014 version; income per capita comes from the UN World Development Indicators
(2014); percentage of the population Catholic as of 1980 from La Porta et al. (1999);
and the share of parties with voluntary gender quotas comes from an original data set.

like a quota likely to be useful, although certainly many countries with low levels of women's representation do not go on to pass a quota (e.g., the United States), and some with high levels of women's representation do (e.g., Spain). The share of women in parliament has also been linked to increases in overall levels of spending (Bolzendahl 2009; Bolzendahl & Brooks 2007), and spending on child care and parental leave (Bonoli & Reber 2010; Kittilson 2008; Profeta 2020).

Economic development and associated increases in women's labor force participation could be associated with quota adoption through their link to increases in women's representation (Iversen & Rosenbluth 2008; Matland 1998; McAllister & Studlar 2002; Tripp & Kang 2008). Many "quota countries" suffer from low levels of women's participation in the workforce, for example, Italy and Spain. Even in Portugal, where the share of women in the labor force is relatively high, the historical lack of women in positions of power was cited as one of the reasons numbers of women in parliament remained low. Center-left (PS) Party member Ana Coucello explains, "In the dictatorship there were practically only men in decision-making, so it was perceived like a man's thing ... nowadays even sometimes it's difficult for women to speak in public, mainly in gatherings where men are in the vast majority."[3]

Women's labor force participation might also be linked to quota adoption through its effect on voter attitudes. Some argue that quota laws are more likely to be adopted in egalitarian political cultures (Lovenduski & Norris 1993). Women's labor force participation has also been found to be an important determinant of women's policy preferences (Iversen & Rosenbluth 2006), which could in turn affect policy outcomes. Both economic development and women's employment are related to policy outcomes. For example, as incomes and government revenues increase, demand for public expenditure should also rise (Wagner's Law). Workforce participation entitles some women to benefits that they would otherwise not be eligible for and increases their need for services to help balance work and family.

Catholicism is also included because of its potential link to women's representation. Catholic culture has been linked to low levels of women's representation in office (Castles 1994; Esping-Andersen 1990). Every country that has passed a quota law in Europe has a strong tradition of Catholicism, from France with 75 percent of the population Catholic as of 1980 to Spain with 96 percent. Catholicism has also been

---

[3] Ana Coucello, personal interview, December 3, 2013, Lisbon, Portugal.

linked to gendered policy outcomes, including family policy and labor market outcomes for women (Castles 1994). In Esping-Andersen's welfare state typology, corporatist welfare states are often characterized by Catholicism, and the traditional male breadwinner family, low labor force participation for women, and relatively low provision of welfare state goods and services are emphasized (Esping-Andersen 1990).

Proportional representation is included because quotas are thought to be more compatible with PR systems where the party presents a list of candidates than with majority systems with lower district magnitude (Matland 2006). Belgium and Portugal both have systems of proportional representation; France is an exception to this rule. Research shows that electoral rules also exert a strong effect on policy outcomes: Majoritarian electoral systems are associated with smaller government spending and smaller welfare states compared to systems of proportional representation (e.g., Iversen & Soskice 2006; Milesi-Ferretti, Perotti, & Rostagno 2002; Persson & Tabellini 2005).

Finally, I include voluntary party quotas because party-level experience with voluntary gender quota provisions might also be linked to adoption of a quota law. In addition to contagion theory, parties that have already passed internal quotas have had the critical debate, making members more likely to be unified in support for a national law. Parties also gain experience in implementing the law and are able to see that it is effective. I expect that voluntary party quotas are linked to policy outcomes mainly through the indirect mechanism of increased women's representation.

To what extent can we treat party quotas and national quota laws as discrete variables? In many cases, use of party quotas preceded quota laws. However, not all countries that have party quotas go on to adopt quota laws. There is also considerable variation in the use of party quotas among countries that pass a quota law. The correlation between quota laws and party quotas is positive at 0.15, but low and not statistically significant.[4] Thus, I treat party and national quotas as distinct phenomena, and consider party quotas an important potential confounder in the relationship between quota laws and policy change.

I considered controlling for several other variables correlated with quota adoption. First, research has highlighted the importance of strong women's movements advocating for change, especially women's sections in the party (Dahlerup 2006; Kittilson 2006). Unfortunately, it is very difficult to measure the presence or strength of women's movements or

---

[4] Point-biserial correlation carried out using Stata package pbis.

party sections across countries over time. The best data available come from Htun and Weldon (2012), who compile measures of the strength and autonomy of feminist women's movements over time in seventy countries. These data show that there was no change in the strength or autonomy of women's movements in Belgium or Portugal before a quota law was passed. In other words, a trend toward strong, autonomous women's movements is not present before quota laws were passed in these cases. My interview data further confirmed that women's movements were not crucial players in these cases.

Second, scholars also point to international information sharing as a key factor in quota adoption (Krook 2006, 2008) – and in my cases, particularly at the European level. Two of the international influences most frequently cited in my interviews were the European Commission and Council of Europe.[5] Because all EU member states are likely to be similarly influenced by these bodies, I do not include this as a matching variable. I return to the question of international influence and women's sections in parties in the subsequent section on balance on other potential confounders.

The matching procedure is carried out using the `MatchIt` package version 2.4-20 in R version 2.14.0. I conduct separate matching procedures for Belgium and Portugal, subsetting the data to countries with elections in the years including and immediately preceding the year in which a quota law was adopted for each case (1994 in Belgium and 2006 in Portugal). I include only one election-year per country.

I drop other "quota countries" before matching. I use nearest neighbor, Mahalanobis matching. Nearest neighbor matching selects the single best control match for each "treated" unit (i.e., Belgium and Portugal). Matching is done using a distance measure, and here the Mahalanobis option is used because it allows for continuous covariates (Ho et al. 2011). The match is selected based on Mahalanobis distance, a generalization of Euclidean distance that accounts for correlations between variables (Rubin 1973). Tables A1.1 and A1.2 present data used in the matching procedures. Matched pairs are in **bold**.

As discussed in the main text, Belgium successfully matches to the case of Austria, and Portugal to Italy. It is useful to briefly discuss balance on other potential confounders here. Turning to the other variables that have been cited as causes of quota adoption in the literature, we can see that both matches are European countries, and thus would have been subject

---

[5] Other international influences were global, for example, CEDAW, Socialist Women International.

TABLE A1.1 Data for matching: Belgium

Country	Election year	% Women in parliament	GNI per capita	PR	Women's labor force participation	% Catholic (1980)	Party quotas (%)
Belgium	**1991**	**9.4**	**28,513**	**1**	**41.81**	**90**	**35**
Australia	1993	8.8	24,411	1	41.74	29.6	0
Austria	**1994**	**21.9**	**29,186**	**1**	**42.81**	**88.8**	**43**
Canada	1993	18	25,412	0	44.74	46.6	63
Denmark	1994	33.5	38,630	1	45.66	0.6	35
Finland	1991	39	25,295	1	47.18	0.1	0
Germany	1994	21.9	29,396	1	NA	35	45
Great Britain	1992	9.2	25,533	0	43.77	13.1	0
Greece	1993	6	15,632	1	37.25	0.4	57
Iceland	1991	23.8	38,706	1	45.77	0.7	38
Ireland	1992	12	20,952	1	NA	95.3	0
Japan	1993	2.67	32,574	1	40.53	0.6	0
Luxembourg	1994	20	51,662	1	36.14	93	0
Netherlands	1994	31.3	31,122	1	41.32	42.6	28
New Zealand	1993	21.2	19,172	1	43.53	18.7	0
Norway	1993	39.4	47,290	1	45.42	0.3	76
Sweden	1991	33.5	29,576	1	47.98	1.4	5
Switzerland	1991	17.5	48,306	1	41.73	52.8	21
United States	1992	11	32,791	0	44.83	30	0

TABLE A1.2 Data for matching: Portugal

Country	Election year	% Women in parliament	GNI per capita	PR	Women's labor force participation	% Catholic (1980)	Party quotas (%)
Portugal	**2005**	**21.3**	**17,994**	**1**	**46.75**	**94.1**	**52**
Australia	2004	24.7	32,379	1	44.65	29.6	40
Canada	2004	21.1	33,704	0	46.61	46.6	50
Denmark	2005	36.9	48,209	1	47.33	0.6	0
Finland	2003	37.5	34,774	1	48.17	0.1	0
Germany	2005	31.8	33,922	1	45.18	35	81
Great Britain	2005	19.7	39,130	0	45.97	13.1	0
Greece	2004	13	21,094	1	40.66	0.4	39
Ireland	2002	13.25	37,004	1	41.65	95.3	0
Italy	**2001**	**9.8**	**30,204**	**1**	**38.74**	**83.2**	**26**
Japan	2005	9	36,615	1	41.35	0.6	0
Luxembourg	2004	23.3	68,354	1	41.96	93	75
Netherlands	2003	36.7	38,146	1	44.17	42.6	33
New Zealand	2005	32.3	25,711	1	46.42	18.7	0
Norway	2001	35.8	61,673	1	46.6	0.3	59
Sweden	2002	45	37,583	1	47.96	1.4	59
Switzerland	2003	25	53,493	1	44.65	52.8	54
United States	2004	14.9	43,615	0	46.18	30	26

to similar influence by the Council of Europe, European Commission, and other European-level and global organizations. Both Austria and Italy also have some political parties with established women's sections, like their counterparts in Belgium and Portugal. In Austria, both the Social Democratic Party and the Christian democratic Austrian People's Party have had a women's section since 1945.[6] In Italy, the Democratic Party of the Left established a women's section in the party in 1991 (Guadagnini 2005).

Interview Methods

The following section details interview methodology, including constructing a sampling frame, interview format and response rate, recording, and compensation strategies for uncertainty.

The purpose of the interviews was to gain knowledge about the determinants of policy outcomes in key areas of interest to women, especially work–family policies, including the role of quotas. In composing the sample frame, I sought a diversity of interview subjects – men and women, politicians, bureaucrats, and activists – who were participants and observers of policy debates about both quotas and work–family policies. Most importantly, I looked for subjects who could offer the best evidence about the implementation of quotas and the evolution of family policies, including past and present party leaders, cabinet members, politicians, and activists. I used parliamentary proceedings and newspaper coverage of key debates, as well as secondary literature, to determine key actors. I also gave interviewees the opportunity to recommend other potential interview subjects. Many times these subjects were already in the sample frame, but some new interviews also resulted from these referrals. All in-person interviews were recorded, with the approval of the interviewee (one interview was not recorded due to technical problems). Audio was transcribed immediately following the interview, along with any other relevant notes or observations. Audio and transcripts of all interviews are available on request for all "on the record" interviews.

The majority of the interviews were semi-structured, with the exception of structured email interviews when in-person interviews were not possible. Most of the interviews were conducted in English. While Austria and Belgium are both countries characterized by very high English

---

[6] http://frauen.spoe.at/ueber-uns;
www.frauenoffensive.at/service/geschichte-der-oesterreichischen-frauenbewegung.html;
and see Köpl 2005.

proficiency, I expected more variation in the cases of Italy and Portugal. Initial emails were sent in both English and native language in these cases (I am proficient in Italian, and used a translator in the case of Portugal). In Portugal, all respondents save for one responded in English, and all interviews were conducted in English. I was unable to conduct one interview with a member of the Communist Party in Portugal because of translator unavailability. In Italy, contacts responded in both Italian and English, and interviews also took place in both languages (often both in the course of the same interview). In this way, interviewees were able to express themselves comfortably in whichever language they preferred. Because interviews were recorded, I could go back, re-listen, and translate into English different portions of the interview as needed.

Table A1.3 reports all interviews sought, obtained, and declined. Interviewees are divided into categories based on country, and then their occupation and party affiliation, with the main groupings being left-wing politicians, right-wing politicians, women's movement activists, and social partners since these are the key actors central to accounts of quotas and policy change for women.

Overall the response rate was just under 50 percent (64/132). Notably, I was unable to obtain any interviews with members of right-wing parties in Italy. I was also unable to obtain any interviews with men in Italy. Response rates for individual countries are: Austria 66 percent (16/24), Belgium 43 percent (17/40), Italy 35 percent (11/31), and Portugal 54 percent (20/37). The gender breakdown of interviews overall is 19 percent men, 81 percent women. One important reason that women are overrepresented is that they are often key actors in debates about work–family policies, and so they are similarly overrepresented in the sample frame. However, it is also the case that in some instances men potential interviewees were less responsive than women (Italy, and to a lesser extent Austria). The gender breakdown for individual countries is as follows: Austria 94 percent women (one man, fifteen women), Belgium 71 percent women (five men, twelve women), Italy 100 percent women (eleven women), Portugal 70 percent women (six men, fourteen women).

Absent interviews with right-wing politicians in Italy, and with men party elites in Italy and Austria, I supplement interview data with parliamentary debates and newspaper coverage. While certainty about individual perspectives cannot be complete, these original sources do provide important missing information, often with verbatim accounts. Pairing interview data with primary source material thus raises confidence that findings are unbiased.

TABLE A1.3 *Interview methods table*

Interviewee	Status	Source	Format	Length	Documentation

Category 1: Left-wing parties

Interviewee	Status	Source	Format	Length	Documentation
Andrea Brunner, SPÖ women's section	Conducted in person 04/22/14	Sample frame and referred by Gisela Wurm	Semi-structured	50 min	Audio recording and transcript available
Irmtraut Karlsson, SPÖ politician	Conducted in person 05/12/14	Sample frame and referred by Andrea Brunner	Semi-structured	60 min	Audio recording and transcript available
Gisela Wurm, SPÖ politician	Conducted via email 04/27/14	Sample frame	Structured	NA	Email transcript available
Ines Stilling, Ministry bureaucrat	Conducted in person 04/22/14	Referred by Julia Valsky	Semi-structured	50 min	Audio recording and transcript available
Julia Valsky, spokesperson for SPÖ Minister	Conducted in person 05/05/14	Substitute in sample frame	Semi-structured	35 min	Audio recording and transcript available
SPÖ Minister's aide	Conducted in person 04/18/14	Substitute in sample frame	Semi-structured	70 min	Confidentiality requested
Berivan Aslan, The Greens politician	Conducted via email 04/01/14	Sample frame	Structured	NA	Email transcript available
Ulrike Lunacek, The Greens politician	Conducted via email 04/25/14	Sample frame	Structured	NA	Email transcript available
Judith Schwentner, The Greens politician	Conducted in person 05/06/14	Sample frame	Semi-structured	45 min	Audio recording and transcript available
SPÖ Minister	Refused 04/17/14	Sample frame			
SPÖ politician 1	Refused 04/01/14	Sample frame			
SPÖ politician 2	Accepted 04/29/14, then no response	Sample frame			

Interviewee	Status	Source	Format	Length	Documentation
Category 2: Right-wing parties					
Claudia Durchschlag, ÖVP politician	Conducted in person 05/05/14	Sample frame and referred by ÖVP politician	Semi-structured	40 min	Audio recording and transcript available
Martina Schenk, Team Stronach politician	Conducted in person 05/07/14	Sample frame	Semi-structured	50 min	Audio recording and transcript available
ÖVP politician	Refused 03/31/14				
FPÖ politician 1	Accepted 05/01/14, then no response	Referred by Andrea Brunner			
FPÖ politician 2	No response	Sample frame			
Category 3: Women's movements, social partners					
Melanie Eckl-Kerber, Fed. Aust. Industries	Conducted in person 05/12/14	Sample frame	Semi-structured	45 min	Audio recording and transcript available
Brigitte Hornyik, activist	Conducted in person 05/08/14	Sample frame	Semi-structured	45 min	Audio recording and transcript available
Ingrid Moritz, activist	Conducted in person 04/30/14	Sample frame	Semi-structured	45 min	Audio recording and transcript available
Maria Rosslhumer, activist	Conducted in person 05/05/14	Sample frame	Semi-structured	45 min	Audio recording and transcript available

Manuela Vollman, abz*austria	Conducted in person 04/30/14	Sample frame	Semi-structured	45 min	Audio recording and transcript available

Belgium

Category 1: Left-wing parties

Anne-Marie Lizin, PS politician	Conducted in person 09/09/13	Sample frame	Semi-structured	55 min	Audio recording and transcript available
Yvan Mayeur, PS politician	Conducted in person 10/17/13	Sample frame	Semi-structured	30 min	Audio recording and transcript available
Louis Tobback, sp.a politician	Conducted in person 09/20/13	Sample frame	Semi-structured	70 min	Audio recording and transcript available
Renaat Landuyt, sp.a politician	Conducted in person 09/23/13	Sample frame	Semi-structured	25 min	Audio recording and transcript available
Vera Claes, sp.a politician	Conducted in person 10/10/13	Sample frame	Semi-structured	60 min	Audio recording and transcript available
Emily Hoyos, ECOLO leader	Conducted in person 09/13/13	Sample frame	Semi-structured	35 min	Audio recording and transcript available
ECOLO politician	No response				
Groen! leader	No response				
PS Minister	Refused 09/19/13	Sample frame			
PS politician 1	Refused 09/04/13	Sample frame			
PS politician 2	Accepted 09/27/13, then no response	Sample frame			
sp.a politician 1	No response	Sample frame			
sp.a politician 2	No response	Sample frame			

TABLE A1.3 *(Continued)*.

Interviewee	Status	Source	Format	Length	Documentation
Category 2: Christian democrats					
Sabine de Bethune, CDV politician	Conducted in person 09/05/13	Sample frame	Semi-structured	80 min	Audio recording and transcript available
Els Van Hoofe, CDV politician	Conducted in person 10/16/13	Sample frame	Semi-structured	75 min	Audio recording and transcript available
Tinneke Huyghe, CDV politician	Conducted in person 10/16/13	Sample frame	Semi-structured	75 min	Audio recording and transcript available
Niki Dheedene, cdH aide	Conducted in person 10/08/13	Referred by cdH Minister 1	Semi-structured	60 min	Audio recording and transcript available
cdH party leader	No response	Sample frame			
cdH Minister 1	Refused 08/29/13	Sample frame			
cdH Minister 2	Refused 10/03/13	Sample frame			
CDV politician 1	Accepted 09/19/13, then unavailable	Sample frame			
CDV politician 2	Accepted 09/05/13, then unavailable	Sample frame			
Category 3: Right-wing parties					
Gerolf Annemans, VB leader	Conducted in person 09/10/13	Sample frame	Semi-structured	55 min	Audio recording and transcript available
Gwendolyn Rutten, Open VLD leader	Conducted in person 10/02/13	Sample frame and referred by Open VLD politician	Semi-structured	50 min	Audio recording and transcript available
Joachim Pohlmann, N-VA official	Conducted in person 09/10/13	Referred by N-VA party leader	Semi-structured	30 min	Audio recording and transcript available

Viviane Teitelbaum, MR politician	Conducted in person 10/23/13	Referred by Anne-Marie Lizin and MR politician 1	Semi-structured	30 min	Audio recording and transcript available
MR politician 1	Refused 10/18/13	Sample frame			
MR politician 2	Accepted 09/16/13, then no response	Sample frame			
Open VLD politician 1	Refused 08/27/13	Sample frame			
Open VLD politician 2	No response	Sample frame			
VB politician	No response	Sample frame			
N-VA party leader	Refused 08/30/13	Sample frame			
N-VA politician 1	No response	Sample frame			
N-VA politician 2	No response	Sample frame			
FDF politician	No response	Sample frame			

Category 4: Women's movements

Serap Altinisik, activist	Conducted in person 10/21/13	Sample frame	Semi-structured	45 min	Audio recording and transcript available
Eveline Cortier, activist	Conducted in person 10/03/13	Sample frame	Semi-structured	50 min	Audio recording and transcript available
Kitty Roggeman, activist	Conducted in person 10/03/13	Referred by Eveline Cortier	Semi-structured	50 min	Audio recording and transcript available
Hedwige Peemans-Poullet, activist	Conducted in person 10/04/13	Referred by Petra Meier and Karen Celis	Semi-structured	70 min	Audio recording and transcript available
Women's movement activist 1	No response	Sample frame			
Women's movement activist 2	No response	Sample frame			

Interviewee	Status	Source	Format	Length	Documentation
Italy					
Category 1: Left-wing parties					
Elsa Fornero, PD Minister	Conducted in person 03/27/14, w/ Skype follow-up	Sample frame	Semi-structured	80 min	Audio recording and transcript available
Cecilia Guerra, PD politician	Conducted in person 04/09/14	Sample frame	Semi-structured	60 min	Audio recording and transcript available
Rosa Calipari, PD politician	Conducted via email 05/19/14	Referred by Simona Lanzoni	Structured	NA	Email transcript available
Valeria Fedeli, PD politician	Conducted via email 05/14/14	Referred by Ludovica Tranquilli Leali	Structured	NA	Email transcript available
Valeria Valente, PD politician	Conducted in person 04/09/14	Sample frame	Semi-structured	50 min	Audio recording and transcript available
Elettra Deiana, PRC, SEL politician	Conducted in person 04/11/14	Sample frame	Semi-structured	120 min	Audio recording and transcript available
DS politician 1	No response	Sample frame			
PD politician 1	Accepted 03/27/14, then unavailable	Sample frame and referred by Elsa Fornero			
PD politician 2	No response	Sample frame			
PD politician 3	No response	Sample frame			
PD politician 4	No response	Sample frame and referred by Elsa Fornero			
PD politician 5	No response	Sample frame			

Participant	Response	Recruitment	Interview type	Duration	Availability
PD politician 6	No response	Referred by Simona Lanzoni			
PRC politician	Accepted 02/25/14, then unavailable	Sample frame then unavailable			
Category 2: Right-wing parties					
FI politician 1	No response	Sample frame			
FI politician 2	No response	Sample frame			
FI politician 3	No response	Sample frame			
FI politician 4	No response	Sample frame			
FI politician 5	No response	Sample frame			
Pdl politician 1	No response	Sample frame			
Pdl politician 2	No response	Sample frame			
Pd politician 3	No response	Sample frame			
LN politician	No response	Sample frame			
UdC politician	Accepted 03/27/14, then unavailable	Sample frame			
Category 3: Other parties					
M5S politician	No response	Sample frame			
SEL politician	No response	Sample frame			
Category 4: Women's movements					
Maria Cimarelli, Working Mothers Italy	Conducted in person 03/25/14	Sample frame	Semi-structured	45 min	Audio recording and transcript available
Ludovica Tranquilli Leali, activist	Conducted in person 03/25/14	Sample frame	Semi-structured	80 min	Audio recording and transcript available

TABLE A1.3 (Continued).

Interviewee	Status	Source	Format	Length	Documentation
Simona Lanzoni, activist	Conducted in person 03/21/14	Sample frame	Semi-structured	50 min	Audio recording and transcript available
Titti Carano, activist	Conducted in person 03/21/14	Sample frame and referred by Ludovica Tranquilli Leali	Semi-structured	75 min	Audio recording and transcript available
Vittoria Tola, activist	Conducted in person 03/15/14	Referred by Simona Lanzoni	Semi-structured	90 min	Audio recording and transcript available
Portugal					
Category 1: Left-wing parties					
Maria de Belém, PS party leader	Conducted in person 11/07/13	Sample frame	Semi-structured	40 min	Audio recording and transcript available
Ana Gomes, PS politician	Conducted in person 12/06/13	Sample frame	Semi-structured	35 min	Audio recording and transcript available
Augusto Santos Silva, PS Minister	Conducted in person 11/12/13	Sample frame	Semi-structured	50 min	Audio recording and transcript available
Elza Pais, PS politician	Conducted in person 11/26/13	Sample frame	Semi-structured	40 min	Audio recording and transcript available
Caterina Marcelino, PS politician	Conducted in person 11/26/13	Sample frame	Semi-structured	40 min	Audio recording and transcript available
Sónia Fertuzinhos, PS politician	Conducted in person 11/22/13	Sample frame	Semi-structured	60 min	Audio recording and transcript available
Sónia Fertuzinhos, PS politician	Conducted via phone 06/02/19	Follow-up	Semi-structured	90 min	Audio recording and transcript available

Vitalino Canas, PS politician	Conducted via email 10/16/13	Sample frame	Structured	NA	Email transcript available
Luís Fazenda, BE politician	Conducted in person 11/05/13	Sample frame	Semi-structured	40 min	Audio recording and transcript available
BE politician 1	No response	Sample frame			
BE politician 2	No response	Sample frame			
BE politician 3	No response	Sample frame			
PS politician 1	No response	Sample frame			
PS politician 2	No response	Sample frame			
PS politician 3	Refused 10/128/13	Sample frame			
PS politician 4	No response	Sample frame			
PS politician 5	No response	Sample frame			
PS politician 6	No response	Sample frame			
PCP politician 1	Refused 10/16/13	Sample frame			
PCP politician 2	Accepted 10/28/13, then unavailable	Sample frame and referred by PCP politician 1			

Category 2: **Right-wing parties**

Helder Amaral, CDS politician	Conducted in person 11/06/13	Sample frame	Semi-structured	40 min	Audio recording and transcript available
João Almeida, CDS politician	Conducted in person 11/20/13	Sample frame	Semi-structured	35 min	Audio recording and transcript available
Teresa Caeiro, CDS politician	Conducted in person 11/05/13	Sample frame	Semi-structured	60 min	Audio recording and transcript available
José Mendes Bota, PSD politician	Conducted in person 11/07/13	Sample frame	Semi-structured	45 min	Audio recording and transcript available

TABLE A1.3 (Continued).

Interviewee	Status	Source	Format	Length	Documentation
Paula Cardoso, PSD politician	Conducted in person 12/05/13	Substitute from sample frame	Semi-structured	35 min	Audio recording and transcript available
Monica Ferro, PSD politician	Conducted in person 12/05/13	Sample frame	Semi-structured	35 min	Audio recording and transcript available
Teresa Morais, PSD Minister	Conducted in person 12/02/13	Substitute from sample frame	Semi-structured	45 min	Notes written w/in 1 hr available
CDS politician 1	No response	Sample frame			
PSD politician 1	Refused 10/10/13	Sample frame			
PSD politician 2	No response	Sample frame			
PSD politician 3	No response	Sample frame			
PSD politician 4	No response	Sample frame			
Category 3: Women's movements					
Ana Coucello, activist	Conducted in person 12/03/13	Referred by Alexandra Silva (EWL)	Semi-structured	145 min	Audio recording and transcript available
Maria José Magalhães, activist	Conducted in person 11/08/13	Sample frame	Semi-structured	60 min	Audio recording and transcript available
Fatima Duarte, bureaucrat	Conducted via email 12/09/13	Sample frame	Structured	NA	Email transcript available
Nora Kiss, activist	Conducted in person 10/30/13	Sample frame	Semi-structured	40 min	Audio recording and transcript available
Regina Tavares da Silva, activist	Conducted in person 11/13/13	Referred by Alexandra Silva (EWL)	Semi-structured	45 min	Audio recording and transcript available

CHAPTER 3

TABLE A3.1 *Countries and years included in survey analysis*

Country	ROG 1 (1985)	ROG 2 (1990)	ROG 3 (1996)	ROG 4 (2006)	FCG 1 (1988)	FCG 2 (1994)	FCG 3 (2002)	FCG 4 (2012)
Australia	✓	✓	✓	✓		✓	✓	✓
Austria					✓	✓	✓	✓
Belgium					✓		✓	✓
Canada		✓	✓		✓			✓
Denmark							✓	✓
France							✓	✓
Germany	✓	✓	✓	✓	✓	✓	✓	✓
Ireland		✓	✓	✓	✓	✓	✓	
Italy	✓	✓	✓		✓	✓		
Japan		✓	✓			✓	✓	✓
Netherlands					✓	✓	✓	✓
New Zealand		✓	✓			✓	✓	
Norway		✓	✓	✓				
Portugal							✓	✓
Spain		✓	✓			✓	✓	✓
Sweden		✓	✓			✓	✓	✓
Switzerland		✓	✓				✓	✓
United Kingdom	✓	✓	✓	✓	✓	✓	✓	✓
United States	✓	✓	✓	✓	✓	✓	✓	✓

Notes: ROG is the ISSP Role of Government survey, and FCG is the ISSP Family and Changing Gender Roles survey.

CHAPTER 4

Details of Matching Procedure

In this section, I describe the selection of five matching variables that might influence the probability of adopting a quota law and party priorities, as well as other variables considered for matching, technical details of the matching process, and diagnostics of the matching procedure.

First, most of the countries that pass quota laws are characterized by low levels of women's representation before the law is passed. The percentage of women in parliament is also perhaps the best proxy available for attitudes toward women in politics (see e.g., Norris 1985), a potential confounder that is very difficult to measure over time. Greater shares of women in political parties are also associated with shifts in party agendas (Kittilson 2011).

Relatedly, left parties are more likely to prioritize women and gender equality – including support for quota laws – than are right parties (Keith & Verge 2016; Kittilson 2006). I thus match on party family to ensure that the parties being compared are similar in ideology. The party family variable also helps to control for international policy diffusion, since similar parties often have close ties to each other across countries which affect both the likelihood of quota adoption and party priorities (Krook 2006, 2008). Third, previous experience with voluntary gender quotas within the party system is likely to increase the chances of a quota law being adopted in that country (Henig 2002; Matland 2005), and potentially also shift party emphasis by increasing numbers of women. Finally, I match on both vote share and year to control for party size and time trends, both of which could be related to women's opportunities in politics and party priorities. For example, smaller, niche parties might be more likely to take up special issues like equality because they are not constrained by a history of emphasizing traditional left-right issues (Kittilson 2011).

While I would ideally like to match on other underlying party and country characteristics, a larger number of covariates will increase the distance between units in the covariate space, meaning that matched pairs will be generally further apart (Nielsen 2014). However, I do adjust for other variables in the post-matching regression analysis, namely: women's labor force participation and GDP per capita (both linked to attitudes toward women, like the matching variable women in the party).

I use nearest neighbor, Mahalanobis matching. Nearest neighbor matching selects the single best control match for each "treated" unit (i.e., party in a country that passes a quota law). Matching is done using a distance measure, and here the Mahalanobis option is used because it allows for continuous covariates (Ho et al. 2011). I use exact matching for party family, as ideology is perhaps the most important identifying characteristic of a party. The matched data thus allow us to compare how quotas affect party priorities across similar types of parties, broadly speaking. The rest of the matches are selected based on Mahalanobis distance (for technical details, see Rubin 1973).

The matching process reduced the multivariate imbalance statistic from 0.95 to 0.75, significantly improving the balance of the sample. Graphical diagnostics of the matching procedure (quantile-quantile plots) demonstrate that matching produces good balance on these covariates overall (see Weeks 2019 for the Q-Q plots). Because the matched data are more balanced on covariates than the full data set, treatment and control units are more comparable, and modelling assumptions (such as which parametric model to use) have less influence on the results of analysis (Ho et al. 2007; King & Zeng 2006). As Nielsen and Sheffield (2009) point out, model dependence is especially likely when observations that have different values on the key variable of interest (here, quota law) also have very different values on other variables. See Weeks (2019) for a table of the matched pairs resulting from the matching procedure.

Summary Statistics

Table A4.1 presents summary statistics for the matched data set (summary statistics for the full data set used for matching can be found in Weeks (2019)). *Equality*, *Welfare State Expansion*, *Vote Share*, and *Right Party* come from the Comparative Manifesto Project (Manifesto Project MRG/MARPOR/MARPOR) Version 2016b (Volkens et al. 2016). *Right Party* includes the parties categorized by MARPOR as Liberal, Christian Democrat, Conservative, or Ethnic and Regional. *Left-Right Position* comes from Lowe et al. (2011)'s log ratio scale. ♀ *Labor Force Participation* comes from OECD Labour Statistics (2017). *Effective no. parties* comes from the Comparative Political Data Set, CPDS 2014 (Armingeon et al. 2014), and *GDP per capita* comes from the Comparative Welfare States Data Set, 2014 (Brady, Huber, & Stephens 2014). *Women in Party* comes from Greene and O'Brien (2016), supplemented by original data collection. Original data for a subset of parties/countries was collected using parliamentary websites, secondary literature, and newspapers, particularly for recent election-years. Original data for *Party Quota*, a binary variable, was compiled using party documents, secondary literature, and correspondence with political party representatives.

TABLE A4.1 *Summary statistics, matched data*

Statistic	N	Mean	St. dev.	Min	Max
Equality	282	5.166	4.400	0.000	23.100
Welfare state expansion	282	8.699	5.384	0.000	31.381
Left–right position	282	−0.406	0.863	−2.944	1.790
Quota law$_{(t-1)}$	282	0.089	0.285	0	1
Quota shock$_{(t-1)}$	282	0.620	0.336	−40	50

TABLE A4.1 *(Continued).*

Statistic	N	Mean	St. dev.	Min	Max
Party quota$_{(t-1)}$	282	19.149	39.417	0	100
♀ Labor force part.$_{(t-1)}$	282	40.86	4.604	26.65	48.42
Vote share$_{(t-1)}$	282	18.147	13.636	0.000	51.287
Effective no. of parties$_{(t-1)}$	282	3.811	1.959	1.690	9.080
GDP per capita$_{(t-1)}$	282	20,465.370	6,651.328	7,072.481	42,817.280
Women in party$_{(t-1)}$	282	14.228	13.502	0.000	97.000
Right party	282	0.450	0.498	0	1

TABLE A4.2 *Summary statistics, work–family policy data*

Statistic	N	Mean	St. dev.	Min	Max
Child care	156	0.320	0.459	0.000	3.185
Family allowances	156	0.434	0.646	0.000	4.348
Gender equality leave	156	0.090	0.354	−0.602	3.822
Quota law$_{(t-1)}$	156	0.288	0.455	0	1
Party quota$_{(t-1)}$	114	42.982	49.724	0.000	100
♀ Labor force part.$_{(t-1)}$	114	43.1	2.6	36.8	47.8
GDP per capita$_{(t-1)}$	114	24,658.880	6,386.738	10,159.950	34,701.820
Fertility rate$_{(t-1)}$	148	1.514	0.175	1.190	1.840
EU membership$_{(t-1)}$	148	0.919	0.274	0.000	1.000

Table A4.2 presents summary statistics for the hand-coded work–family policy data. The following parties are included:

Austria:
The Greens
Austrian social democrats (SPÖ)
Austrian People's Party (ÖVP)
Freedom Party (FPÖ)
Belgium:
Ecologists (ECOLO)
Green (Agalev/Groen!)
Francophone Socialist Party (PS)
Flemish Socialist Party (sp.a)
Christian People's Party (PSC/cdH)
Christian democratic and Flemish (CVP/CD&V)

Open Flemish Liberals and Democrats (PVV/VLD/Open VLD)
New Flemish Alliance (NV-A)
Flemish Block/Flemish Interest (VB)
Italy:
Democratic Party (PDS/DS/PD)
Go Italy/People of Freedom
(FI/PdL)
5 Star Movement (M5S), Northern League (LN)
National Alliance (AN)
Portugal:
Portuguese Communist Party (PCP)
Left Bloc (BE)
Socialist Party (PS)
Social democratic Center-Popular Party (CDS-PP)
Social democratic party (PSD-PP)

Regression Models

TABLE A4.3 *Effects of quota laws on policy priorities*

	Dependent variable			
	Equality (1)	Welfare expansion (3)	Women in party$_{(t-1)}$ (2)	Equality (4)
Quota law$_{(t-1)}$	5.643*** (1.481)	1.596 (2.374)	−7.764 (4.076)	5.674*** (1.487)
Women in party$_{(t-1)}$				0.004 (0.025)
Party quota$_{(t-1)}$	0.004 (0.009)	−0.003 (0.012)	0.064** (0.021)	0.004 (0.010)
♀ Labor force part.$_{(t-1)}$	0.085 (0.211)	0.179 (0.232)	0.415 (0.391)	0.083 (0.212)
Vote share$_{(t-1)}$	0.011 (0.031)	−0.129* (0.055)	0.074 (0.106)	0.010 (0.032
Effective no. of parties$_{(t-1)}$	−0.134 (0.586)	0.079 (0.652)	0.091 (1.074)	−0.135 (0.589)
Log(GDP per capita$_{(t-1)}$	−10.864** (3.384)	−2.471 (4.147)	−8.770 (6.737)	−10.829** (3.378)
Constant	105.961*** (30.129)	13.345 (37.313)	67.903 (62.278)	105.686*** (30.119)

TABLE A4.3 *(Continued).*

	Equality	Welfare expansion	Women in party$_{(t-1)}$	Equality
	(1)	(3)	(2)	(4)
Observations	282	282	282	282
R^2	0.651	0.551	0.721	0.651
Adjusted R^2	0.500	0.357	0.6	0.497
Year fixed effects	Yes	Yes	Yes	Yes
Party fixed effects	Yes	Yes	Yes	Yes

*$p < 0.05$; **$p < 0.01$; ***$p < 0.001$
Note: Robust standard errors clustered around election in parentheses.

TABLE A4.4 *Effects of quota laws on work–family policy priorities*

	Family allowances (1)	Child care (2)	Gender equality leave (3)
Quota law$_{(t-1)}$	−4.456**	13.712**	16.120*
	(2.108)	(5.386)	(9.637)
Party quota$_{(t-1)}$	0.001	0.002	−0.000
	(0.002)	(0.002)	(0.001)
♀ Labor force part.$_{(t-1)}$	0.374	−1.354**	−1.646
	(0.242)	(0.6330)	(1.083)
Log(GDP per capita$_{(t-1)}$)	3.214*	−11.211**	−13.532*
	(1.652)	(4.657)	(7.889)
Fertility rate$_{(t-1)}$	11.396**	−30.049**	−33.442
	(5.570)	(12.077)	(20.996)
EU membership$_{(t-1)}$	2.012***	−2.365*	−1.804
	(0.759)	(1.318)	(2.016)
Constant	−65.942*	215.124**	255.434*
	(33.812)	(85.868)	(151.651)
Year fixed effects	Yes	Yes	Yes
Party fixed effects	Yes	Yes	Yes
Observations	114	114	114
R^2	0.575	0.687	0.630
Adjusted R^2	0.294	0.480	0.385

Note: *$p < 0.1$; **$p < 0.05$; ***$p < 0.01$
Robust standard errors clustered around election in parentheses.

Notes: The number of observations in Table A4.4 is reduced from 156 to 114 due to missingness in several covariates (GDP per capita, Party Quota, and Women's Labor Force Participation).

Robustness Checks

TABLE A4.5 *Regression results, "quota shock" (1–2) and tests of common trends (3–4)*

	Equality	Welfare expansion	Equality	Equality
	Dependent variable			
	(1)	(2)	(3)	(4)
Quota shock$_{(t-1)}$	0.030	0.005		
	(0.040)	(0.056)		
Quota law$_{(t-2)}$			6.277**	
			(1.950)	
Quota law$_{(t-1)}$			4.698*	1.381
			(1.972)	(1.102)
Quota law			−1.059	
			(1.207)	
Quota law$_{(t+1)}$			0.080	
			(1.497)	
Quota law$_{(t+2)}$			1.182	
			(1.467)	
Quota law$_{(t+3)}$			−0.580	
			(1.729)	
Party quota$_{(t-1)}$	0.008	−0.002	0.000	0.002
	(0.009)	(0.012)	(0.007)	(0.398)
♀ Labor force part.$_{(t-1)}$	0.117	0.188	0.158	−0.105*
	(0.226)	(0.230)	(0.211)	(0.043)
Vote share$_{(t-1)}$	0.001	−0.132*	0.006	0.019
	(0.031)	(0.054)	(0.029)	(0.647)
Effective no. of parties$_{(t-1)}$	−0.168	0.069	−0.200	−0.225
	(0.574)	(0.658)	(0.656)	(7.530)
Log(GDP per capita$_{(t-1)}$)	−12.268***	−2.874	−11.094**	−11.210***
	(3.519)	(4.005)	(3.513)	(0.341)
Constant	117.736***	16.745	104.984***	−324.993
	(33.016)	(35.916)	(30.777)	(584.659)
Observations	282	282	282	282
R^2	0.63	0.550	0.667	0.718
Adjusted R^2	0.469	0.355	0.510	0.502
Year fixed effects	Yes	Yes	Yes	Yes

TABLE A4.5 *(Continued)*.

	Dependent variable			
	Equality	Welfare expansion	Equality	Equality
	(1)	(2)	(3)	(4)
Party fixed effects	Yes	Yes	Yes	Yes
Party-specific time trends	No	No	No	Yes

$^*p < 0.05; ^{**}p < 0.01; ^{***}p < 0.001$
Note: Robust standard errors clustered around election in parentheses.

TABLE A4.6 *Effects of quota laws on work–family policy priorities, no controls*

	Dependent variable		
	Family allowances (1)	Child care (2)	Gender equality leave (3)
Quota law$_{(t-1)}$	−0.026	0.236***	0.278***
	(0.091)	(0.066)	(0.045)
Constant	0.151	0.082	−0.121
	(0.159)	(0.135)	(0.104)
Year fixed effects	Yes	Yes	Yes
Party fixed effects	Yes	Yes	Yes
Observations	156	156	156
R^2	0.511	0.414	0.331
Adjusted R^2	0.312	0.174	0.058

Note: $^*p < 0.1; ^{**}p < 0.05; ^{***}p < 0.01$
Robust standard errors clustered around election in parentheses.

CHAPTER 5

Sources and Summary Statistics for Data Used in Analysis

TABLE A5.1 *Summary statistics, 22 countries*

Variable	M	SD	Min	Max	N	Data source
Overall family policy spending	2.0	1.06	0.15	4.45	687	OECD SOCX
Family allowances spending	0.89	0.56	0.08	2.76	687	OECD SOCX
Parental leave spending	0.23	0.23	0	1	690	OECD SOCX
Old age benefits	7.05	2.47	2.38	15.06	687	OECD SOCX
Education spending	4.83	1.10	1.59	7.62	485	CDPS 2018
Health care spending	5.63	1.15	2.42	8.61	648	CDPS 2018
Overall social spending	21.15	4.99	9.74	34.65	687	CDPS 2018
Gender equality leave	29.6	40.9	-24	152.5	560	Derived from OECD EMP
Maternity leave	16.4	9.6	0	52	560	OECD EMP
Paid parental leave	41.1	37.1	0	161	560	OECD EMP
Father-specific leave	4.95	9.26	0	52	560	OECD EMP
Quota law$_{(t-1)}$	0.05	0.22	0	1	687	Own data
Quota shock$_{(t-1)}$	0.31	1.7	0	1	687	Own data
% Women in parliament$_{(t-2)}$	19.1	12.10	0	47.3	687	CDPS 2018
Log GDP per capita$_{(t-2)}$	9.9	0.68	7.8	11.7	687	World Bank
Women's labor force part.$_{(t-2)}$	74.9	12.9	38.2	94.5	687	OECD
Left government$_{(t-2)}$	34.3	38.8	0	100	687	CPDS 2018
Party quota$_{(t-2)}$	19.74	25.96	0	92	687	Own data
Fertility rate$_{(t-2)}$	1.7	0.28	1.13	3.21	687	World Bank
EU membership$_{(t-2)}$	0.61	0.48	0	1	687	EU 2018

Notes:

OECD SOCX is the OECD social expenditures database, accessed in November 2018.

OECD EMP is the OECD employment database, accessed in November 2018.

CPDS 2018 is the Comparative Political Dataset, 1960–2016, 2018 version (Armingeon et al. 2018).

EU 2018 is the list of EU member states available from the European Union on europa.eu (2018).

Original data on party quotas were compiled using secondary literature, party documents, and correspondence with political party representatives (for further details, see Weeks 2016).

Regression Models

TABLE A5.2 *Determinants of family policy spending*

	(1) Allowances	(2) Leave	(3) Overall family
Quota law$_{(t-1)}$	−0.335*	0.033	−0.142
	(0.142)	(0.039)	(0.109)
Log GDP per capita$_{(t-2)}$	−0.042	0.154**	0.406
	(0.239)	(0.074)	(0.301)
Women's labor force part.$_{(t-2)}$	−0.0001	−0.003	0.005
	(0.0117)	(0.003)	(0.016)
Left government$_{(t-2)}$	−0.001	0.00001	0.0001
	(0.000)	(0.0001)	(0.0004)
Party quota$_{(t-2)}$	0.002	0.000	0.000
	(0.002)	(0.000)	(0.002)
Fertility rate$_{(t-2)}$	−0.315	0.051	−0.266
	(0.196)	(0.060)	(0.254)
EU membership$_{(t-2)}$	−0.083	−0.173***	−0.508***
	(0.098)	(0.057)	(0.149)
Constant	2.529	−1.378**	−1.549
	(2.255)	(0.660)	(2.632)
Observations	687	690	687
R^2	0.813	0.888	0.914
Adjusted R^2	0.794	0.876	0.905
Country fixed effects	Yes	Yes	Yes
Year fixed effects	Yes	Yes	Yes

*$p < 0.1$; **$p < 0.05$; ***$p < 0.01$
Note: Analysis carried out using R version 3.4.2. Standard errors (in parentheses) clustered by country.

TABLE A5.3 *Determinants of duration of leave policy (weeks)*

	(1) Gender equality leave	(2) Maternity	(3) Paid parental	(4) Father specific
Quota law$_{(t-1)}$	19.307***	−4.647*	9.054*	5.606*
	(6.197)	(2.444)	(4.621)	(3.252)
Log GDP per capita$_{(t-2)}$	8.013	6.980**	25.441**	−10.449
	(16.456)	(2.914)	(10.745)	(9.523)

	(1) Gender equality leave	(2) Maternity	(3) Paid parental	(4) Father specific
Women's labor	−1.259*	0.165	−1.030**	−0.064
force part.$_{(t-2)}$	(0.651)	(0.233)	(0.446)	(0.271)
Left government$_{(t-2)}$	−0.023	−0.004	−0.036	0.009
	(0.040)	(0.008)	(0.033)	(0.012)
Party quota$_{(t-2)}$	−0.070	−0.031	−0.129*	0.028
	(0.0927)	(0.023)	(0.074)	(0.038)
Fertility rate$_{(t-2)}$	−20.438	2.975	−13.209	−4.254
	(16.840)	(6.166)	(11.854)	(7.663)
EU membership$_{(t-2)}$	−20.248**	2.684	−22.981***	5.417
	(9.002)	(3.724)	(6.876)	(6.049)
Constant	40.222	−83.877**	−153.319*	109.664
	(167.486)	(38.435)	(85.565)	(103.806)
Observations	560	560	560	560
R^2	0.911	0.867	0.939	0.546
Adjusted R^2	0.901	0.853	0.933	0.497
Country fixed effects	Yes	Yes	Yes	Yes
Year fixed effects	Yes	Yes	Yes	Yes

*$p < 0.1$; **$p < 0.05$; ***$p < 0.01$
Note: Analysis carried out using R version 3.4.2. Standard errors (in parentheses) clustered by country.

TABLE A5.4 *Determinants of other spending*

	(1) Overall social	(2) Health	(3) Old age	(4) Education
Quota law$_{(t-1)}$	1.142	0.061	0.947	0.448
	(1.280)	(0.148)	(0.605)	(0.320)
Log GDP per	1.338	0.628	−0.060	0.333
capita$_{(t-2)}$	(2.377)	(0.612)	(1.092)	(0.351)
Women's labor	−0.138	0.006	−0.095***	0.035
force part.$_{(t-2)}$	(0.0845)	(0.016)	(0.035)	(0.025)
Left government$_{(t-2)}$	0.003	0.001	0.002	0.001*
	(0.004)	(0.001)	(0.002)	(0.001)
Party quota$_{(t-2)}$	0.006	−0.002	0.005*	−0.002
	(0.013)	(0.004)	(0.009)	(0.004)
Fertility rate$_{(t-2)}$	−2.036	0.191	−2.163*	0.179
	(2.119)	(0.637)	(1.295)	(0.553)
EU membership$_{(t-2)}$	−1.001	−0.372	−0.005	0.397
	(1.424)	(0.480)	(0.702)	(0.329)
Constant	12.157	−2.401	14.176	−0.765
	(22.378)	(5.164)	(10.680)	(3.468)

Appendix

TABLE A5.4 *(Continued)*.

	(1) Overall social	(2) Health	(3) Old age	(4) Education
Observations	687	696	687	485
R^2	0.846	0.799	0.841	0.825
Adjusted R^2	0.831	0.780	0.825	0.793
Country fixed effects	Yes	Yes	Yes	Yes
Year fixed effects	Yes	Yes	Yes	Yes

$^*p < 0.1$; $^{**}p < 0.05$; $^{***}p < 0.01$

Note: Analysis carried out using R version 3.4.2. Standard errors (in parentheses) clustered by country.

TABLE A5.5 *Regression results: Quota shocks*

	Dependent variable	
	Allowances (spending) (1)	Gender equality leave (weeks) (2)
Quota shock$_{(t-1)}$	−0.053***	2.189**
	(0.010)	(0.982)
Log GDP per	−0.026	4.846
capita$_{(t-2)}$	(0.248)	(16.179)
Women's labor	−0.003	−0.969
force part.$_{(t-2)}$	(0.011)	(0.643)
Left government$_{(t-2)}$	−0.001	−0.023
	(0.001)	(0.041)
Party quota$_{(t-2)}$	0.002	−0.089
	(0.002)	(0.094)
Fertility rate$_{(t-2)}$	−0.320*	−16.931
	(0.189)	(19.700)
EU membership$_{(t-2)}$	−0.108	−19.874**
	(0.101)	(8.760)
Constant	2.548	43.447
	(2.317)	(165.410)
Observations	687	560
R^2	0.816	0.907
Adjusted R^2	0.798	0.897
Country fixed effects	Yes	Yes
Year fixed effects	Yes	Yes

Note: $^*p < 0.1$; $^{**}p < 0.05$; $^{***}p < 0.01$

Robustness Checks

TABLE A5.6 *Regression results with no controls (1–2), and country-specific time trends (3–4)*

	Dependent variable			
	Allowances (spending) (1)	Gender equality leave (weeks) (2)	Allowances (spending) (3)	Gender equality leave (weeks) (4)
Quota law$_{(t-1)}$	−0.345**	17.609**	0.028	11.705**
	(0.149)	(7.807)	(0.085)	(5.895)
Log GDP per capita$_{(t-2)}$			−0.240*	14.178
			(0.145)	(9.463)
Women's labor force part.$_{(t-2)}$			−0.009	0.116
			(0.011)	(0.574)
Left government$_{(t-2)}$			−0.001	−0.033
			(0.001)	(0.036)
Party quota$_{(t-2)}$			0.003***	−0.023
			(0.001)	(0.067)
Fertility rate$_{(t-2)}$			0.357**	5.484
			(0.168)	(14.187)
EU membership$_{(t-2)}$			0.077	9.710
			(0.068)	(9.097)
Constant	1.474***	−9.762**	−115.007***	272.737
	(0.085)	(4.098)	(21.091)	(976.750)
Observations	687	560	687	560
R^2	0.802	0.899	0.935	0.956
Adjusted R^2	0.785	0.890	0.926	0.949
Country fixed effects	Yes	Yes	Yes	Yes
Year fixed effects	Yes	Yes	Yes	Yes
Country-specific time trend	No	No	Yes	Yes

Note: $^*p < 0.1$; $^{**}p < 0.05$; $^{***}p < 0.01$

References

Abadie, Alberto, Alexis Diamond & Jens Hainmueller. 2010. "Synthetic control methods for comparative case studies: Estimating the effect of California's tobacco control program." *Journal of the American Statistical Association* 105(490):493–505.

Abadie, Alberto, Alexis Diamond & Jens Hainmueller. 2011. "Synth: An R package for synthetic control methods in comparative case studies." *Journal of Statistical Software* 42(13):1–17.

Abadie, Alberto, Alexis Diamond & Jens Hainmueller. 2014. "Comparative politics and the synthetic control method." *American Journal of Political Science*: 495–510. http://dx.doi.org/10.1111/ajps.12116

Abadie, Alberto & Javier Gardeazabal. 2003. "The economic costs of conflict: A case study of the Basque Country." *American Economic Review* 93(1):113–132.

Abendschön, Simone & Stephanie Steinmetz. 2014. "The gender gap in voting revisited: Women's party preferences in a European context." *Social Politics* 21(2):315–344.

Abrams, Burton A & Russell F Settle. 1999. "Women's suffrage and the growth of the welfare state." *Public Choice* 100(3):289–300.

Adams, Greg D. 1997. "Abortion: Evidence of issue evolution." *American Journal of Political Science* 41:718–737.

Adams, James, Andrea B Haupt & Heather Stoll. 2009. "What moves parties? The role of public opinion and global economic conditions in Western Europe." *Comparative Political Studies* 42(5):611–639.

Adams, James, Michael Clark, Lawrence Ezrow & Garrett Glasgow. 2004. "Understanding change and stability in party ideologies: Do parties respond to public opinion or to past election results?" *British Journal of Political Science* 34(4):589–610.

Adams, James, Michael Clark, Lawrence Ezrow & Garrett Glasgow. 2006. "Are niche parties fundamentally different from mainstream parties? The causes and the electoral consequences of Western European parties' policy shifts, 1976–1998." *American Journal of Political Science* 50(3):513–529.

Adams, James, Samuel Merrill III & Bernard Grofman. 2005. *A unified theory of party competition: A cross-national analysis integrating spatial and behavioral factors.* Cambridge University Press.

Addabbo, Tindara, Valentina Cardinali, Dino Giovannini & Sara Mazzucchelli. 2016. "Italy Country Note [2018], in Blum, S., Koslowski, A., Macht, A. and Moss, P. (eds.) International Review of Leave Policies and Research 2018. Available at: http://www.leavenetwork.org/lp_and_r_reports."

Adema, Willem 2014. "Society at a Glance." *OECD.*

Adema, Willem, Pauline Fron & Maxime Ladaique. 2011. 'Is the European welfare state really more expensive?' Indicators on Social Spending, 1980–2012; and a Manual to the OECD Social Expenditure Database (SOCX)," OECD Social, Employment and Migration Working Papers, No. 124, OECD Publishing, Paris, https://doi.org/10.1787/5kg2d2d4pbf0-en.

Albers, Isabel & Anja Otte. March 20, 2004. "Interview: Laurette Onkelinx staat pal voor de PS." *De Standaard.*

Aldrich, John H. 1995. *Why parties? The origin and transformation of political parties in America.* University of Chicago Press.

Alesina, Alberto & Edward Glaeser. 2004. *Fighting poverty in the US and Europe: A world of difference.* Oxford University Press.

Alesina, Alberto & Paola Giuliano. 2011. "Preferences for redistribution." In *Handbook of social economics.* Benhabib, Jess, Bisin, Alberto, and Jackson, Matthew O. eds. Vol. 1. Elsevier. pp. 93–131.

Alexiadou, Despina. 2015. "Ideologues, partisans, and loyalists: Cabinet ministers and social welfare reform in parliamentary democracies." *Comparative Political Studies* 48(8):1051–1086.

Allan, James P & Lyle Scruggs. 2004. "Political partisanship and welfare state reform in advanced industrial societies." *American Journal of Political Science* 48(3):496–512.

Allen, Peter & David Cutts. 2018. "How do gender quotas affect public support for women as political leaders?" *West European Politics* 41(1):147–168.

Allen, Peter, David Cutts & Rosie Campbell. 2016. "Measuring the quality of politicians elected by gender quotas–are they any different?" *Political Studies* 64(1):143–163.

Allen, Peter & Sarah Childs. 2019. "The grit in the oyster? Women's parliamentary organizations and the substantive representation of women." *Political Studies* 67(3):618–638.

Alonso, Sonia & Sara Claro da Fonseca. 2012. "Immigration, left and right." *Party Politics* 18(6):865–884.

Anderson, Miriam J & Liam Swiss. 2014. "Peace accords and the adoption of electoral quotas for women in the developing world, 1990–2006." *Politics & Gender* 10(1):33–61.

Anesi, Vincent & Philippe De Donder. 2009. "Party formation and minority ideological positions." *The Economic Journal* 119(540):1303–1323.

Annesley, Claire & Francesca Gains. 2010. "The core executive: Gender, power and change." *Political Studies* 58(5):909–929.

Annesley, Claire, Isabelle Engeli & Francesca Gains. 2015. "The profile of gender equality issue attention in Western Europe." *European Journal of Political Research* 54(3):525–542.

Annesley, Claire, Karen Beckwith & Susan Franceschet. 2019. *Cabinets, ministers, and gender.* Oxford University Press.

Anzia, Sarah F & Christopher R Berry. 2011. "The Jackie (and Jill) Robinson effect: Why do congresswomen outperform congressmen?" *American Journal of Political Science* 55(3):478–493.

Ararat, Melsa, Mine H Aksu & Ayse Tansel Cetin. 2010. "The impact of board diversity on boards' monitoring intensity and firm performance: Evidence from the Istanbul Stock Exchange." *SSRN 1572283.*

Araújo, Clara & Ana Isabel García. 2006. *Latin America: The experience and the impact of quotas in Latin America.* In Dahlerup, Drude. 2006, Women, quotas and politics, ed. Drude Dahlerup New York: Routledge. http://www.loc.gov/catdir/toc/ecip0512/2005012587.html.

Armingeon, Klaus, Virginia Wenger, Fiona Wiedemeier, Christian Isler, Laura Knöpfel, David Weisstanner and Sarah Engler. 2018. Comparative Political Data Set 1960–2016. Bern: Institute of Political Science, University of Berne.

Armingeon, Klaus, Christian Isler, Laura Knöpfel, David Weisstanner & Sarah Engler. 2014. *Codebook: Comparative political data set 1960–2014.* Institute of Political Science, University of Bern.

Armingeon, Klaus, Christian Isler, Laura Knöpfel, David Weisstanner & Sarah Engler. 2016. *Codebook: Comparative political data set 1960–2016.* Institute of Political Science, University of Berne. https://www.cpds-data.org/images/Update2018/Codebook-CPDS-1960-2016-Update-2018.pdf.

Arriola, Leonardo R & Martha C Johnson. 2014. "Ethnic politics and women's empowerment in Africa: Ministerial appointments to executive cabinets." *American Journal of Political Science* 58(2):495–510.

Atchison, Amy. 2015. "The impact of female cabinet ministers on a female-friendly labor environment." *Journal of Women, Politics & Policy* 36(4):388–414.

Atchison, Amy & Ian Down. 2009. "Women cabinet ministers and female-friendly social policy." *Poverty & Public Policy* 1(2):1–23.

Atchison, Amy L & Ian Down. 2019. "The effects of women officeholders on environmental policy." *Review of Policy Research* 36(6):805–834.

Attanasio, Orazio, Hamish Low & Virginia Sanchez-Marcos. 2008. "Explaining changes in female labor supply in a life-cycle model." *The American Economic Review* 98(4):1517–1552.

Austen-Smith, David 2000. "Redistributing income under proportional representation." *Journal of Political Economy* 108(6):1235–1269.

Austen-Smith, David & Michael Wallerstein. 2006. "Redistribution and affirmative action." *Journal of Public Economics* 90(10):1789–1823.

Bachrach, Peter & Morton S Baratz. 1962. "Two faces of power." *American Political Science Review* 56(4):947–952.

Bækgaard, Martin & Ulrik Kjaer. 2012. "The gendered division of labor in assignments to political committees: Discrimination or self-selection in Danish local politics?" *Politics & Gender* 8(4):465–482.

Bagues, Manuel & Pamela Campa. 2021. "Can gender quotas in candidate lists empower women? Evidence from a regression discontinuity design." *Journal of Public Economics* 194:104315.

Baker, Michael & Kevin Milligan. 2008. "How does job-protected maternity leave affect mothers' employment?" *Journal of Labor Economics* 26(4):655–691.

Baldez, Lisa 2004. "Elected bodies: The gender quota law for legislative candidates in Mexico." *Legislative Studies Quarterly* 29(2):231–258.

Baldez, Lisa. 2011. "The UN Convention to Eliminate All Forms of Discrimination Against Women (CEDAW): A new way to measure women's interests." *Politics & Gender* 7(3):419–423.

Ban, Radu & Vijayendra Rao. 2008. "Tokenism or agency? The impact of women's reservations on village democracies in south India." *Economic Development and Cultural Change* 56(3):501–530.

Barber, Michael, Daniel M Butler & Jessica Preece. 2016. "Gender inequalities in campaign finance." *Quarterly Journal of Political Science* 11(2):219–248.

Bardhan, Pranab K, Dilip Mookherjee & Monica Parra Torrado. 2010. "Impact of political reservations in West Bengal local governments on anti-poverty targeting." *Journal of Globalization and development* 1(1). https://doi.org/10.2202/1948-1837.1025.

Barnes, Samuel H. 1977. *Representation in Italy: Institutionalized tradition and electoral choice*. University of Chicago Press.

Barnes, Tiffany. 2016. *Gendering legislative behavior*. Cambridge University Press.

Barnes, Tiffany D & Diana Z O'Brien. 2018. "Defending the realm: The appointment of female defense ministers worldwide." *American Journal of Political Science* 62(2):355–368.

Barnes, Tiffany D & Erin C Cassese. 2017. "American party women: A look at the gender gap within parties." *Political Research Quarterly* 70(1):127–141.

Barnes, Tiffany D & Mirya R Holman. 2020. "Gender quotas, women's representation, and legislative diversity." *The Journal of Politics* 82(4):1271–1286.

Barnes, Tiffany D & Stephanie M Burchard. 2013. "'Engendering' politics: The impact of descriptive representation on women's political engagement in Sub-Saharan Africa." *Comparative Political Studies* 46(7):767–790.

Baron, Reuben M & David A Kenny. 1986. "The moderator–mediator variable distinction in social psychological research: Conceptual, strategic, and statistical considerations." *Journal of Personality and Social Psychology* 51(6):1173.

Bartel, Ann P, Maya Rossin-Slater, Christopher J Ruhm, Jenna Stearns & Jane Waldfogel. 2018. "Paid family leave, fathers' leave-taking, and leave-sharing in dual-earner households." *Journal of Policy Analysis and Management* 37(1):10–37.

Bartolini, Stefano & Peter Mair. 2007. *Identity, competition and electoral availability: The stabilisation of European electorates 1885–1985*. ECPR Press.

Bauer, Gretchen & Hannah Evelyn Britton. 2006. *Women in African parliaments.* Lynne Rienner.

Bauer, Gretchen & Jennie E Burnet. 2013. Gender quotas, democracy, and women's representation in Africa: Some insights from democratic Botswana and autocratic Rwanda. In *Women's studies international forum.* Vol. 41. Elsevier. pp. 103–112.

Baum, Michael & Ana Espírito-Santo. 2012. "Portugal's quota-parity law: An analysis of its adoption." *West European Politics* 35(2):319–342.

Bawn, Kathleen, Martin Cohen, David Karol et al. 2012. "A theory of political parties: Groups, policy demands and nominations in American politics." *Perspectives on Politics* 10(3):571–597.

Beall, Victoria & Tiffany D Barnes. 2020. "Mapping right-wing women's policy priorities in Latin America." *Journal of Women, Politics, and Policy* 41(1): 36–65.

Beaman, Lori, Esther Duflo, Rohini Pande & Petia Topalova. 2011. Political reservation and substantive representation: Evidence from Indian village councils. In *India policy forum.* Vol. 7. National Council of Applied Economic Research. pp. 159–201.

Beaman, Lori, Raghabendra Chattopadhyay, Esther Duflo, Rohini Pande & Petia Topalova. 2009. "Powerful women: Does exposure reduce bias?" *The Quarterly Journal of Economics* 124(4):1497–1540.

Beckwith, Karen. 2011. "Interests, issues, and preferences: Women's interests and epiphenomena of activism." *Politics & Gender* 7(3):424–429.

Beckwith, Karen. 2014. Plotting the path from one to the other: Women's interests and political representation. In *Representation: The case of women.* Escobar-Lemmon, Maria C., and Michelle M. Taylor-Robinson, eds Oxford University Press. pp. 19–40.

Bego, Ingrid. 2014. "Accessing power in new democracies: The appointment of female ministers in postcommunist Europe." *Political Research Quarterly* 67(2):347–360.

Belgium Flemish Christian Democrats. 2007. "Samen Werken aan Morgen." Electoral program. https://docplayer.nl/2047408-Federaal-verkiezingsprogramma-10-juni-2007.html.

Benabou, Roland. 1996. Inequality and growth. In *NBER macroeconomics annual 1996.* Vol. 11. MIT Press. pp. 11–92.

Benoit, Kenneth & Michael Laver 2006. *Party policy in modern democracies.* Routledge.

Beramendi, Pablo, Silja Häusermann, Herbert Kitschelt & Hanspeter Kriesi. 2015. *The politics of advanced capitalism.* Cambridge University Press.

Bergemann, Annette & Regina T Riphahn. 2011. "The introduction of a short-term earnings-related parental leave benefit system and differential effects on employment intentions." *Schmollers Jahrbuch: Journal of Applied Social Science Studies/Zeitschrift für Wirtschafts-und Sozialwissenschaften* 131(2):315–325.

Bergman, Torbjörn, Wolfgang C Müller, Kaare Strøm & Magnus Blomgren. 2003. "Democratic delegation and accountability: Cross-national patterns." In *Delegation and accountability in parliamentary democracies.* Kaare Strøm,

Wolfgang C. Müller, and Torbjörn Bergman eds Oxford University Press. 107–218. https://madoc.bib.uni-mannheim.de/6772/.

Bergqvist, Christina & Ann-Cathrine Jungar. 2000. Adaptation or diffusion of the Swedish gender model? In *Gendered policies in Europe*. Springer. pp. 160–179.

Bergqvist, Christina, Elin Bjarnegård & Pär Zetterberg. 2018. "The gendered leeway: Male privilege, internal and external mandates, and gender-equality policy change." *Politics, Groups, and Identities* 6(4):576–592.

Bernhard, Rachel, Shauna Shames & Dawn Langan Teele. 2021. "To emerge? Breadwinning, motherhood, and women's decisions to run for office." *American Political Science Review* 115(2):379–394.

Bertocchi, Graziella. 2011. "The enfranchisement of women and the welfare state." *European Economic Review* 55(4):535–553.

Bertrand, Marianne, Esther Duflo & Sendhil Mullainathan. 2004. "How much should we trust differences-in-differences estimates?" *The Quarterly Journal of Economics* 119(1):249–275.

Besley, Timothy, Olle Folke, Torsten Persson & Johanna Rickne. 2017. "Gender quotas and the crisis of the mediocre man: Theory and evidence from Sweden." *American Economic Review* 107(8):2204–2242.

Besley, Timothy, Rohini Pande & Vijayendra Rao. 2005. "Political selection and the quality of government: Evidence from South India." https://ssrn.com/abstract=821152.

Besley, Timothy & Stephen Coate. 1997. "An economic model of democracy." *Quarterly Journal of Economics* 112(1):85–114.

Betz, Timm, David Fortunato & Diana Z O'Brien. 2021. "Women's descriptive representation and gendered import tax discrimination." *American Political Science Review* 115(1):307–315.

Bhavnani, Rikhil R. 2009. "Do electoral quotas work after they are withdrawn? Evidence from a natural experiment in India." *American Political Science Review* 103(1):23–35.

Bird, Karen. 2005. "The political representation of visible minorities in electoral democracies: A comparison of France, Denmark, and Canada." *Nationalism and Ethnic Politics* 11(4):425–465.

Bird, Karen. 2014. "Ethnic quotas and ethnic representation worldwide." *International Political Science Review* 35(1):12–26.

Bjarnegård, Elin & Pär Zetterberg. 2014. "Why are representational guarantees adopted for women and minorities? Comparing constituency formation and electoral quota design within countries." *Representation* 50(3): 307–320.

Blau, Francine D & Lawrence M Kahn. 2013. "Female labor supply: Why is the United States falling behind?" *American Economic Review* 103(3): 251–256.

Bleich, Erik & Robert Pekkanen. 2013. "How to report interview data." *Interview Research in Political Science* 1:84–105.

Blondel, Jean & Ferdinand Müller-Rommel. 1993. *Governing together: The extent and limits of joint decision-making in Western European cabinets*. St. Martin's Press.

Blum, Sonja. 2010. "Between instrument tinkering and policy renewal: Reforms of parental leave in Germany and Austria." *German Policy Studies/Politikfeldanalyse* 6(3):83–118.

Blum, Sonja. 2014. "No need to reinvent the wheel: Family policy transfers in Germany and Austria." *Policy Studies* 35(4):357–376.

Boeckmann, Irene, Joya Misra & Michelle J Budig. 2015. "Cultural and institutional factors shaping mothers' employment and working hours in postindustrial countries." *Social Forces* 93(4):1301–1333.

Bolzendahl, Catherine. 2009. "Making the implicit explicit: Gender influences on social spending in twelve industrialized democracies, 1980–99." *Social Politics: International Studies in Gender, State & Society* 16(1):40–81.

Bolzendahl, Catherine & Clem Brooks. 2007. "Women's political representation and welfare state spending in 12 capitalist democracies." *Social Forces* 85(4):1509–1534.

Bonoli, Giuliano & Frank Reber. 2010. "The political economy of childcare in OECD countries: Explaining cross-national variation in spending and coverage rates." *European Journal of Political Research* 49(1):97–118.

Bordignon, Fabio. 2014. "Matteo Renzi: A 'Leftist Berlusconi' for the Italian democratic party?" *South European Society and Politics* 19(1):1–23.

Bornschier, Simon. 2010. *Cleavage politics and the populist right: The new cultural conflict in Western Europe.* Temple University Press.

Brady, David, Evelyne Huber & John D Stephens. 2014. "Comparative welfare states data set." *University of North Carolina and WZB Berlin Social Science Center.* https://mdl.library.utoronto.ca/collections/numeric-data/comparative-welfare-states-dataset-2014-ed.

Bratton, Kathleen A & Leonard P Ray. 2002. "Descriptive representation, policy outcomes, and municipal day-care coverage in Norway." *American Journal of Political Science* 46(2):428–437.

Broockman, David E. 2013. "Black politicians are more intrinsically motivated to advance blacks' interests: A field experiment manipulating political incentives." *American Journal of Political Science* 57(3):521–536.

Brulé, Rachel E. 2020. *Women, power, and property: The paradox of gender equality laws in India.* Cambridge University Press.

Budge, Ian. 2001. *Mapping policy preferences: Estimates for parties, electors, and governments, 1945–1998.* Vol. 1. Oxford University Press.

Budge, Ian, David Robertson & Derek Hearl. 1987. *Ideology, strategy and party change: Spatial analyses of post-war election programmes in 19 democracies.* Cambridge University Press.

Burden, Barry C. 2007. *Personal roots of representation.* Princeton University Press.

Burgoon, Brian. 2012. "Partisan embedding of liberalism how trade, investment, and immigration affect party support for the welfare state." *Comparative Political Studies* 45(5):606–635.

Burnet, Jennie E. 2011. "Women have found respect: Gender quotas, symbolic representation, and female empowerment in Rwanda." *Politics & Gender* 7(3):303–334.

Burrell, Barbara. 1994. *A woman's place is in the house*. University of Michigan Press.

Busemeyer, Marius R & Erik Neimanns. 2017. "Conflictive preferences towards social investments and transfers in mature welfare states: The cases of unemployment benefits and childcare provision." *Journal of European Social Policy* 27(3):229–246.

Bush, Sarah Sunn. 2011. "International politics and the spread of quotas for women in legislatures." *International Organization* 65(1):103–137.

Campbell, Andrea Louise. 2003. *How policies make citizens: Senior political activism and the American welfare state*. Princeton University Press.

Campbell, Andrea Louise. 2012. "Policy makes mass politics." *Annual Review of Political Science* 15:333–351.

Campbell, Rosie, Sarah Childs & Joni Lovenduski. 2010. "Do women need women representatives?" *British Journal of Political Science* 40(1):171–194.

Carey, John M. 2007. "Competing principals, political institutions, and party unity in legislative voting." *American Journal of Political Science* 51(1):92–107.

Carnes, Nicholas. 2012. "Does the numerical underrepresentation of the working class in Congress matter?" *Legislative Studies Quarterly* 37(1):5–34.

Casey, Logan S & Andrew Reynolds. 2015. *Standing out: Transgender and gender variant candidates and elected officials around the world*. LGBTQ Representation and Rights Initiative, University of North Carolina.

Castles, Francis G. 1994. "On religion and public policy: Does Catholicism make a difference?" *European Journal of Political Research* 25(1):19–40.

Catalano, Ana 2009. "Women acting for women? An analysis of gender and debate participation in the British House of Commons 2005–2007." *Politics & Gender* 5(1):45–68.

Caul, Miki. 1999. "Women's representation in parliament: The role of political Parties." *Party Politics* 5(1):79–98.

Cavaillé, Charlotte & Kris-Stella Trump. 2015. "The two facets of social policy preferences." *The Journal of Politics* 77(1):146–160.

Cederman, Lars-Erik, Andreas Wimmer & Brian Min. 2010. "Why do ethnic groups rebel? New data and analysis." *World Politics* 62(1):87–119.

Celis, Karen. 2006. "Substantive representation of women: The representation of women's interests and the impact of descriptive representation in the Belgian parliament (1900–1979)." *Journal of Women, Politics & Policy* 28(2):85–114.

Celis, Karen. 2007. "Substantive representation of women: The representation of women's interests and the impact of descriptive representation in the Belgian parliament (1900–1979)." *Journal of Women, Politics & Policy* 28(2):85–114.

Celis, Karen. 2008. "Studying women's substantive representation in legislatures: When representative acts, contexts and women's interests become important." *Representation* 44(2):111–123.

Celis, Karen & Sarah Childs. 2014. *Gender, conservatism and political representation*. ECPR Press.

Celis, Karen & Sarah Childs. 2020. *Feminist democratic representation*. Oxford University Press.

Celis, Karen & Silvia Erzeel. 2015. "Beyond the usual suspects: Non-left, male and non-feminist MPs and the substantive representation of women." *Government and Opposition* 50(1):45–64.

Chattopadhyay, Raghabendra & Esther Duflo. 2003. "Women as policy makers: Evidence from a India-wide randomized policy experiment." *NBER Working Paper* 8615.

Chattopadhyay, Raghabendra & Esther Duflo. 2004. "Women as policy makers: Evidence from a randomized policy experiment in India." *Econometrica* 72(5):1409–1443.

Chen, Li-Ju. 2010. "Do gender quotas influence women's representation and policies?" *The European Journal of Comparative Economics* 7(1):13–60.

Childs, Sarah & Mona Lena Krook. 2009. "Analysing women's substantive representation: From critical mass to critical actors." *Government and Opposition* 44(2):125–145.

Childs, Sarah. 2004. "A feminised style of politics? Women MPs in the House of Commons." *The British Journal of Politics & International Relations* 6(1):3–19.

Childs, Sarah & Julie Withey. 2004. "Women representatives acting for women: Sex and the signing of early day motions in the 1997 British parliament." *Political Studies* 52(3):552–564.

Childs, Sarah & Karen Celis. 2018. "Conservatism and women's political representation." *Politics and Gender* 14(1):5–26.

Claveria, Silvia. 2014. "Still a 'male business'? Explaining women's presence in executive office." *West European Politics* 37(5):1156–1176.

Clayton, Amanda. 2018. "Do gender quotas really reduce bias? Evidence from a policy experiment in Southern Africa." *Journal of Experimental Political Science* 5(3):182–194.

Clayton, Amanda. 2021. "How do electoral gender quotas affect policy?" *Annual Review of Political Science* 24:235–252.

Clayton, Amanda, Cecilia Josefsson, Robert Mattes & Shaheen Mozaffar. 2019. "In whose interest? Gender and mass–elite priority congruence in Sub-Saharan Africa." *Comparative Political Studies* 52(1):69–101.

Clayton, Amanda, Cecilia Josefsson & Vibeke Wang. 2014. "Present without presence? Gender, quotas and debate recognition in the Ugandan parliament." *Representation* 50(3):379–392.

Clayton, Amanda & Pär Zetterberg. 2018. "Quota shocks: Electoral gender quotas and government spending priorities worldwide." *The Journal of Politics* 80(3):916–932.

Clayton, Amanda B. 2015. "Electoral gender quotas, female leadership, and women's political engagement: Evidence from a randomized policy experiment." *Comparative Political Studies* 48(3):333–369.

Cole, Alistair & Brian Doherty. 1995. Pas comme les autres–the French Greens at the crossroads. In *The Green challenge: The development of Green parties in Europe*. Routledge. pp. 33–47.

Collins, Caitlyn. 2019. *Making motherhood work*. Princeton University Press.

Corder, J Kevin & Christina Wolbrecht. 2016. *Counting women's ballots.* Cambridge University Press.

Cowell-Meyers, Kimberly. 2016a. "Do women's parties improve the lot of women? Theorizing impact, strategy and system in assessing the effect of women's parties." Paper presented at the American Political Science Association Annual Conference.

Cowell-Meyers, Kimberly. 2016b. "Women's political parties in Europe." *Politics & Gender* 12(1):1–27.

Criscitiello, Annarita. 1994. The political role of cabinet ministers in Italy. In *Cabinet ministers and parliamentary government.* CUP Archive. pp. 187–200.

Crowder-Meyer, Melody. 2013. "Gendered recruitment without trying: How local party recruiters affect women's representation." *Politics & Gender* 9(4):390–413.

Cusack, Thomas, Torben Iversen & Philipp Rehm. 2006. "Risks at work: The demand and supply sides of government redistribution." *Oxford Review of Economic Policy* 22(3):365–389.

Czibor, Eszter & Silvia Dominguez Martinez. 2019. "Never too late: Gender quotas in the final round of a multistage tournament." *The Journal of Law, Economics, and Organization* 35(2):319–363.

Dahlerup, Drude 2006. *Women, quotas and politics.* Vol. 10. Routledge.

Dahlerup, Drude & Lenita Freidenvall. 2005. "Quotas as a 'fast track' to equal representation for women: Why Scandinavia is no longer the model." *International Feminist Journal of Politics* 7(1):26–48.

Dallinger, Ursula. 2010. "Public support for redistribution: What explains cross-national differences?" *Journal of European Social Policy* 20(4):333–349.

Dalton, Russell J. 1985. "Political parties and political representation: Party supporters and party elites in nine nations." *Comparative Political Studies* 18(3):267–299.

Dalton, Russell J. 2009. "Economics, environmentalism and party alignments: A note on partisan change in advanced industrial democracies." *European Journal of Political Research* 48(2):161–175.

De Paola, Maria, Vincenzo Scoppa & Rosetta Lombardo. 2010. "Can gender quotas break down negative stereotypes? Evidence from changes in electoral rules." *Journal of Public Economics* 94(5–6):344–353.

De Paola, Maria, Vincenzo Scoppa & Marco Alberto De Benedetto. 2014. "The impact of gender quotas on electoral participation: Evidence from Italian municipalities." *European Journal of Political Economy* 35:141–157.

Devisscher, Stephanie & Debbie Sanders. 2007. Ageing and life-course issues: The case of the career break scheme (Belgium) and the life-course regulation (Netherlands). In *Modernising social policy for the new life course.* OECD. p. 117.

Devlin, Claire & Robert Elgie. 2008. "The effect of increased women's representation in parliament: The case of Rwanda." *Parliamentary Affairs* 61(2):237–254.

Dewan, Torun & Rafael Hortala-Vallve. 2011. "The three As of government formation: Appointment, allocation, and assignment." *American Journal of Political Science* 55(3):610–627.

Dix, Robert H. 1989. "Cleavage structures and party systems in Latin America." *Comparative Politics* 22(1):23–37.

Dolezal, Martin. 2010. "Exploring the stabilization of a political force: The social and attitudinal basis of green parties in the age of globalization." *West European Politics* 33(3):534–552.

Dovi, Suzanne. 2007. "Theorizing women's representation in the United States." *Politics & Gender* 3(3):297–319.

Downs, Anthony. 1957. *An economic theory of democracy*. Harper and Row.

Dustmann, Christian & Uta Schönberg. 2012. "Expansions in maternity leave coverage and children's long-term outcomes." *American Economic Journal: Applied Economics* 4(3):190–224.

Duverger, Maurice. 1955. *The political role of women*. UNESCO.

Eagly, Alice H & Blair T Johnson. 1990. "Gender and leadership style: A meta-analysis." *Psychological Bulletin* 108(2):233.

Edlund, Lena & Rohini Pande. 2002. "Why have women become left-wing? The political gender gap and the decline in marriage." *The Quarterly Journal of Economics* 117(3):917–961.

Edwards, Martin S & Frank C Thames. 2007. "District magnitude, personal votes, and government expenditures." *Electoral Studies* 26(2):338–345.

Eger, Maureen A & Nate Breznau. 2017. "Immigration and the welfare state: A cross-regional analysis of European welfare attitudes." *International Journal of Comparative Sociology* 58(5):440–463.

Emmenegger, Patrick & Philip Manow. 2014. "Religion and the gender vote gap: Women's changed political preferences from the 1970s to 2010." *Politics & Society* 42(2):166–193.

Enelow, James M & Melvin J Hinich. 1984. *The spatial theory of voting: An introduction*. Cambridge University Press Archive.

Ennser-Jedenastik, Laurenz. 2017. "How women's political representation affects spending on family benefits." *Journal of Social Policy* 46(3):563–581.

Erhardt, Niclas L, James D Werbel & Charles B Shrader. 2003. "Board of director diversity and firm financial performance." *Corporate Governance: An International Review* 11(2):102–111.

Erhel, Christine & Mathilde Guergoat-Larivière. 2013. "Labor market regimes, family policies, and women's behavior in the EU." *Feminist Economics* 19(4):76–109.

Esaiasson, Peter & Knut Heidar. 2000. *Beyond Westminster and Congress: The Nordic experience*. Ohio State University Press.

Escobar-Lemmon, Maria & Michelle M Taylor-Robinson. 2005. "Women ministers in Latin American government: When, where, and why?" *American Journal of Political Science* 49(4):829–844.

Esping-Andersen, Gosta. 1990. *The three worlds of welfare capitalism*. Vol. 6. Polity Press.

Esping-Andersen, Gosta. 1999. *Social foundations of postindustrial economies*. Oxford University Press.

Esping-Andersen, Gøsta. 2002. *Why we need a new welfare state*. Oxford University Press.

Espírito-Santo, Ana. 2018. From electoral to corporate board quotas. In *Transforming gender citizenship: The irresistible rise of gender quotas in Europe*. Cambridge University Press. p. 216.

Espírito-Santo, Ana, André Freire & Sofia Serra-Silva. 2020. "Does women's descriptive representation matter for policy preferences? The role of political parties." *Party Politics* 26(2):227–237.

Espírito-Santo, Ana & Edalina Rodrigues Sanches. 2019. "Who gets what? The interactive effect of MPs' sex in committee assignments in Portugal." *Parliamentary Affairs* 73(2), 450–472.

Esteve-Volart, Berta & Manuel Bagues. 2012. "Are women pawns in the political game? Evidence from elections to the Spanish Senate." *Journal of Public Economics* 96(3-4):387–399.

Estevez-Abe, Margarita, Torben Iversen & David Soskice. 2001. Social protection and the formation of skills: A reinterpretation of the welfare state. In *Varieties of capitalism: The institutional foundations of comparative advantage*. Oxford University Press. p. 145. European Commission. 2017. "Women in the labour market factsheet."

Ezrow, Lawrence. 2007. "The variance matters: How party systems represent the preferences of voters." *Journal of Politics* 69(1):182–192.

Fernandes, Jorge M. 2016. "Intra-party delegation in the Portuguese legislature: Assigning committee chairs and party coordination positions." *The Journal of Legislative Studies* 22(1):108–128.

Fernandes, Jorge M, Lopes da Fonseca & Miguel Won. 2021. "Closing the gender gap in legislative debates: The role of gender quotas." *Political Behavior*. https://doi.org/10.1007/s11109-021-09737-3.

Ferrara, Federico & J Timo Weishaupt. 2004. "Get your act together: Party performance in European parliament elections." *European Union Politics* 5(3):283–306.

Ferreira, Fernando & Joseph Gyourko. 2011. "Does gender matter for political leadership? The case of US mayors." *Journal of Public Economics* 112:24–39.

Ferrera, Maurizio. 2005. Welfare states and social safety nets in Southern Europe. In *Welfare state reform in Southern Europe*. Routledge. pp. 14–36.

Finseraas, Henning. 2009. "Income inequality and demand for redistribution: A multilevel analysis of European public opinion." *Scandinavian Political Studies* 32(1):94–119.

Fox, Richard L & Jennifer L Lawless. 2004. "Entering the arena? Gender and the decision to run for office." *American Journal of Political Science* 48(2):264–280.

Fox, Richard L & Jennifer L Lawless. 2010. "If only they'd ask: Gender, recruitment, and political ambition." *The Journal of Politics* 72(2):310–326.

Franceschet, Susan & Jennifer M Piscopo. 2008. "Gender quotas and women's substantive representation: Lessons from Argentina." *Politics & Gender* 4(3):393–425.

Franceschet, Susan, Mona Lena Krook & Jennifer M Piscopo. 2012. *The impact of gender quotas*. Oxford University Press.

Fraser, Nancy. 2012. "Feminism, capitalism, and the cunning of history." In *Citizenship Rights*, Shaw, J., and Štiks, I. (eds.). (2013). (1st ed.). Routledge. *https://halshs.archives-ouvertes.fr/halshs-00725055/*

Fréchette, Guillaume R, Francois Maniquet & Massimo Morelli. 2008. "Incumbents' interests and gender quotas." *American Journal of Political Science* 52(4):891–909.

Frymer, Paul. 2010. *Uneasy alliances: Race and party competition in America.* Princeton University Press.

Fuchs, Dieter & Hans-Dieter Klingemann. 1990. The left-right schema. In *Continuities in political action: A longitudinal study of political orientations in three western democracies.* De Gruyter. pp. 203–234.

Funk, Kendall D & Andrew Q Philips. 2019. "Representative budgeting: Women mayors and the composition of spending in local governments." *Political Research Quarterly* 72(1):19–33.

Funk, Patricia & Christina Gathmann. 2008. "Gender gaps in policy making: Evidence from direct democracy in Switzerland." *Political Research Quarterly* 72(1):19–33.

Galligan, Yvonne, Sara Clavero & Marina Calloni. 2007. *Gender politics and democracy in post-socialist Europe.* Barbara Budrich.

Gatto, Malu AC. 2016. "Endogenous institutionalism and the puzzle of gender quotas: insights from Latin America." Doctoral Dissertation, University of Oxford, UK.

Gatto, Malu AC. 2017. Gender quotas, legislative resistance and non-legislative reform. In *Law and policy in Latin America.* Springer. pp. 239–255.

Gaventa, John. 1982. *Power and powerlessness: Quiescence and rebellion in an Appalachian valley.* University of Illinois Press.

Gelb, Joyce. 1989. *Feminism and politics: A comparative perspective.* University of California Press.

Gemenis, Kostas. 2013. "What to do (and not to do) with the comparative manifestos project data." *Political Studies* 61(suppl 1):3–23.

Genovese, Federica, Pia Wassmann & Gerald Schneider. 2014. "The Eurotower strikes back: Crises, adjustments and Europe's austerity protests." *Comparative Political Studies* 939–967.

George, Alexander L & Andrew Bennett. 2005. *Case studies and theory development in the social sciences.* MIT Press.

Gerring, John. 2006. *Case study research: Principles and practices.* Cambridge University Press.

Gerring, John. 2007. "Is there a (viable) crucial-case method?" *Comparative Political Studies* 40(3):231–253.

Giger, Nathalie. 2009. "Towards a modern gender gap in Europe? A comparative analysis of voting behavior in 12 countries." *The Social Science Journal* 46(3):474–492.

Gilens, Martin, Paul M Sniderman & James H Kuklinski. 1998. "Affirmative action and the politics of realignment." *British Journal of Political Science* 28(1):159–183.

Gingrich, Jane & Ben W. Ansell. 2015. The dynamics of social investment: Human capital, activation, and care. In *The politics of advanced capitalism*. Cambridge University Press. pp. 282–304.

Glynn, Adam N & Nahomi Ichino. 2014. "Increasing inferential leverage in the comparative method: Placebo tests in small-n research." *Sociological Methods & Research* 45(3):598–629.

Gontcharova, Natalie. 2018. "Ivanka Trump says she wants to 'go beyond parental leave'." *Refinery29*. www.refinery29.com/en-gb/2018/07/204207/paid-family-leave-ivanka-trump-kirsten-gillibrand

Górecki, Maciej A & Michał Pierzgalski. 2022. "Legislated candidate quotas and women's descriptive representation in preferential voting systems." *European Journal of Political Research* 61(1):154–174.

Gornick, Janet C, Marcia K Meyers & Katherin E Ross. 1997. "Supporting the employment of mothers: Policy variation across fourteen welfare states." *Journal of European Social Policy* 7(1):45–70.

Gottfried, Heidi & Jacqueline O'Reilly. 2002. "Reregulating breadwinner models in socially conservative welfare systems: Comparing Germany and Japan." *Social Politics: International Studies in Gender, State & Society* 9(1):29–59.

Gottlieb, Jessica, Guy Grossman & Amanda Lea Robinson. 2016. "Do men and women have different policy preferences in Africa? Determinants and implications of gender gaps in policy prioritization." *British Journal of Political Science* 48(3):611–636.

Greene, Zachary & Diana Z O'Brien. 2016. "Diverse parties, diverse agendas? Female politicians and the parliamentary party's role in platform formation." *European Journal of Political Research* 55(3):435–453.

Greene, Zachary & Matthias Haber. 2016. "Leadership competition and disagreement at party national congresses." *British Journal of Political Science*: 46(3):611–632.

Grose, Christian R. 2011. *Congress in black and white: Race and representation in Washington and at home*. Cambridge University Press.

Guadagnini, Marila. 2005. Gendering the debate on political representation in Italy: A difficult challenge. In *State feminism and political representation*. Cambridge University Press. pp. 130–152.

Haider-Markel, Donald P. 2010. *Out and running: Gay and lesbian candidates, elections, and policy representation*. Georgetown University Press.

Harbers, Imke, Catherine E de Vries & Marco R Steenbergen. 2013. "Attitude variability among Latin American publics: How party system structuration affects left/right ideology." *Comparative Political Studies* 46(8):947–967.

Harmel, Robert & Lars Svåsand. 1997. "The influence of new parties on old parties' platforms: The cases of the progress parties and Conservative parties of Denmark and Norway." *Party Politics* 3(3):315–340.

Harmel, Robert, Uk Heo, Alexander Tan & Kenneth Janda. 1995. "Performance, leadership, factions and party change: An empirical analysis." *West European Politics* 18(1):1–33.

Hartlapp, Miriam. 2009. "Implementation of EU social policy directives in Belgium: What matters in domestic politics?" *European Integration* 31(4):467–488.

Haupt, Andrea B. 2010. "Parties' responses to economic globalization: What is left for the left and right for the right?" *Party Politics* 16(1):5–27.

Häusermann, Silja. 2006. "Changing coalitions in social policy reforms: The politics of new social needs and demands." *Journal of European Social Policy* 16(1):5–21.

Häusermann, Silja. 2010. *The politics of welfare state reform in continental Europe: Modernization in hard times*. Cambridge University Press.

Häusermann, Silja & Hanspeter Kriesi. 2015. What do voters want? Dimensions and configurations in individual-level preferences and party choice. In *The politics of advanced capitalism*. Cambridge University Press. pp. 202–230.

Haussman, Melissa & Birgit Sauer. 2007. *Gendering the state in the age of globalization: Women's movements and state feminism in postindustrial democracies.* Rowman & Littlefield.

Hawkesworth, Mary. 2003. "Congressional enactments of race–gender: Toward a theory of raced–gendered institutions." *American Political Science Review* 97(4):529–550.

Hayes, Bernadette C, Ian McAllister & Donley T Studlar. 2000. "Gender, postmaterialism, and feminism in comparative perspective." *International Political Science Review* 21(4):425–439.

Hazan, Reuven Y. 2001. *Reforming parliamentary committees: Israel in comparative perspective*. Ohio State University Press.

Heath, Michelle Roseanna, Leslie A Schwindt-Bayer & Michelle M Taylor-Robinson. 2005. "Women on the sidelines: Women's representation on committees in Latin American legislatures." *American Journal of Political Science* 49(2):420–436.

Henig, Simon. 2002. *Women and political power: Europe since 1945*. Routledge.

Hideg, Ivona, Anja Krstic, Raymond NC Trau & Tanya Zarina. 2018. "The unintended consequences of maternity leaves: How agency interventions mitigate the negative effects of longer legislated maternity leaves." *Journal of Applied Psychology* 103:1155.

Hinojosa, Magda & Miki Caul Kittilson. 2020. *Seeing women, strengthening democracy: How women in politics foster connected citizens*. Oxford University Press.

Ho, Daniel E, Kosuke Imai, Gary King & Elizabeth A Stuart. 2007. "Matching as nonparametric preprocessing for reducing model dependence in parametric causal inference." *Political Analysis* 15(3):199–236.

Ho, Daniel E, Kosuke Imai, Gary King & Elizabeth Stuart. 2011. "MatchIt: Nonparametric preprocessing for parametric causal inference." *Journal of Statistical Software* 42:1–28.

Höhmann, Daniel & Mary Nugent. 2021. "Male MPs, electoral vulnerability and the substantive representation of women's interests." *European Journal of Political Research*. https://doi.org/10.1111/1475-6765.12472.

Holman, Mirya R. 2014. "Sex and the city: Female leaders and spending on social welfare programs in US municipalities." *Journal of Urban Affairs* 36(4):701–715.

Htun, Mala. 2004. "Is gender like ethnicity? The political representation of identity groups." *Perspectives on Politics* 2:439–458.

Htun, Mala, Marina Lacalle & Juan Pablo Micozzi. 2013. "Does women's presence change legislative behavior? Evidence from Argentina, 1983–2007." *Journal of Politics in Latin America* 5(1):95–125.

Htun, Mala & Mark P Jones. 2002. Engendering the right to participate in decision-making: Electoral quotas and women's leadership in Latin America. In *Gender and the politics of rights and democracy in Latin America*, Basingstoke: Palgrave. pp. 32–56.

Htun, Mala & S Laurel Weldon. 2012. "The civic origins of progressive policy change: Combating violence against women in global perspective, 1975–2005." *American Political Science Review* 106(3):548–569.

Htun, Mala & S Laurel Weldon. 2018. *The logics of gender justice: State action on women's rights around the world*. Cambridge University Press.

Hu, Li-tze & Peter M Bentler. 1999. "Cutoff criteria for fit indexes in covariance structure analysis: Conventional criteria versus new alternatives." *Structural Equation Modeling: A Multidisciplinary Journal* 6(1):1–55.

Huber, Evelyne & John D Stephens. 2000. "Partisan governance, women's employment, and the social democratic service state." *American Sociological Review* 65(3):323–342.

Huber, Evelyne & John D Stephens. 2001. *Development and crisis of the welfare state: Parties and policies in global markets*. University of Chicago Press.

Hughes, Melanie M. 2011. "Intersectionality, quotas, and minority women's political representation worldwide." *American Political Science Review* 105(3):604–620.

Hughes, Melanie M, Mona Lena Krook & Pamela Paxton. 2015. "Transnational women's activism and the global diffusion of gender quotas." *International Studies Quarterly* 59(2):357–372.

Hwang, Carl-Philip & Anders G Broberg. 2014. The historical and social context of child care in Sweden. In *Child care in context: Cross-cultural perspectives*. Psychology Press. pp. 27–53.

Imai, Kosuke, Gary King & Elizabeth A Stuart. 2008. "Misunderstandings between experimentalists and observationalists about causal inference." *Journal of the Royal Statistical Society: Series A (Statistics in Society)* 171(2):481–502.

Imai, Kosuke, Gary King & Olivia Lau. (2008). "Toward A Common Framework for Statistical Analysis and Development." *Journal of Computational and Graphical Statistics* 17(4):892–913.

Imai, Kosuke, Luke Keele & Dustin Tingley. 2010. "A general approach to causal mediation analysis." *Psychological Methods* 15(4):309.

Indridason, Indridi H & Christopher Kam. 2005. "The timing of cabinet reshuffles in five Westminster parliamentary systems." *Legislative Studies Quarterly* 30(3):327–363.

Inglehart, Ronald F. 2008. "Changing values among western publics from 1970 to 2006." *West European Politics* 31(1–2):130–146.

Inglehart, Ronald & Pippa Norris. 2000. "The developmental theory of the gender gap: Women's and men's voting behavior in global perspective." *International Political Science Review* 21(4):441–463.

International Labor Office (ILO). 2016. *Women at work: Trends 2016.*

Iversen, Torben & David Soskice. 2001. "An asset theory of social policy preferences." *American Political Science Review* 95(4):875–894.

Iversen, Torben & David Soskice. 2006. "Electoral institutions and the politics of coalitions: Why some democracies redistribute more than others." *American Political Science Review* 100(2):165.

Iversen, Torben & Frances Rosenbluth. 2008. "Work and power: The connection between female labor force participation and female political representation." *Annual Review of Political Science* 11:479–495.

Iversen, Torben & Frances McCall Rosenbluth. 2010. *Women, work, and politics: The political economy of gender inequality.* Yale University Press.

Iversen, Torben & Frances Rosenbluth. 2006. "The political economy of gender: Explaining cross-national variation in the gender division of labor and the gender voting gap." *American Journal of Political Science* 50(1):1–19.

Jaumotte, Florence. 2003. "Female labour force participation: Past trends and main determinants in OECD countries." OECD Working Paper No. 376. https://ssrn.com/abstract=2344556 orhttp://dx.doi.org/10.2139/ssrn.2344556.

Jensenius, Francesca R. 2017. *Social justice through inclusion: The consequences of electoral quotas in India.* Oxford University Press.

Josefsson, Cecilia. 2020. "Adaptive resistance: Power struggles over gender quotas in Uruguay." PhD thesis. Statsvetenskapliga institutionen, Uppsala universitet.

Judd, Charles M & David A Kenny. 1981. "Process analysis estimating mediation in treatment evaluations." *Evaluation Review* 5(5):602–619.

Judd, Charles M & David A Kenny. 2010. Data analysis in social psychology: Recent and recurring issues. In *Handbook of social psychology.* Fiske, Susan T., Daniel T. Gilbert, and Gardner Lindzey, eds. John Wiley & Sons. 2, pp. 115–142.

Kahn, Sarah. 2021. "Count me out: Women's unexpressed preferences in Pakistan." *Unpublished manuscript.*

Kanter, Rosabeth Moss. 1977. *Men and women of the corporation.* Vol. 5049. Basic Books.

Kathlene, Lyn 1994. "Power and influence in state legislative policymaking: The interaction of gender and position in committee hearing debates." *American Political Science Review* 88(3):560–576.

Katzenstein, Mary Fainsod & Carol McClurg Mueller. 1987. *The women's movements of the United States and Western Europe consciousness, political opportunity, and public policy.* Temple University Press.

Keith, Daniel James & Tània Verge. 2016. "Nonmainstream left parties and women's representation in Western Europe." *Party Politics* 24(4): 397–409.

Kerevel, Yann. 2019. "Empowering women? Gender quotas and women's political careers." *The Journal of Politics* 81(4):1167–1180.

Kerevel, Yann P & Lonna Rae Atkeson. 2013. "Explaining the marginalization of women in legislative institutions." *The Journal of Politics* 75(4): 980–992.

King, Gary & Langche Zeng. 2006. "The dangers of extreme counterfactuals." *Political Analysis* 14(2):131–159.

King, Gary & Richard Nielsen. 2016. "Why propensity scores should not be used for matching." *Political Analysis* 27(4):435–454.

Kitschelt, Herbert. 2000a. "Linkages between citizens and politicians in democratic polities." *Comparative Political Studies* 33(6–7):845–879.

Kitschelt, Herbert. 1994. *The transformation of European social democracy.* Cambridge University Press.

Kitschelt, Herbert. 2000b. "Citizens, politicians, and party cartellization: Political representation and state failure in post-industrial democracies." *European Journal of Political Research* 37(2):149–179.

Kitschelt, Herbert P. 1988. "Left-libertarian parties: Explaining innovation in competitive party systems." *World Politics* 40(2):194–234.

Kittilson, Miki Caul. 2006. *Challenging parties, changing parliament: Women and elected office in contemporary Western Europe.* Ohio State University Press.

Kittilson, Miki Caul. 2008. "Representing women: The adoption of family leave in comparative perspective." *The Journal of Politics* 70(2):323–334.

Kittilson, Miki Caul. 2011. "Women, parties and platforms in post-industrial democracies." *Party Politics* 17(1):66–92.

Kittilson, Miki Caul & Leslie A Schwindt-Bayer. 2012. *The gendered effects of electoral institutions: Political engagement and participation.* Oxford University Press.

Klingemann, Hans-Dieter. 2006. *Mapping policy preferences II: Estimates for parties, electors, and governments in Eastern Europe, European Union, and OECD 1990–2003.* Vol. 2. Oxford University Press on Demand.

Klingemann, Hans-Dieter, Richard I Hofferbert, Ian Budge et al. 1994. *Parties, policies, and democracy.* Westview Press.

Koch, Michael T & Sarah A Fulton. 2011. "In the defense of women: Gender, office holding, and national security policy in established democracies." *The Journal of Politics* 73(1):1–16.

Kolinsky, Eva. 1988. "The West German Greens – A women's party?" *Parliamentary Affairs* 41(1):129–148.

Köpl, Regina. 2005. Gendering political representation: Debates and controversies in Austria. In *State feminism and political representation.* Cambridge University Press. pp. 20–40.

Korpi, Walter. 1983. *The democratic class struggle.* Routledge.

Korpi, Walter & Joakim Palme. 2003. "New politics and class politics in the context of austerity and globalization: Welfare state regress in 18 countries, 1975–95." *American Political Science Review* 97(3):425–446.

Kriesi, Hanspeter. 1998. "The transformation of cleavage politics: The 1997 Stein Rokkan lecture." *European Journal of Political Research* 33(2):165–185.

Kriesi, Hanspeter, Edgar Grande, Romain Lachat et al. 2006. "Globalization and the transformation of the national political space: Six European countries compared." *European Journal of Political Research* 45(6):921–956.

Kriesi, Hanspeter, Edgar Grande, Romain Lachat et al. 2008. *West European politics in the age of globalization.* Cambridge University Press.

Krook, Mona Lena. 2006. "Reforming representation: The diffusion of candidate gender quotas worldwide." *Politics & Gender* 2(3):303–327.

Krook, Mona Lena. 2008. Campaigns for candidate gender quotas: A new global women's movement? In *Women's movements: Flourishing or in abeyance.* Routledge. 22, pp. 105–115.

Krook, Mona Lena. 2009. *Quotas for women in politics: Gender and candidate selection reform worldwide.* Oxford University Press.

Krook, Mona Lena. 2015. "Empowerment versus backlash: Gender quotas and critical mass theory." *Politics, Groups, and Identities* 3(1):184–188.

Krook, Mona Lena & Diana Z O'Brien. 2012. "All the president's men? The appointment of female cabinet ministers worldwide." *The Journal of Politics* 74(3):840–855.

Krook, Mona Lena, Joni Lovenduski & Judith Squires. 2009. "Gender quotas and models of political citizenship." *British Journal of Political Science* 39(4):781–803.

La Porta, Rafael, Florencio Lopez-de Silanes, Andrei Shleifer & Robert Vishny. 1999. "The quality of government." *Journal of Law, Economics, and Organization* 15(1):222–279.

Lambert, Priscilla A. 2008. "The comparative political economy of parental leave and child care: Evidence from twenty OECD countries." *Social Politics: International Studies in Gender, State & Society* 15(3):315–344.

Latura, Audrey. 2021. "Private benefits, public origins: Employer childcare in liberal welfare regimes." *Working paper.* https://scholar.harvard.edu/audreylatura/private-public.

Latura, Audrey & Ana Catalano Weeks. "Corporate Board Quotas and Gender Equality Policies in the Workplace." Forthcoming, *American Journal of Political Science.*

Laver, Michael & Kenneth A Shepsle. 1996. *Making and breaking governments: Cabinets and legislatures in parliamentary democracies.* Cambridge University Press.

Laver, Michael. 2003. *Estimating the policy position of political actors.* Routledge.

Lawless, Jennifer L & Richard Logan Fox. 2005. *It takes a candidate: Why women don't run for office.* Cambridge University Press.

Leston-Bandeira, Cristina & Tiago Tibúrcio. 2012. "Developing links despite the parties–parliament and citizens in Portugal." *The Journal of Legislative Studies* 18(3–4):384–402.

Levitsky, Steven. 2003. *Transforming labor-based parties in Latin America: Argentine Peronism in comparative perspective.* Cambridge University Press.

Lewis, Jane. 1992. "Gender and the development of welfare regimes." *Journal of European Social Policy* 2(3):159–173.

Lichter, Daniel T & David J Eggebeen. 1994. "The effect of parental employment on child poverty." *Journal of Marriage and the Family* 56(3):633–645.

Lindert, Peter H. 1996. "What limits social spending?" *Explorations in Economic History* 33(1):1–34.

Lipset, Seymour Martin. 1960. *Political man: the social bases of politics.* Doubleday.

Lipset, Seymour Martin & Stein Rokkan. 1967. *Party systems and voter alignments*. New York: Free Press.

Lloren, Anouk, Jan Rosset & Reto Wüest. 2015. "Descriptive and substantive representation of poor citizens in Switzerland." *Swiss Political Science Review.* 21(2):254–260.

Lobo, Marina Costa. 2001. "The role of political parties in Portuguese democratic consolidation." *Party Politics* 7(5):643–653.

Loll, Dana & Kelli Stidham Hall. 2019. "Differences in abortion attitudes by policy context and between men and women in the world values survey." *Women & Health* 59(5):465–480.

Lott, Jr, J John & Lawrence W Kenny. 1999. "Did women's suffrage change the size and scope of government?" *Journal of Political Economy* 107(6):1163–1198.

Lovenduski, Joni. 2001. "Women and politics: Minority representation or critical mass?" *Parliamentary Affairs* 54(4):743–758.

Lovenduski, Joni & Pippa Norris. 1993. *Gender and party politics*. Sage.

Lowe, Will, Kenneth Benoit, Slava Mikhaylov & Michael Laver. 2011. "Scaling policy preferences from coded political texts." *Legislative Studies Quarterly* 36(1):123–155.

Lyall, Jason. 2014. "Why armies break: Explaining mass desertion in conventional war." SSRN 2524561 (2016).

Madrigal, Róger, Francisco Alpízar & Achim Schlüter. 2011. "Determinants of performance of community-based drinking water organizations." *World Development* 39(9):1663–1675.

Magni, Gabriele & Andrew Reynolds. 2021. "Voter preferences and the political underrepresentation of minority groups: Lesbian, gay, and transgender candidates in advanced democracies." *The Journal of Politics* 83(4): 1199–1215.

Manow, Philip. 2009. "Electoral rules, class coalitions and welfare state regimes, or how to explain Esping-Andersen with Stein Rokkan." *Socio-Economic Review* 7(1):101–121.

Mansbridge, Jane. 1999. "Should blacks represent blacks and women represent women? A contingent 'yes'." *The Journal of Politics* 61(3):628–657.

Mansbridge, Jane. 2003. "Rethinking representation." *American Political Science Review* 97(4):515–528.

Mansbridge, Jane. 2015. "Should workers represent workers?" *Swiss Political Science Review* 21(2):261–270.

Mansergh, Lucy & Robert Thomson. 2007. "Election pledges, party competition, and policymaking." *Comparative Politics* 39(3):311–329.

Marks, Gary, Liesbet Hooghe, Moira Nelson & Erica Edwards. 2006. "Party competition and European integration in the East and West: Different structure, same causality." *Comparative Political Studies* 39(2):155–175.

Marques-Pereira, Berengere & Catherine Gigante. 2001. "The political representation of women: quotas at parity?" *Center for Socio-Political Research and Information (CRISP)*. https://doi.org/10.3917/cris.1723.0005.

Martin, Lanny W. 2004. "The government agenda in parliamentary democracies." *American Journal of Political Science* 48(3):445–461.

Matland, Richard E. 1998. "Women's representation in national legislatures: Developed and developing countries." *Legislative Studies Quarterly* 23(1):109–125.

Matland, Richard E. 2005. The Norwegian experience of gender quotas. In *The implementation of quotas: European experiences*. International Institute for Democracy and Electoral Assistance, IDEA, 2005. p. 64.

Matland, Richard E. 2006. Electoral quotas: Frequency and effectiveness. In *Women, quotas and politics*. Routledge. pp. 275–292.

Matland, Richard E & Donley T Studlar. 1996. "The contagion of women candidates in single-member district and proportional representation electoral systems: Canada and Norway." *The Journal of Politics* 58(3):707–733.

Matsunaga, Masaki. 2015. "How to factor-analyze your data right: Do's, don'ts, and how-to's." *International Journal of Psychological Research* 3(1):97–110.

Matthews, Donald R. 1984. "Legislative recruitment and legislative careers." *Legislative Studies Quarterly*: 9(4)547–585.

Mayhew, David R. 1974. *Congress: The electoral connection*. Yale University Press.

Mazur, Amy G. 2002. *Theorizing feminist policy*. Oxford University Press.

McAllister, Ian & Donley T Studlar. 2002. "Electoral systems and women's representation: A long-term perspective." *Representation* 39(1):3–14.

McDonald, Michael D & Ian Budge. 2005. *Elections, parties, democracy: Conferring the median mandate*. Oxford University Press.

Desvaux, Georges and Sandrine Devillard. McKinsey, Company &. 2008. *Women matter: Female leadership, a competitive edge for the future*. McKinsey.

Meguid, Bonnie M. 2005. "Competition between unequals: The role of mainstream party strategy in niche party success." *American Political Science Review* 99(3):347–359.

Meguid, Bonnie M. 2008. *Party competition between unequals: Strategies and electoral fortunes in Western Europe*. Cambridge University Press.

Meier, Petra. 2004. "The mutual contagion effect of legal and party quotas: A Belgian perspective." *Party Politics* 10(5):583–600.

Meier, Petra. 2012. "From laggard to leader: Explaining the Belgian gender quotas and parity clause." *West European Politics* 35(2):362–379.

Meier, Petra. 2013. "Quotas, quotas everywhere: From party regulation to gender quotas for corporate management boards. Another case of contagion." *Representation* 49(4):453–466.

Mendelberg, Tali, Christopher F Karpowitz & Nicholas Goedert. 2013. "Does descriptive representation facilitate women's distinctive voice? How gender composition and decision rules affect deliberation." *American Journal of Political Science* 58(2):91–306.

Merla, Laura, Dimitri Mortelmans & Bernard Fusulier. 2018. "Belgium country note." *International Review on Leave Policies and Related Research* (14):66–74. http://www.leavenetwork.org/lp_and_r_reports/.

Milanovic, Branko. 2000. "The median-voter hypothesis, income inequality, and income redistribution: An empirical test with the required data." *European Journal of Political Economy* 16(3):367–410.

Milesi-Ferretti, Gian Maria, Roberto Perotti & Massimo Rostagno. 2002. "Electoral systems and public spending." *The Quarterly Journal of Economics* 117(2):609–657.

Miller, Grant. 2008. "Women's suffrage, political responsiveness, and child survival in American history." *The Quarterly Journal of Economics* 123(3):1287–1327.

Moene, Karl Ove & Michael Wallerstein. 2001. "Inequality, social insurance, and redistribution." *American Political Science Review* 95(4):859–874.

Morel, Nathalie. 2007. "From subsidiarity to 'free choice': Child-and elder-care policy reforms in France, Belgium, Germany and the Netherlands." *Social Policy & Administration* 41(6):618–637.

Moreno, Luis. 2006. "The model of social protection in Southern Europe." *Revue française des Affaires sociales* (5):73–95. https://doi.org/10.3917/rfas.en605.0073.

Morgan-Collins, Mona. 2021. "The electoral impact of newly enfranchised groups: The case of women's suffrage in the United States." *Journal of Politics* 83(1), 150–165.

Morgan, Jana. 2015. Gender and the Latin American voter. In *The Latin American voter*. University of Michigan Press. pp. 143–167.

Morgan, Kimberly J. 2006. *Working mothers and the welfare state: Religion and the politics of work-family policies in Western Europe and the United States.* Stanford University Press.

Morgan, Kimberly J. 2013. "Path shifting of the welfare state: Electoral competition and the expansion of work-family policies in Western Europe." *World Politics* 65(1):73–115.

Mosley, Layna. 2013. *Interview research in political science.* Cornell University Press.

Moss, Peter & Margaret O'Brien. 2019. United Kingdom: Leave policy and an attempt to take a new path. In *Parental leave and beyond: Recent international developments, current issues and future directions*. Policy Press. p. 57.

Moss, Peter & Fred Deven. 2015. "Leave policies in challenging times: Reviewing the decade 2004–2014." *Community, Work & Family* 18(2):137–144.

Moss, Peter & Fred Deven. 2019. "Leave policies in Europe: Current policies, future directions." *International Journal of Sociology and Social Policy* 40(5/6): 429–440.

Mughan, Anthony & Pamela Paxton. 2006. "Anti-immigrant sentiment, policy preferences and populist party voting in Australia." *British Journal of Political Science* 36(2):341–358.

Müller, Wolfgang C. 1994. Models of government and the Austrian cabinet. In *Cabinet ministers and parliamentary government*. CUP Archive. pp. 15–34.

Müller, Wolfgang C. 2004. "The parliamentary election in Austria, November 2002." *Electoral Studies* 2(23):346–353.

Murray, Rainbow. 2010. "Second among unequals? A study of whether France's 'quota women' are up to the job." *Politics & Gender* 6(1):93–118.

Murray, Rainbow. 2012. "Parity in France: a 'dual track' solution to women's under-representation." *West European Politics* 35(2):343–361.

Murray, Rainbow, Mona Lena Krook & Katherine AR Opello. 2012. "Why are gender quotas adopted? Party pragmatism and parity in France." *Political Research Quarterly* 65(3):529–543.

Naldini, Manuela. 2004. *Family in the Mediterranean welfare states*. Routledge.

Naurin, Elin. 2014. "Is a promise a promise? Election pledge fulfilment in comparative perspective using Sweden as an example." *West European Politics* 37(5):1046–1064.

Neto, Octávio Amorim & Marina Costa Lobo. 2009. "Portugal's semi-presidentialism (re) considered: An assessment of the president's role in the policy process, 1976–2006." *European Journal of Political Research* 48(2):234–255.

Niederle, Muriel & Lise Vesterlund. 2008. "Gender differences in competition." *Negotiation Journal* 24(4):447–463.

Nielsen, Rich & John Sheffield. 2009. "Matching with time-series cross-sectional data." *Polmeth XXVI. Yale University.* http://citeseerx.ist.psu.edu/viewdoc/download?doi=10.1.1.510.7097&rep=rep1&type=pdf.

Nielsen, Richard A. 2014. "Case selection via matching." *Sociological Methods & Research* 45(3):569–597.

Nieuwenhuis, Rense, Ariana Need & Henk Van Der Kolk. 2012. "Institutional and demographic explanations of women's employment in 18 OECD countries, 1975-1999." *Journal of Marriage and Family* 74(3):614–630.

Niven, David. 1998. "Party elites and women candidates: The shape of bias." *Women & Politics* 19(2):57–80.

Norris, Pippa. 1985. "Women's legislative participation in Western Europe." *West European Politics* 8(4):90–101.

Norris, Pippa. 1995. *Political recruitment: Gender, race and class in the British Parliament*. Cambridge University Press.

Norris, Pippa. 2003. The gender gap: Old challenges, new approaches. In *Women and American politics: New questions, new directions*. Oxford University Press on Demand. pp. 146–172.

Norris, Pippa. 2005. *Radical right: Voters and parties in the electoral market*. Cambridge University Press.

Norris, Pippa. 2007. "Opening the door: Women leaders and constitution-building in Iraq and Afghanistan." In *Women Who Lead*. Barbara Kellerman (ed.). Jossey Bass. pp. 197–226.

O'Brien, Diana Z. 2018. "'Righting' conventional wisdom: Women and right parties in established democracies." *Politics & Gender* 14(1):27–55.

O'Brien, Diana Z & Johanna Rickne. 2016. "Gender quotas and women's political leadership." *American Political Science Review* 110(1):112–126.

O'Brien, Diana Z. 2012. Quotas and qualifications in Uganda. In *The impact of gender quotas*. Oxford University Press. pp. 57–71.

O'Connor, Julia S. 1999. "Employment equality strategies in liberal welfare states." In Gender and welfare state regimes. Oxford University Press.

O'Regan, Valerie R. 2000. *Gender matters: Female policymakers' influence in industrialized nations*. Greenwood.

Olken, Benjamin A. 2010. "Direct democracy and local public goods: Evidence from a field experiment in Indonesia." *American Political Science Review* 104(2):243–267.

Orloff, Ann. 1996. "Gender in the welfare state." *Annual Review of Sociology* 22(1):51–78.

Orloff, Ann Shola. 1993. "Gender and the social rights of citizenship: The comparative analysis of gender relations and welfare states." *American Sociological Review* 58(3):303–328.

Osborne, Jason W & Anna B Costello. 2009. "Best practices in exploratory factor analysis: Four recommendations for getting the most from your analysis." *Pan-Pacific Management Review* 12(2):131–146.

Osborne, Martin J & Al Slivinski. 1996. "A model of political competition with citizen-candidates." *The Quarterly Journal of Economics* 111(1): 65–96.

Palici di Suni, Elisabetta. 2012. "Gender parity and quotas in Italy: A convoluted reform process." *West European Politics* 35(2):380–394.

Pansardi, Pamela & Michelangelo Vercesi. 2017. "Party gate-keeping and women's appointment to parliamentary committees: Evidence from the Italian case." *Parliamentary Affairs* 70(1):62–83.

Parsons, Craig & Till Weber. 2011. "Cross-cutting issues and party strategy in the European Union." *Comparative Political Studies* 44(4):383–411.

Patnaik, Ankita. 2019. "Reserving time for daddy: The consequences of fathers' quotas." *Journal of Labor Economics* 37(4):1009–1059.

Paxton, Pamela & Melanie M Hughes. 2015. "The increasing effectiveness of national gender quotas, 1990–2010." *Legislative Studies Quarterly* 40(3):331–362.

Paxton, Pamela, Melanie M Hughes & Matthew A Painter. 2010. "Growth in women's political representation: A longitudinal exploration of democracy, electoral system and gender quotas." *European Journal of Political Research* 49(1):25–52.

Paxton, Pamela Marie, Melanie M Hughes & Tiffany Barnes. 2020. *Women, politics, and power: A global perspective*. Rowman & Littlefield.

Perrigo, Sarah. 1996. "Women and change in the labour party 1979–1995." *Parliamentary Affairs* 49(1):116–129.

Persson, Torsten & Guido Enrico Tabellini. 2005. *The economic effects of constitutions*. MIT Press.

Pfau-Effinger, Birgit. 2004. "Socio-historical paths of the male breadwinner model: An explanation of cross-national differences." *The British Journal of Sociology* 55(3):377–399.

Pierson, Paul. 2000. "Increasing returns, path dependence, and the study of politics." *American Political Science Review* 94(2):251–267.

Pinto, António Costa & Pedro Tavares de Almeida. 2008. Portugal: The primacy of "independents." In *The selection of ministers in Europe*. Routledge. pp. 165–176.

Pischke, Jörn-Steffen. 2005. "Empirical methods in applied economics: Lecture notes." http://econ.lse.ac.uk/staff/spischke/ec524/evaluation3.pdf

Piscopo, Jennifer M. 2011. "Rethinking descriptive representation: Rendering women in legislative debates." *Parliamentary Affairs* 64(3):448–472.

Piscopo, Jennifer M. 2016. "Democracy as gender balance: The shift from quotas to parity in Latin America." *Politics, Groups, and Identities* 4(2): 214–230.

Piscopo, Jennifer M & Susan Clark Muntean. 2018. "Corporate quotas and symbolic politics in advanced democracies." *Journal of Women, Politics & Policy* 39(3):285–309.

Pitlik, Hans & Ludek Kouba. 2015. "Does social distrust always lead to a stronger support for government intervention?" *Public Choice* 163(3–4): 355–377.

Plümper, Thomas, Vera E Troeger & Eric Neumayer. 2019. "Case selection and causal inferences in qualitative comparative research." *PloS One* 14(7):e0219727.

Pontusson, Jonas. 2015. "Introduction to the debate: Does descriptive misrepresentation by income and class matter?" *Swiss Political Science Review* 21(2):207–212.

Portugal Socialist Party. 2011. "Defender Portugal, Construir o Futuro." Electoral program. URL: https://ps.pt/wp-content/uploads/2021/03/2011.5.jun_PS_Programa.Eleitoral.2011-2015.Defender.Portugal.Construir.o.Futuro.pdf

Prillaman, Soledad. 2021. "Why women mobilize: Dissecting and dismantling India's political gender gap." *Book manuscript.*

Profeta, Paola. 2020. *Gender equality and public policy: Measuring progress in Europe.* Cambridge University Press.

Profeta, Paola & Eleanor F. Woodhouse. 2022. "Electoral rules, women's representation and the qualification of politicians." *Comparative Political Studies.* doi:10.1177/00104140211047414.

Ramalho, Maria do Rosário Palma, Petra Foubert & Susanne Burri. 2015. "The implementation of parental leave directive 2010/18 of in 33 European countries." *European Union.* https://data.europa.eu/doi/10.2838/957478.

Rehavi, Marit M. 2007. "Sex and politics: Do female legislators affect state spending." Unpublished manuscript.

Reynolds, Andrew. 1999. "Women in the legislatures and executives of the world." *World Politics* 51(4):547–572.

Reynolds, Andrew. 2013. "Representation and rights: The impact of LGBT legislators in comparative perspective." *American Political Science Review* 107(2):259–274.

Rigon, Massimiliano & Giulia Tanzi. 2012. "Does gender matter for public spending? Empirical evidence from Italian municipalities." Bank of Italy Temi di Discussione Working Paper 862. https://econpapers.repec.org/paper/bdiwptemi/td_5f862_5f12.htm

Rille-Pfeiffer, Christiane, Helene Dearing & Andrea E Schmidt. 2018. "Austria country note." *International Review on Leave Policies and Related Research* (14):66–74. http://www.leavenetwork.org/lp_and_r_reports/.

Ripley, Amanda. 2005. "Equal time: Gender quotas have helped European women get ahead in politics. But can the law put women in all-male boardrooms? Gender equality's final frontier." *Time Europe.* http://content.time.com/time/subscriber/article/0,33009,485708,00.html.

Roemer, John E. 1998. "Why the poor do not expropriate the rich: An old argument in new garb." *Journal of Public Economics* 70(3):399–424.

Rogers, William. 1994. "Regression standard errors in clustered samples." *Stata Technical Bulletin* 3(13): 1–32.

Rønsen, Marit & Marianne Sundström. 1996. "Maternal employment in Scandinavia: A comparison of the after-birth employment activity of Norwegian and Swedish women." *Journal of Population Economics* 9(3):267–285.

Rosenthal, Cindy Simon. 1998. *When women lead: Integrative leadership in state legislatures.* Oxford University Press on Demand.

Rovny, Jan. 2012. "Who emphasizes and who blurs? Party strategies in multidimensional competition." *European Union Politics* 13(2):269–292.

Rubin, Donald B. 1973. "Matching to remove bias in observational studies." *Biometrics* 29(1):159–183.

Rueda, David. 2005. "Insider–outsider politics in industrialized democracies: The challenge to social democratic parties." *American Political Science Review* 99(1):61–74.

Rueda, David & Jonas Pontusson. 2010. "Individual preferences for redistribution in Western Europe: Self-interest, political articulation, altruism and identity." *Unpublished manuscript* www.yale.edu/leitner/resources/papers/RuedaYale2010.pdf.

Ruedin, Didier. 2009. "Ethnic group representation in a cross-national comparison." *The Journal of Legislative Studies* 15(4):335–354.

Rule, Wilma. 1987. "Electoral systems, contextual factors and women's opportunity for election to parliament in twenty-three democracies." *The Western Political Quarterly* 40(3):477–498.

Rule, Wilma. 1994. "Parliaments of, by, and for the people: Except for women?" *Contributions in Political Science* 338:15–30.

Rule, Wilma & Joseph Francis Zimmerman. 1994. *Electoral systems in comparative perspective: Their impact on women and minorities.* No. 338, Greenwood.

Sabatier, Paul A & Christopher Weible. 2014. *Theories of the policy process.* Westview Press.

Sacchet, Teresa. 2008. "Beyond numbers: The impact of gender quotas in Latin America." *International Feminist Journal of Politics* 10(3):369–386.

Sanbonmatsu, Kira. 2006. *Where women run: Gender and party in the American states.* University of Michigan Press.

Sapiro, Virginia. 1981. "Research frontier essay: When are interests interesting? The problem of political representation of women." *American Political Science Review* 75(3):701–716.

Sartori, Giovanni. 1968. "Representational systems." *International Encyclopedia of the Social Sciences* 13:470–475.

Scheve, Kenneth & David Stasavage. 2006. "Religion and preferences for social insurance." *Quarterly Journal of Political Science* 1(3):255–286.

Scheve, Kenneth F & Matthew J Slaughter. 2001. "Labor market competition and individual preferences over immigration policy." *Review of Economics and Statistics* 83(1):133–145.

Schreiber, Ronnee. 2002. "Injecting a woman's voice: Conservative women's organizations, gender consciousness, and the expression of women's policy preferences." *Sex Roles* 47(7–8):331–342.

Schwarz, Peter. 2012. "Tax disincentives and female employment in Organisation for Economic Co-operation and Development (OECD) countries." *Journal of European Social Policy* 22(1):17–29.

Schwindt-Bayer, Leslie A. 2006. "Still supermadres? Gender and the policy priorities of Latin American legislators." *American Journal of Political Science* 50(3):570–585.

Schwindt-Bayer, Leslie A. 2009. "Making quotas work: The effect of gender quota laws on the election of women." *Legislative Studies Quarterly* 34(1):5–28.

Seawright, Jason & John Gerring. 2008. "Case selection techniques in case study research a menu of qualitative and quantitative options." *Political Research Quarterly* 61(2):294–308.

Sen, Maya & Omar Wasow. 2016. "Race as a 'bundle of sticks': Designs that estimate effects of seemingly immutable characteristics." *Annual Review of Political Science* 19:499–522.

Sénac-Slawinski, Réjane. 2008. "Justifying parity in France after the passage of the so-called parity laws and the electoral application of them: The 'ideological tinkering' of political party officials (UMP and PS) and women's NGOs." *French Politics* 6(3):234–256.

Shin, Ki-young. 2016. "Challenges and new strategies of women's local party in Japan: What does it represent and how does it sustain its electoral success?" Paper presented at the American Political Science Association Annual Meeting.

Shorrocks, Rosalind. 2018. "Cohort change in political gender gaps in Europe and Canada: The role of modernization." *Politics & Society* 46(2):135–175.

Shugart, Matthew Soberg. 1998. "The inverse relationship between party strength and executive strength: A theory of politicians' constitutional choices." *British Journal of Political Science* 28(1):1–29.

Shwindt-Bayer, Leslie A & Renato Corbetta. 2004. "Gender turnover and roll-call voting in the US house of representatives." *Legislative Studies Quarterly* 29(2):215–229.

Siaroff, Alan. 2000. "Women's representation in legislatures and cabinets in industrial democracies." *International Political Science Review* 21(2):197–215.

Simon, Rita J & Jean M Landis. 1989. "A report: Women's and men's attitudes about a woman's place and role." *The Public Opinion Quarterly* 53(2):265–276.

Skeije, Hege 1993. *Gender and party politics*. Sage, 1993.

Skjeie, Hege. 1991. "The rhetoric of difference: On women's inclusion into political elites." *Politics & Society* 19(2):233–263.

Skorge, Øyvind Søraas & Magnus Bergli Rasmussen. 2021. "Volte-face on the welfare state: Social partners, knowledge economies, and the expansion of work-family policies." *Politics & Society*: https://doi.org/10.1177/00323292211014371.

Smith, Tom W & Jaesok Son. 2013. "Trends in public attitudes towards abortion." *The National Opinion Research Center.*

Smooth, Wendy. 2011. "Standing for women? Which women? The substantive representation of women's interests and the research imperative of intersectionality." *Politics & Gender* 7(3):436–441.

Somer-Topcu, Zeynep. 2009. "Timely decisions: The effects of past national elections on party policy change." *The Journal of Politics* 71(1): 238–248.

Spoon, Jae-Jae, Sara B Hobolt & Catherine E De Vries. 2014. "Going green: Explaining issue competition on the environment." *European Journal of Political Research* 53(2):363–380.

Strøm, Kaare. 1998. "Parliamentary committees in European democracies." *The Journal of Legislative Studies* 4(1):21–59.

Strøm, Kaare. 2000. "Delegation and accountability in parliamentary democracies." *European Journal of Political Research* 37(3):261–290.

Stuart, Elizabeth A. 2010. "Matching methods for causal inference: A review and a look forward." *Statistical Science: A Review Journal of the Institute of Mathematical Statistics* 25(1):1.

Studlar, Donley T, Ian McAllister & Bernadette C Hayes. 1998. "Explaining the gender gap in voting: A cross-national analysis." *Social Science Quarterly:* 79(4):779–798.

Svaleryd, Helena. 2009. "Women's representation and public spending." *European Journal of Political Economy* 25(2):186–198.

Svallfors, Svaleryd. 1997. "Worlds of welfare and attitudes to redistribution: A comparison of eight western nations." *European Sociological Review* 13(3):283–304.

Swers, Michele L. 1998. "Are women more likely to vote for women's issue bills than their male colleagues?" *Legislative Studies Quarterly* 23(3):435–448.

Swers, Michele L. 2002. *The difference women make: The policy impact of women in Congress.* University of Chicago Press.

Swers, Michele L. 2005. "Connecting descriptive and substantive representation: An analysis of sex differences in cosponsorship activity." *Legislative Studies Quarterly* 30(3):407–433.

Tarrow, Sidney. 2010. "The strategy of paired comparison: Toward a theory of practice." *Comparative Political Studies* 43(2):230–259.

Teele, Dawn Langan. 2018. "How the west was won: Competition, mobilization, and women's enfranchisement in the United States." *The Journal of Politics* 80(2):442–461.

Teigen, Mari. 2012. Gender quotas on corporate boards: On the diffusion of a distinct national policy reform. In *Firms, boards and gender quotas: Comparative perspectives.* Emerald Group. pp. 115–146. https://doi.org/10.1108/S0195-6310(2012)0000029008.

Thames, Frank C. 2017. "Understanding the impact of electoral systems on women's representation." *Politics & Gender* 13(3):379–404.

Thomas, Sue. 1994. *How women legislate.* Oxford University Press.

Thomassen, Jacques. 2012. "The blind corner of political representation." *Representation* 48(1):13–27.

Thomson, Robert, Terry Royed, Elin Naurin et al. 2012. "The program-to-policy linkage: A comparative study of election pledges and government policies in ten countries." Paper presented at the American Political Science Association Annual Meeting.

Timmermans, Arco. 1994. Cabinet ministers and policy-making in Belgium: The impact of coalitional constraints. In *Cabinet ministers and parliamentary government*. CUP Archive. pp.106–107.

Tingley, Dustin, Teppei Yamamoto, Kentaro Hirose, Luke Keele & Kosuke Imai. 2014. "Mediation: R package for causal mediation analysis." *Journal of Statistical Software* 59(5).

Tripp, Aili Mari & Alice Kang. 2008. "The global impact of quotas on the fast track to increased female legislative representation." *Comparative Political Studies* 41(3):338–361.

Ueda, Michiko. 2008. "The impact of minority representation on policy outcomes: Evidence from the US States." Social Science Working Paper, 1284. California Institute of Technology, Pasadena, CA. (Unpublished) https://resolver.caltech.edu/CaltechAUTHORS:20170728-142011149.

Vaes, Benedict. April 15, 2005. "Politique - La majorite violette serre quelques boulons avant de s'en aller affronter les prochains orages Bon vent social, sans souffle politique Independants: les projets sur la table Pluie de cadeaux pour ceux qui font des bebes." *Le Soir*.

Vaes, Benedict. March 12, 2007. "Politique Du climat a la famille, le SP.A propose un nouveau modele social: Un an de conge parental par enfant." *Le Soir*.

Valdini, Melody E. 2019. *The inclusion calculation: Why men appropriate women's representation*. Oxford University Press.

Van de Wardt, Marc, Catherine E De Vries & Sara B Hobolt. 2014. "Exploiting the cracks: Wedge issues in multiparty competition." *The Journal of Politics* 76(4):986–999.

Van der Brug, Wouter & Joost Van Spanje. 2009. "Immigration, Europe and the 'new' cultural dimension." *European Journal of Political Research* 48(3):309–334.

Van Kersbergen, Kees. 2003. *Social capitalism: A study of Christian democracy and the welfare state*. Routledge.

Van Roe, Filip. 2013. "Als Minister Moet Je Soms Drie Dagen Geen Krant Lezen." *Knack*.

Vandeweyer, Jessie & Ignace Glorieux. 2008. "Men taking up career leave: An opportunity for a better work and family life balance?" *Journal of Social Policy* 37(2):271–294.

Vega, Arturo & Juanita M Firestone. 1995. "The effects of gender on congressional behavior and the substantive representation of women." *Legislative Studies Quarterly* 20(2):213–222.

Verba, Sidney, Kay L Schlozman & Henry E Brady. 1995. *Voice and equality: Civic voluntarism in American politics*. Harvard University Press.

Verge, Tania. 2012. "Institutionalising gender equality in Spain: From party quotas to electoral gender quotas." *West European Politics* 35(2):395–414. www.tandfonline.com/doi/abs/10.1080/01402382.2011.648014.

Verge, Tania & Emanuela Lombardo. 2015. "The differential approach to gender quotas in Spain: Regulated politics and self-regulated corporate boards." *EUI Department of Law Research Paper* 2015/24.

Vliegenthart, Rens & Stefaan Walgrave. 2011. "Content matters: The dynamics of parliamentary questioning in Belgium and Denmark." *Comparative Political Studies* 44(8):1031–1059.

Volkens, Andrea, Pola Lehmann, Theres Matthieß et al. 2016. "The manifesto project dataset-codebook." *Manifesto Project (MRG/ CMP/MARPOR). Version 2016a. Wissenschaftszentrum Berlin für Sozialforschung (WZB).* https://manifesto-project.wzb.eu/down/data/2016a/ codebooks/codebook_MPDataset_MPDS2016a.pdf.

von Steinitz M Steinitz. 2010. "Wahl: Christine Marek." *Wienerin.* https://wienerin.at/wahl-christine-marek

Von Wahl, Angelika. 2006. "Gender equality in Germany: Comparing policy change across domains." *West European Politics* 29(3):461–488.

Walgrave, Stefaan, Frédéric Varone & Patrick Dumont. 2006. "Policy with or without parties? A comparative analysis of policy priorities and policy change in Belgium, 1991 to 2000." *Journal of European Public Policy* 13(7):1021–1038.

Wall, Karin & Anna Escobedo. 2009. Portugal and Spain: Two pathways in Southern Europe. In *The politics of parental leave policies: Children, parenting, gender and the labour market.* Policy Press. pp. 207–226.

Wall, Karin & Mafalda Leitão. 2018. "Portugal country note." *International Review of Leave Policies and Research 2018.* http://www.leavenetwork.org/lp_and_r_reports/

Walsh, Joan. 2015. "EXCLUSIVE: 'That's outrageous! And incorrect and sexist!': Sen. Gillibrand unloads to Salon." *Salon.* https://www.salon.com/2015/02/09/exclusive_%E2%80%9Cthat%E2%80% 99s_outrageous_and_incorrect_and_sexist%E2%80%9D_sen_gillibrand_ unloads_to_salon/.

Wängnerud, Lena. 2009. "Women in parliaments: Descriptive and substantive representation." *Annual Review of Political Science* 12:51–69.

Wängnerud, Lena. 2000. "Testing the politics of presence: Women's representation in the Swedish Riksdag." *Scandinavian Political Studies* 23(1): 67–91.

Wängnerud, Lena. 2005. Sweden: A step-wise development. In *Women in parliament: Beyond numbers.* International Institute for Democracy and Electoral Assistance (International IDEA). pp. 238–248.

Washington, Ebonya L. 2008. "Female socialization: how daughters affect their legislator fathers' voting on women's issues." *The American Economic Review* 98(1):311–332.

Weeks, Ana Catalano. 2016. "Identity and policymaking: The policy impact of gender quota laws." PhD thesis, Harvard University. http://nrs.harvard.edu/ urn-3:HUL.InstRepos:33493419

Weeks, Ana Catalano. 2018. "Why are gender quota laws adopted by men? The role of inter-and intraparty competition." *Comparative Political Studies* 51(14):1935–1973.

Weeks, Ana Catalano. 2019. "Quotas and party priorities: Direct and indirect effects of quota laws." *Political Research Quarterly* 72(4):849–862.

Weeks, Ana Catalano, Bonnie Meguid, Miki Kittilson & Hilde Coffé. Forthcoming. "When do Männerparteien elect women? Radical right populist parties and strategic descriptive representation." *American Political Science Review.*

Weeks, Ana Catalano & Lisa Baldez. 2015. "Quotas and qualifications: The impact of gender quota laws on the qualifications of legislators in the Italian parliament." *European Political Science Review* 7(1):119–144.

Welch, Susan. 1985. "Are women more liberal than men in the US Congress?" *Legislative Studies Quarterly* 10(1):125–134.

Weldon, S Laurel. 2002. "Beyond bodies: Institutional sources of representation for women in democratic policymaking." *Journal of Politics* 64(4):1153–1174.

Wiliarty, Sarah Elise. 2010. *The CDU and the politics of gender in Germany: Bringing women to the party*. Cambridge University Press.

Wiliarty, Sarah Elise. 2011. "Gender and energy policy making under the first Merkel government." *German Politics* 20(3):449–463.

Williams, Rick L. 2000. "A note on robust variance estimation for cluster-correlated data." *Biometrics* 56(2):645–646.

Wucherpfennig, Julian, Nils W Metternich, Lars-Erik Cederman & Kristian Skrede Gleditsch. 2012. "Ethnicity, the state, and the duration of civil war." *World Politics* 64(1):79–115.

Xydias, Christina. 2009. "Women representing women: Examining the effects of gender quotas." Paper presented at the American Political Science Association Annual Meeting.

Xydias, Christina. 2013. "Mapping the language of women's interests: Sex and party affiliation in the Bundestag." *Political Studies* 61(2):319–340.

Xydias, Christina. 2014. "Women's rights in Germany: Generations and gender quotas." *Politics & Gender* 10(1):4–32.

Xydias, Christina V. 2007. "Inviting more women to the party: Gender quotas and women's substantive representation in Germany." *International Journal of Sociology* 37(4):52–66.

Young, Iris Marion. 1997. "Deferring group representation." *Nomos* 39:349–376.

Zetterberg, Pär 2008. "The downside of gender quotas? Institutional constraints on women in Mexican state legislatures." *Parliamentary Affairs* 61(3):442–460.

Zetterberg, Pär. 2009. "Do gender quotas foster women's political engagement? Lessons from Latin America." *Political Research Quarterly* 62(4):715–730.

Index

www.ingramcontent.com/pod-product-compliance
Ingram Content Group UK Ltd.
Pitfield, Milton Keynes, MK11 3LW, UK
UKHW041848270225
455670UK00004B/104